AN ILLUSTRATED HISTORY
OF
TRAINS
in
TROUBLE
ALAN EARNSHAW
A CENTURY OF
BRITISH RAILWAY
DISASTERS
1868-1968
ALAN EARNSHAW
Atlantic

PUBLISHED BY:
ATLANTIC TRANSPORT PUBLISHERS
TREVITHICK HOUSE • WEST END • PENRYN TR10 8HE

ISBN: 0 906899 69 9

DESIGN AND REPRODUCTION:
BARNABUS DESIGN AND REPRO • TRURO • CORNWALL

PRINTED BY:
AMADEUS PRESS LIMITED • HUDDERSFIELD • WEST YORKSHIRE

British Cataloguing in Publication Data
A catalogue record for this book is available from the British Library

CONTENTS

INTRODUCTION

When *Trains In Trouble* was first devised by Atlantic Transport Publishers back in 1980, I do not think anyone could have ever foreseen how popular this little picture album would become. It was certainly never intended that it would turn into a series of four books, and not in our wildest dreams did we consider there would ever be a demand for eight volumes - yet the books' popularity has never diminished and interest in the subject has remained strong. Its originator Arthur Trevena was a dedicated GWR enthusiast and skilled model-maker, and it was these interests which had led to his study of railway safety matters. His concept was an album which would provide pictorial illustrations to Tom Rolt's excellent book, *Red For Danger*, which had been first published by John Lane in 1955. It was through a mutual friend of Tom Rolt's, that Arthur first made contact with me in 1979, with a request to loan one of my pictures of the 1916 Penistone Viaduct accident. I was pleased to help not only with that, but also with some of the research for the second volume. It was at this time that I first met the Kenneth Hoole, upon who's mantle the authorship of the series would fall after Arthur's passing in 1981. Ken Hoole's first and foremost interest was in the North Eastern Railway, but second to this was his study of railway accidents which went back to his reading of a newspaper report into the accident at Hull Paragon station in February 1927. Yet, Ken knew he could not possibly research all the accidents in the UK, so I was asked to carry on my photographic research work from Volume 2, by concentrating on incidents which occurred on the western side of Britain. The fourth volume went on sale in 1983 and there the series came to its apparent end; yet as the original stocks became depleted, popular demand led to a re-print of the first four books in 1989, accompanied by two new volumes under my authorship. At the time of planning that fifth volume, a conscious decision was made to change the content of the books, so that they went much deeper into the subject than the short captions and interesting pictures presented in the earlier volumes. This work was accomplished and our readers immediately showed their appreciation for Volume 5, by requesting details of when more books would follow. Sadly this period coincided with the death of Ken Hoole, and was a time when my own health was far from what it should have been. A friend jokingly suggested to me at the time that I'd better hurry up and write the next instalment in the series, as the going rate was just two books for each of the three authors. I was therefore greatly relieved when Atlantic's then managing editor, David Jenkinson commissioned two more books in the series.

When we reached the eighth book in 1993, it seemed as though we had definitely come to the end of the road, but our readers continued to demand more information. As a consequence of this interest, and in a desire to make *Trains In Trouble* into a comprehensive reference book; it was decided to produce a single hard-back version of the original paper-backs, and substantially enlarge the material therein. To enable this revision to take place, a number of substantial changes have had to be made, including the decision to discard trivial incidents and anything post-1968, particularly if we wanted to expand the text on many of the accidents in the first four books. Reflecting back on those earlier publications, it is easy to conclude that there were too many areas of white space and that the simple captions did not fully do justice to the very serious subject of railway safety. In altering the original text of Arthur Trevena and Ken Hoole, I must state that this is in no way a reflection on what they have previously presented. It is merely a change in the expectations of our readers which has resulted in the amended presentation and extended information. Accordingly, I have spent the past two years reading up the official reports on these accidents, studying news reports and endeavouring to understand the lessons which should have been learnt from them. In itself, this work has spawned separate magazine article series, in which subjects such as Accidents in Post War Britain, Modern Traction and Automated Train Control/Advance Warning Systems have been covered. With this, there has come a wide range of correspondence from all over the world, leading to information being forwarded on a variety of accident subjects. Even as I write this introduction, I have received a telephone call from Turkey by someone interested in the subject who had valuable information to impart. To this gentleman, and all the hundreds of others who have written to me, may I extend my sincere thanks and gratitude. *Trains in Trouble* is a tribute to you, and in many ways this is your book as much as it is mine.

But why is it that there is such a fascination in this subject, and why is this interest so universal? Whenever I am invited to visit a television or radio studio to offer 'expert comment' on a modern accident, I am usually asked this question. Fortunately this is usually put to me 'off air', because I do not think I have ever been able to answer the question with any degree of accuracy. For over 15 years I have been involved in researching, writing and recording the history of British railway accidents. Yet, even with this background I am unable to determine where reader fascination in the subject springs from. I am only convinced that it is not from an interest in the macabre, as not one single letter or enquiry has ever displayed a ghoulish trait in its origination or content. One common area of appreciation for the subject comes from the railway modelling fraternity, for accident pictures often reveal bits of locomotives and

PICTURE LEFT *A view of the accident at Staplehurst, in which ten of Charles Dickens' co-travellers regretfully lost their lives when the 'Up Tidal' train was derailed over the Beult Viaduct. The disaster was due to gangers replacing the longitudinal timbers on three low viaducts in the section from Ashford to Staplehurst in the intervals when the line was quiet. However, on 9th June when the rail over the Beult Viaduct was broken after the 2.51pm Up train had passed by, the foreman platelayer had misread the timetable and not made allowances for the 'Tidal' express. As the train was doing in excess of 50mph as it travelled along the dead-straight section from Headcorn station, the driver had little chance to react when he saw the lookout-signalman, who had been posted some 554 yards from the site of the work as opposed to the specified 1,000 yards. The train had slowed to about 30 mph when it reached the 'broken' track, but No.199's momentum carried it on over the break before it came to a halt on the west bank. Though some of the coaches remained upright, the bulk of the train crashed over the viaduct parapet dropping into the river below. In addition to the fatalities, forty other passengers sustained some form of injury. Dickens was particularly fortunate, his First-class coach being the one pictured here standing by itself on the viaduct.* PHOTOGRAPH; KENT COUNTY LIBRARY SERVICE.

PICTURE BELOW *As we will discuss later, the railway line from Huddersfield to Penistone was no stranger to accidents. Like the disaster at Springwood Junction in 1858, the majority of these were runaways, and over the years a whole series of such accidents occurred as wagons escaped from Berry Brow, Honley and Brockholes. In 1952 a number of loaded coal wagons ran away from Honley, and to prevent a repetition of 1858 were diverted into the goods yard at Lockwood. In one of the roads a rake of five 'Shock' wagons were located and the runaways were put into that road, unfortunately the stationary wagons were not able to withstand the impact and they spilled down into Swan Lane, bringing down a signal post in the process.* PHOTOGRAPH; HUDDERSFIELD EXAMINER

rolling stock that ordinary photographs cannot capture. The underside of an overturned loco, the interior of a smashed goods van, the exposed view of the inside of a wrecked coach; all have their admirers. Similarly, a good number of railway preservation groups have also written to me asking for a copy of a particular print, because it happened to reveal a facet of construction which they wanted to emulate in a restoration process. Others have expressed appreciation for coverage of a particular accident, because it happened to involve a piece of railway history in which they were interested; such interest might vary from the geographic to the mechanical. For example, an amazing number of people are interested in accidents to BR Standard locomotive classes; conversely, some locations seem to have an almost magnetic attraction to disasters and students of railway history in those particular areas wish to know why. Yet it is the growing number of people who share with me a desire to study the overall lessons that can be learnt from railway accidents, which seems to be the most common denominator in the interest in this subject. All around the country, both employees within the rail industry and students of transport history, are writing to ask (or comment on) 'what is to be learned from history'. In fact, this very question was even asked of me by a Transport Minister over lunch at Westminster a couple of years back, so one must assume that this fascination in railway accidents and disasters comes from not the macabre, but a genuine desire to improve railway safety. It can not be denied that railway safety is an emotive issue, and as we slip and slide towards rail privatisation a good many people are asking how safe the railway system will really be once it has entered private hands. Confidence within the industry is a matter of debate, for at the present time there is an almost equal divide between those who believe that the system has attained a good all-round level of safety, and others who feel that the railways are poised on a knife-edge with worn-out areas of infrastructure (particularly signalling) lurking as a hidden menace between the apparently calm waters. It is not our place to moralise on that debate, nor to take any sides! Yet, having witnessed the aftermath of the 1995 Aisgill accident I do feel that some very pointed questions ought to be asked. I had watched the first of the two 'Sprinter' trains involved in that collision pass my study window in the glowing dusk, reflecting with some pride that the trains were still getting through even though Appleby was cut in half by the swollen River Eden. When I saw the second pass, I began to get alarmed, and wondered why on earth they were still running trains up into the mountains on such a vile night. Then, when I heard of the accident shortly afterwards, I wondered if even now we have yet learned the lessons that 170 years of railway history have tried to teach us? Worst still, are we ignoring these 'signals from the past'? For example, on lines such as the Settle & Carlisle Railway where landslides have been common occurrences for many years - should trains have been running in such adverse conditions as those which prevailed that night? Railway accidents will still continue to happen, and two have taken place in the weeks when this book was in its final course of preparation! But are such accidents freak occurrences or are there more serious underlying causes which have not yet been rooted out (or worse still covered over in the Government's mad rush to hive off the railway network into the private sector)? Let us hope that by continuing the debate through *Trains In Trouble* and with articles on historic accidents in magazines like *BackTrack*, we can keep the issue in focus and avoid the matter of railway safety being swept under the carpet.

Alan Earnshaw,
Appleby-in-Westmorland, May 1996.

LEARNING THE LESSONS

Where man and machinery come together, there is the inevitable risk of mishap and injury. When other factors such as speed and impetus, adverse weather, mechanical or civil engineering failures and, above all human error are added, the ingredients for disaster are prepared. From the very early days of the railways, the management and workmen employed thereon were faced with numerous obstacles which had to be overcome. From a primitive machine designed to replace horse-haulage, to high speed trains running in excess of 100 miles per hour, Britain's railways came a very long way in a remarkably short period of time. Progress was not lightly achieved however, and many mistakes occurred along the way. It was a very large learning curve, and undoubtedly mistakes, faults and omissions which seem downright negligent in hindsight, might be viewed more correctly as teething problems which occurred along the way; indeed many of the changes and improvements to the railways only came about because of accidents and disasters. From the time that the unfortunate Mr. Huskisson was knocked down and killed during the Rainhill Trials on 15th September 1830, railway operators were faced with the implications of careful management, safety of the public, and prevention of accidents.

An early problem that was encountered, centred round people having to come to terms with the new technology, as for example was experienced where highways of various kinds crossed the railway. In 1833 a collision which took place on the Leicester & Swannington Railway at Bagworth between a train and a cart loaded with farm produce, is reputed to have been instrumental in the provision of whistles on locomotives. How these would be needed in the years that followed! In 1840 an Act of Parliament empowered the Board of Trade to appoint Railway Inspecting Officers, a group of men that were recruited from the Corps of Royal Engineers. Their two-fold purpose was to inspect newly built railway lines and report on the worthiness prior to operation, and to investigate the causes of accidents. A further Act confirmed additional powers in 1842, but the first enquiry carried out by an Inspector came about as a result of derailment caused by a casting falling from a truck on the Leeds & Selby Railway at Howden on 7th August 1840. In the months and years that followed, they examined incidents like the major landslide at Sonning Cutting on Christmas Eve 1841, and bridge collapses such as those at Tonbridge and Dee Bridge in 1846 and 1847 respectively. Another 1847 failure was examined at Southall where a broken wheel derailed a goods train. Boiler explosions were commonplace, as we shall discuss later, and so were collisions with wagons left on the line. One such incident befell a train from Exeter at Shrivenham station on 10th May 1848, when two porters pushed a cattle truck and a horse box on to the main line. This obstruction was not noticed by the policeman (the early name for signalmen) who was located at the far end of the platform, and he signalled the express through the station. Six people died as a result of this mishap.

Remains of the train sketched an hour and a half after the accident at Abergale.

Rear-end collisions were also quite prevalent in those days, primarily because trains were operated on what was known as a time-lapse system. Basically, when trains were let into a particular section of track by a policeman or pointsman, it was (theoretically) known how long it would take them to reach the other end. A little extra time was added for a safety margin, whereupon the next train would be sent into the section. Unfortunately trains often broke down, stalled or were otherwise delayed in the section and accidents occurred as a result. Two such frightening incidents occurred in the North-west of England within a few years of each other, these being at Bootle in 1849 and at Frodsham two years later. Throughout the long list of accidents investigated by the Railway Inspectorate, we find reference after reference where the Inspectors request, suggest, demand and even plead for improvements to be brought about. For years their request was 'Lock, Block and Brake', referring to the inter-locking of signals and point mechanisms, block working to replace the time-lapse system and continuous braking for trains. Some of the companies acted quickly, but in other instances the requests were ignored for years, the classic example concerning the provision of Advance Warning or Automatic Train Control systems. Installation of such invaluable warning equipment came about after the Slough accident in 1900. Although many railways dabbled and experimented in its introduction, only the Great Western Railway had the courage to begin a wide-scale implementation of this much needed safety measure; their subsequent accident record demonstrates that their faith and expenditure was not misplaced. Elsewhere the issue dragged on through the pre-Grouping and Grouped eras, and it was not fully resolved until long after nationalisation of the railway network in 1948. Installation of the equipment took much, much longer, with 70 years elapsing from Slough before anything like a near satisfactory national system was in operation. Whilst ATC/AWS is a classic case of not learning, some lessons were learnt much more quickly.

Derailments were a frequent cause of accidents, as we note in the example of Staplehurst in 1865 when a train carrying the great Charles Dickens was derailed and part of it fell in to the River Beult killing ten people; this incident so badly affected the novelist that he was never the same man again. Problems were also experienced with runaway trains, such as the accident which resulted when a rake of coal wagons escaped from Honley station in the West Riding of Yorkshire on 17th June 1858. The wagons ran out of control for 6 miles before they collided with a Leeds-Manchester train at Springwood Junction near Huddersfield, a third-class brake coach took the full force of the impact and three passengers lost their lives with a further 11 being seriously injured. Eight years later a similar problem occurred at Round Oak, but this time it was a passenger train which ran away and 14 passengers died. The most infamous runaway however occurred at the start of our 'Hundred Years Of Railway

Accidents' when a simple sequence of events led to what was the greatest loss of life in a railway accident up to that time.

On the morning of 20th August 1868 a pick-up goods train called at the Flintshire Oil Works at Saltney near Chester, where two loaded wagons were awaiting collection. Each wagon contained 25 casks of paraffin, giving a combined load of nearly 8 tons of fuel. The train picked up more trucks along the way, and when it left Abergele at 12.15pm it was comprised of 43 wagons. At 12.24pm, having reached Landulas, a decision was taken to shunt the train, but there was insufficient room to fit it into the Llysfaen Lime Sidings in one go. However, by dividing the train it was felt that there was sufficient room to shunt it clear, but the station-master ordered some more movements to be carried out even though the down Irish Mail was imminently due. This was in strict contravention of the LNWR's standing rules which stated 'Goods trains when likely to be overtaken by a passenger train must be shunted at stations where there are fixed signals at least ten minutes before such a passenger train is due.' The freight engine now began to move three timber wagons out of the sidings, leaving a brake van and 6 wagons standing on the main line without their brakes having first been pinned down. As the main line had a gradient of 1:147 which increased to 1:100 nearer Abergele, the potential for disaster should have been really obvious! The movement of the timber wagons involved a manoeuvre known as fly-shunting, which was a far from accurate procedure that involved a brakesman running alongside the wagons to drop their brakes. Sadly the man failed to accomplish this and the timber trucks cannoned into the unbraked wagons standing on the main line which, in turn, overcame the hand-brake on the guard's van. The force of the impact started the stationary wagons rolling down the incline with the timber trucks following close behind; the freight train driver decided to give chase to try and catch them up, but to no avail. Down the incline the trucks rolled, gathering speed as they entered a long sweeping curve! One and three quarter miles west of Abergele the Irish Mail was storming up the grade at 40mph. The runaways smashed into the passenger train and the casks of paraffin were strewn around the site, quickly igniting when their contents made contact with the hot coals that spilled from the locomotive's firebox. Thirty-two passengers died in the conflagration which followed, as it was then common practice to lock coach doors before trains departed from a station. The passengers thus had no means of escaping. The inspector was critical of the whole operation, yet just five years later the whole thing was repeated at Stairfoot, near Barnsley, but this time the disaster was not attended by fire.

Despite extensive research we have been unable to find suitable illustrations of the accident at Abergele, as the bulk of 'news' pictures around this time were merely line drawings and lithographs, of the type made famous by the *London Evening News*. However, as the 1860s drew to their end photography became more common, and our last section in this preliminary introduction is a classic example of an early railway accident picture. The issue of an engine's ability to stay on the track, was one of the great arguments in the battle of the gauges. It had been long contended that Brunel's broad gauge was more stable than the 4' 8½" gauge promoted by the Stephenson's (and others) which later became the standard gauge. The statistics tend to confirm the argument for broad gauge as, mile for mile, the standard gauge systems had substantially higher derailment figures. The stability of the broad gauge was dramatically illustrated on 5th November 1868, when the GWR locomotive *Rob Roy* smashed into the back of a cattle train at Awse Junction near Newnham but, as our picture shows, it remained reasonably upright. By way of contrast, many of the illustrations which follow will clearly show us what could happen when a standard gauge engine overturned even at a relatively slow speed. Yet the battle of the gauges was eventually won out in favour of 4'8½", but as we will see in those early years locomotives built to this gauge were inherently susceptible to derailment when they met with any solid object.

BOILER EXPLOSIONS 1840 - 1909

PICTURE ABOVE *The ferocity and devastating power of un-harnessed live steam is clearly demonstrated in this picture of NER No.218 which exploded at Holbeck station, near Leeds on 27th July 1875. The 2-4-0 has been literally ripped apart and as it stands at the old Leeds Northern Railway works, the power behind this blast is clearly depicted.* PHOTOGRAPH; THE LATE KENNETH HOOLE COLLECTION

It might seem incredible to report that in the early days of railways, one of the most common group of accidents is notable by the fact that locomotives literally blew themselves to bits. Whilst man had harnessed steam for motive power, it remains arguable that he had not fully realised the tremendous potency of live steam and the dangers it posed. Construction of those early boilers was, to say the least, haphazardous and their subsequent maintenance was even worse. Then, when it came to operation, further dangers were introduced by drivers and firemen tampering with safety valves in an attempt to optimise their locomotive's performance. Some years ago, whilst on a visit to the spring manufacturing company George Salter of West Bromwich, I was shown one of their early boiler safety valves. At the top of the valve a knurled nut was provided to make minor adjustments. On inspection it was only too evident that such a device could easily be used to increase boiler pressure in an attempt to 'improve' the performance of the early, under-powered locomotives. Sadly, such tampering quite often led to frightening incidents. Just a few miles from Salter's factory stands Bromsgrove station, which is located at the foot of the infamous Lickey Incline and where, in November 1840, an awful explosion occurred. Although we have no proof that the two enginemen had tampered with the safety valve on their experimental engine named *Eclipse*, such practices were common amongst crews working the Lickey. Sadly no-one knows because both enginemen lost their lives and were buried in the local church-yard. A more readily proven case of safety-valve tampering is recorded at Hemerdon Incline on the South Devon Railway in June 1849, where a broad gauge engine *Goliah*[sic] suffered a collapsed firebox crown after its valves were screwed down to release at more than twice the normal working pressure. Yet it was not just safety valve problems which caused boiler explosions, as corrosion and wear also took their toll in days when boiler examinations were nowhere near as frequent as they ought to have been. On 8th July 1861 a locomotive exploded whilst running near Newbold Revel with the Irish Mail at 40 mph, killing the fireman as a result. From the remains of the fragments which showered Easenhall Bridge it was discovered that the boiler barrel had worn down to no more than 1/16" thick. Although it had been re-tubed just three years earlier, no-one had noticed (or acted on) the corrosion to the barrel. The locomotive boiler which blew up at Westbourne Park in November 1862 had not been examined in seven years, whilst that on the Midland Railway locomotive which exploded at Colne in May 1864 had seen its boiler pressure *officially* raised to 140lbs. Just four days after this incident, a Great Northern engine succeeded in not only blowing itself up, but demolishing the entire roof and footbridge at Farringdon Street station; examination revealed that the boiler barrel was 'little thicker than an egg-shell.' Whilst this is by no means an exhaustive list of early boiler failures, it is representative. The problems were addressed in a number of ways, for example stronger plate steel became available through the Bessemer and Seimen manufacturing processes, so corrosion gradually became less of a problem.

PICTURE LEFT *Remaining with the North Eastern we travel a few miles north of Leeds, to Alne on the East Coast Main Line. In 1877 0-6-0 No.510 was working a Darlington - Normanton freight train when it stopped at Alne station to take on water from the column at the end of the platform. As it stood there its boiler suddenly exploded and parts of the engine were thrown as far as 539 feet (164.5 metres) from where it had been standing. With its twisted tubing showing like the entrails of a disembowelled animal, the 0-6-0 stands outside Darlington Works awaiting attention.*

PHOTOGRAPH; THE LATE KENNETH HOOLE COLLECTION

Picture Above *Despite the introduction of tamper-proof safety valves it was still common practice amongst enginemen to rig the valves so that they did not blow off until the boiler was at a much greater pressure than they were intended to operate at, and thereby improve their engine's performance. This was commonly seen on freight workings, where drivers would do all that they could to squeeze an extra few pounds of tractive effort from their locomotive. The habit died hard, but in its continued practice many enginemen also died as their charges blew up around them. A typical case in point is the disaster at Lewes on 27th September 1879, when LBSCR No.174 blew up in the station. The 2-4-0 was hauling the London - Hastings passenger train and had just got the 'right-away' when the firebox suddenly blew-up. The exploding locomotive showered the station with boiling water, steam, soot, coal and ballast as it was blown off the rails whilst its smokebox door shot across the tracks. The body of the unfortunate driver was thrown forcefully on to the roof of the second coach, but his fireman survived although he was severely injured, as was the train's guard who was caught by flying debris. On examination it was discovered that the safety valves had been reset to blow off at 140lb when the limit was 120lb psi, the pressure the explosion had actually occurred at.*
Photograph; The late Arthur Trevena Collection

Picture Right *The graves of Driver William Scaife and Fireman Joseph Rutherford lay side by side in Bromsgrove Church, as close together in death has they would have worked in life. The illustrations on the tombstones depict the American 4-2-0 Norris locomotives which were built for the Birmingham & Gloucester Railway by Norris of Philadelphia. However, these engines are incorrectly depicted here, as Scaife and Rutherford's engine was not of this type.*
Photograph; H.M. Lidell

Coupled to manufacturing advances came more frequent boiler examination and hydraulic testing, so boilers gradually became much safer. A new type of safety valve devised by Ramsbottom at Crewe brought even greater improvement as, theoretically, these new valves could not be tampered with. Even so, when errors were made in maintenance, such as on the Rhymney Railway in 1909, engine boilers could still blow up with disastrous results. We will discuss another such incident, a boiler explosion at Buxton in greater detail later, but for now the accompanying pictures will serve to illustrate how railways were still suffering fifty years after their inception.

THE TAY BRIDGE DISASTER

North British Railway
28th December 1879

Whilst mechanical requirements were being addressed in the fields of locomotives and rolling stock, major problems were being tackled in the field of civil engineering. Bigger and more ambitious projects were being promoted, in an era of what can only be called incredible optimism. Naturally, the successful projects bestowed great accolades upon their engineers and designers, and none was more favoured than Thomas Bouch who received a knighthood from Queen Victoria for his work on the bridge across the Firth of Tay. Unfortunately, his short period of glory was soon to turn to tragedy and vilification.

Our story begins on the last week of 1879, when an off-shore gale raging in the North Sea was sending ships scurrying to the safety of the ports. On the morning of Sunday 28th December, the wind turned and the gale began blowing hard inshore. By the early evening wind speeds had reached well over 80 mph and passengers on the afternoon service to Dundee had to face the rigours of a rough crossing over the Forth to Burntisland. A North British 4-4-0 express locomotive, No. 224, conveyed them northwards, stopping at St. Fort station at around 7pm for a ticket inspection. In addition to the crew of six, 69 passengers remained on board as the driver collected the token for crossing the single line bridge from the St. Fort signalman. Hindsight tells us that the train should have been held at this point whilst the wind subsided, but it was allowed to go on even though the ferocity of the gale was so great that the signalman had to crawl back to his 'box on all-fours after handing over the token. Into the very teeth of the storm No.224 went on, but as it climbed towards the centre section the signalman noticed sparks coming from beneath the train wheels. Just then a sudden gust of even greater strength swept up the estuary, and when he looked again the train was no longer to be seen. When the block instruments went dead, he hoped against hope that No. 224 had made the other side. Meanwhile anxious officials in Dundee, concerned about the non-arrival and the sudden loss of the telegraph, prayed that the train was still on the south shore. About 10pm a steamer managed to battle across the Tay, and the worst fears were confirmed.

The extent of the disaster was revealed at first light, when it was seen that three whole sections of the high bridge had fallen into the swirling waters of the Tay taking the train and all the souls aboard with it. If the death of the passengers was instantaneous, then that affecting Sir Thomas was not - it was to linger slowly and painfully for the next ten months. He, as designer, was made the scapegoat and received the villification and ostracism associated with it. He was pilloried at the public enquiry, and though many historians now feel that he only deserved a fraction of the blame, the damning report said: "We find that the bridge was badly designed, badly constructed, and badly maintained and that its downfall was due to inherent defects in the structure which

Picture Left
Viewed shortly after the accident, the high girders of Bouch's Tay Bridge lay in the waters of the firth imprisoning inside them the wrecked remains of the 5.20pm from Burntisland. It is in stark contrast from 27th June 1879, when the bridge was crossed in triumphant procession by Queen Victoria on her return from Balmoral.

Picture Below Left
This view shows the remains of the 4-4-0 express locomotive, No. 224, which might be said to be one of the unluckiest victims of the Tay Bridge Disaster. This engine had been pressed into working the 5.20pm service in place of the normal 0-4-2T 'Ladybank' which had broken down. In due course No.224 was repaired, but as it began to suffer freak, unexplainable minor accidents, drivers would have nothing to do with it. It was much the same on transfer to Edinburgh, where it was given the unofficial name The Dipper. *With the reluctance of Scottish drivers to work this engine growing as its catalogue of minor accidents continued, No. 224 was transferred to the Waverley line, but once again it was difficult to get Scottish crews to work the engine. It then moved back to the ECML route, but no driver would take her across the Tay until one brave man ran her across the new bridge into Dundee on 28th December 1908, 28 years to the day since it fell into the waters below. Following its relegation to more menial duties No.224 became widely employed on the Borders Counties Railway south of Riccarton where Englishmen were given the task of driving it. Ironically, the engine was to suffer two major (though non-serious) derailments in the years which followed, but it was not scrapped until 1919.*

must sooner or later have brought it down. For these defects, both in design, construction, and maintenance Sir Thomas Bouch is in our opinion mainly to blame". However, many of the issues surrounding this accident have, to my mind at least, never received a satisfactory answer. Mysteries such as the 'comet-like' shower of sparks seen coming from the ill-fated train, have yet to be fully explained. Bouch contended that they were caused by a derailment of the rear coaches which he speculated had been blown off the tracks. He also presented information which showed that the Astronomer Royal had provided inaccurate wind-speed estimates, which turned out to be far lower than those which prevailed on the Forth at certain times. Furthermore he also pointed out that much of the cast-iron work was far below the standards he had set, but the magnitude of the defects in the girders was hidden from him by the foundry management who filled in the holes with putty and then covered them with paint. There was a further point which he also demonstrated, which showed that NBR drivers were racing across the bridge at speeds far higher than he (and the Board of Trade) had prescribed. Literally his already weakened bridge was being battered by train speeds and wind speeds which it was never designed for. Yet his arguments were dismissed at the Public Inquiry, even though there was good reason to give him the benefit of the doubt, as later events tended to show his theories about the disaster were probably right. In our subsequent accounts of a bridge failure at Norwood Junction, and high wind speeds at Owencarrow we will consider two of these issues again. However, both these happened later in railway history and too late for Sir Thomas. As a broken man he became another victim of both the Tay Bridge and Victorian optimism; he died at Moffat on 29th October 1880, just a few months after the enquiry ended.

PICTURE ABOVE *When the fallen girders from the Tay Bridge were eventually recovered from the Tay, it was found that they had fallen to the east side of the structure. They settled on their eastern face on the bed of the Firth of Tay, still with some of the coaches encapsulated within their framework. In this view the girders are standing on their side, with the base of the single track bridge standing vertically on the right. It is also worth mentioning that during the course of the construction that one section of the high girders had already fallen into the Tay and been badly buckled as a result, and this story is told in Volume 5 of* BackTrack *on pages 232 - 240, under the title, Sir Thomas Bouch, Hero or Villain.*

PICTURE LEFT *A collection of tickets which were gathered up by William Friend at St. Fort station just before the train crossed the ill-fated bridge. These were handed over to Robert Morris, and later used in a display to raise funds for the victims of the disaster.*

PICTURE INSET *The fob watch of the train guard which was recovered after the disaster.*

PHOTOGRAPHS: ALL THE LATE ARTHUR TREVENA COLLECTION

THE WYE VALLEY

Near Chepstow

Great Western Railway

16th February 1880

The route through the Wye Valley from Chepstow to Monmouth must be ranked as one of the loveliest of the lost Welsh lines. Today only a stub of the line remains from Wye Valley Junction to a quarry near Tidenham, to where it was cut back after the branch to Tintern Quarry closed a few years ago. The line north of Tintern closed in 1964, and this picturesque route faded into oblivion. Yet, along with its beauty and charm, there were hidden dangers on this heavily engineered line and on 16th February 1880 this feature resulted in a spectacular derailment. At 1pm the pick-up goods train to Chepstow departed from Monmouth and was just 1½ miles from its destination when it hit a huge boulder which had slipped on to the track. The rock was part of the foundations of a retaining wall on the Coleford, Monmouth, Usk & Pontypool Railway which had been built higher up the hillside. As the engine rounded a bend the driver and fireman failed to see the obstruction in their path and they hit it at a speed of around 32 mph. The open-cabbed engine derailed and overturned, pinning the driver beneath his charge, fortunately he was freed by members of the train crew and found not to be too badly injured. Interestingly, the engine which was already 10 years old at the time of the accident was taken back to the GWR's Wolverhampton Works and there rebuilt - it was to be good for another 50 years of service, and was not withdrawn until 1930. Today the site of the accident is just recognisable as a former railway line, and thanks to a friendly farmer we were able to visit the scene whilst on holiday in the area in the spring of 1996. Like so many scenes of disaster, little remains in evidence today at this tranquil pastoral scene where birds sing and butterflies flutter. Even the farmer who took us to the site had no idea that this was once the scene of a disaster.

PHOTOGRAPH; L&GRP COLLECTION

MARSHALL MEADOWS

North British and North Eastern Railways

10th August 1880

The operation of the Anglo-Scottish services along the East Coast Main Line fell to a consortium of three companies, these were the Great Northern, the North Eastern and the North British railways. By the last quarter of the 19th century the route was being transformed from a simple rail corridor, to a main trunk route where services were based on the cornerstones of speed, reliability, comfort and safety. Yet not all was as well as it seemed, for a series of financial shortages had resulted in a number of cut-backs and deferrals. In the year following the Tay Bridge Disaster the NBR were having a hard time of things one way or another, and what it could least do with was yet another serious accident, but this is exactly what happened at Marshall Meadows on 10th August 1880. On the day in question an ECML express was being worked south by NER 2-4-0 No.178, and it was running at speed just north of Berwick on Tweed. At the point where the railway entered a shallow cutting, work had been undertaken on a series of track problems which had been associated with water getting beneath the permanent way. Spot repairs had been carried out to pack 'pumping' sleepers and more comprehensive work was under way when the engine ran over the defective track at speed. The engine's wheels lifted from the track, and it became derailed within the narrow confines of the excavation. Thus derailed, the wheels bit deeply into the ballast and the train was slewed round violently. The coaches then piled up around the engine which was now coming to rest almost at right-angles to the track, and as they did so the wooden bodies split open killing the footplate crew and a guard who was riding as a passenger.

PHOTOGRAPH; THE LATE KENNETH HOOLE COLLECTION

SEVENOAKS

South Eastern Railway
7th June 1884

Having considered accident ingredients such as boiler explosions, civil engineering failures, track maintenance and driver error, we are now going to look at another of the most common ingredients in the field of railway safety; the issues concerning signalling and signalman error. To do this we move from the Scottish borders to the 'Garden of England', Kent where a fearful collision occurred at Sevenoaks (Tub Hill) station. At a little after 1.30am on 6th June 1884 the stillness of the night was suddenly shattered when a double-headed express goods train from Deal overtook, and then ran into the rear of a slow moving goods train. The circumstances which led to the accident were both curious and tragic, as they were responsible for the death of the footplate crew on the leading express engine. The slow goods was an up train from Folkestone which was booked to stop for water at Sevenoaks at 12.20am, but it had arrived there about an hour late. It was just coming to halt when the collision occurred, so there can be no doubt that the culprits were the signalmen who allowed the express-goods train to run forward at 25mph under clear signals. The Deal train, hauled by 0-6-0s, Nos. 1 and 294, was also late and had been due to pass Sevenoaks at 12.40am. Therefore, the crew of the leading engine, expecting the Folkestone train to have long since left, may have been anticipating a clear road. Yet even though the signals were off, the tail-lights of the near-stationary train could have been seen at a distance of 600 yards and this should have been more than ample time for a diligent crew to make an emergency brake application.

The investigation reached the opinion that the collision was due to a mistake by a signalman at Hildenboro', who omitted to send the proper block signal for the Folkestone train and; that his error was compounded by the signalman at Sevenoaks No. 2 cabin, who should have been more prompt in putting his signals to danger after this train passed him. Prior to this collision, the SER had largely been accident-free for a long period, but this was in no way thanks to its signalling system which the report considered as highly unsatisfactory. The practice of clearing the line directly a train arrived, and then leaving it clear for the next one, as opposed to adopting the more universal policy of setting signals at danger behind a passing train was, the Inspector concluded, likely to lead to accidents. The inter-locking of signals and telegraph equipment employed on the system was also subject of adverse criticism.

ABOVE *The two 0-6-0s of the express-goods train derailed at Sevenoaks, with No. 294 and the tender of No. 1 pitched over onto their sides. Number 1 was re-boilered as a result of this collision, but it was withdrawn just six years later in 1890, whilst number 294 (just five years old) at the time of the accident, lasted until 1909.*
PHOTOGRAPH; THE LATE ARTHUR TREVENA COLLECTION

BELOW *General view of the scene, looking over Tub Hill station with wreckage of the Folkestone goods train brake van scattered across the platforms. The guard in this van saw the express over-taking his train and was able to jump out in time.*
PHOTOGRAPH; SOUTHERN RAILWAY OFFICIAL COLLECTION, COURTESY KENT LIBRARY SERVICE.

PENISTONE; BULLHOUSE COLLIERY

Manchester, Sheffield & Lincolnshire Railway 16th July 1884

On 16th July the 12.40pm from Manchester to London and Grimsby was running down through the Don Valley towards Sheffield when it was suddenly derailed at Bullhouse Colliery two miles west of Penistone. A Cheshire Lines Committee horse-box behind the engine remained upright, but the five GNR coaches which formed the London portion (and came next) were all thrown down a steep embankment and wrecked. The next five vehicles were MS&L coaches bound for Grimsby, and these suffered less severe damage from the derailment. Nineteen passengers were killed on the spot and five more died later in hospital, the last lingering in a critical condition until 6th August. A further 64 people were injured, many of them seriously, so it became of vital importance to discover what it was that caused the derailment of the Gorton-built 4-4-0, No.434. A detailed examination revealed that the Retford-based engine was suffering from an unseen fracture in the crank-axle, which engineering techniques of the day would have been hard pressed to detect. Actually, failures of this kind were problems which occurred with more frequency than might be otherwise assumed (247 in 1883 alone) but such fractures usually occurred without any serious mishap.

Unfortunately, a combination of speed (about 50 mph), gradient (1:124) and track radius (40 chains) all combined to deadly affect and exploited the mechanical defect in a most catastrophic way. When the fracture came, it could not have occurred in a worse possible location as a long, low embankment lay dead ahead. As the damaged running gear of the engine broke up the permanent way behind it, the speed of the train, the incline and the curvature of the track all served to catapult the unfortunate train down the left-hand side of the embankment. It was a true accident, which even the Inspector had to conclude 'was one which could not have been foreseen or prevented'. The growing flaw in the web of the crank could have been detected by the spectographic or ultra-sonic examinations which are common-place within the engineering world today, but back then it was a case of visual examination. As a consequence of Bullhouse, the Inspector recommended more stringent inspections for moving parts such as crank-axles; this took the practical application of taking down locomotives' big-ends on a weekly basis, rather than at the

monthly inspection as had previously been the practice. There also came the telling words that this 'should lead locomotive engineers to consider carefully the relative advantages of engines with inside cylinders and crank-axles, as compared with engines with outside cylinders and straight axles; of steel axles as compared with iron axles; and of cranks hooped with wrought-iron bands, as compared with having the additional strength provided by an increase of metal in the webs of the crank itself.' From the adversity, tragedy and heroism that were experienced at Bullhouse, the railways would become a significantly safer place as new technology was applied to rectify problems of fast-moving metal parts. Even so, disaster was not to be eliminated from the railways around Penistone, and less than a year later another serious accident befell the MS&LR on 1st January 1885. Whilst that accident is not covered in this book, we must regretfully remain at Penistone for our next accident.

PHOTOGRAPHS: ALL THE LATE ARTHUR TREVENA COLLECTION

PENISTONE

Manchester, Sheffield & Lincolnshire Railway 30th March 1899

The third disaster at Penistone occurred on 30th March 1889, when an excursion train was derailed in circumstances curiously similar to the Bullhouse tragedy and just less than five years later. In view of this it seems opportune to take this accident out of chronological sequence, and look at the events which claimed one passenger's life and injured 61 others. This time the mechanical failure was the fracture of the leading axle of engine No. 188, in which had developed a large crescent-shaped flaw on the seat of the left wheel. This flaw had grown in the 619,414 miles that the engine had run since it was built, but another, smaller flaw was also found on the shoulder seat of the right wheel. Both of these flaws might have been detected if the wheels had been removed at No. 188's previous overhaul, just three months earlier but this was not done and the axle subsequently failed as the up special from Liverpool/Southport to King's Cross left Dunford Bridge station. Actually, the engine quickly rerailed itself on a set of trailing points, but it was smashing the rail chairs as it went along. As No. 183 drew its train of 19 coaches through Huddersfield Junction at the east end of the station, an alert signalman saw sparks coming from the front of the train and he threw all his signals to danger. He thought that the engine was obviously trailing some component or other, but before the crew could bring No.188 to a complete halt it had pitched off the rails and 17 coaches were derailed. Thankfully the signalman's alert action helped the excursion train driver realise that something was quite wrong. Having slowed and drastically reduce his speed in accord with the signals, he was thus better able to take preventative action in the sequence of events which followed. In addition, by throwing all his signals to danger he was able to warn the driver of a down mail which was approaching at speed. Although this train smashed into the wreckage, it did so at a very low speed and was relatively unharmed. As will be imagined, several aspects of this accident were uncannily similar to those in the 1884 accident; meanwhile Penistone is a location to which we will return yet again. Sadly, this was only one of the many MS&L's troubles in this part of the country, for on 16th September 1877 they had sustained a serious accident at Hexthorpe when the driver of a Manchester - Hull train overran signals which were set at danger. Having done this it then crashed into the rear of a special Doncaster Races' train which was standing at a ticket, platform killing 25 people as a result.

PHOTOGRAPH; BARNSLEY METROPOLITAN COUNCIL LIBRARY & ARCHIVE SERVICE

WATH

Midland Railway
27th August 1887

Throughout *Trains In Trouble*, we will come across a number of accidents caused by trains over-running boards (signals), and from this we might conclude that it was not an isolated phenomenon. Indeed, as we will see later with the Cudworth accident, two such incidents occurred on the Midland Railway just a few miles apart in South Yorkshire inside a few years. It was however, an even more common occurrence than the accident statistics suggest, as trains 'slid past the boards' all too often. This was a serious offence as far as the railways were concerned, and drivers were fined heavily for such infringements of the rules. As these offences carried a fine and a disciplinary caution on the driver's record card, many went unreported, particularly where a signalman took the view that 'no harm had been done' and did not enter the error in his train register. Yet when these offences led to accidents, the results were usually spectacular as the first of our two Midland accidents in South Yorkshire reveal. This was at Wath-on-Dearne, where a six-coach passenger train overran the boards and smashed into the rear of a Leeds-bound 33-wagon coal train as it was being shunted to allow the express to pass.

As the freight train was being set-back the leading draw-bar on the 22nd wagon broke, the train became divided and the series of events which followed led to 17 passengers and five railwaymen sustaining nasty injuries. After the train had broken in two, the guard made a hand signal to the 'box, which the Wath station signalman took to mean that they had cleared the Manvers Main section and he sent the 'out of section' signal. Manvers Main then offered him the express, but he did not accept it and kept both his distant and home signals 'on'. As the crew of the coal train tried to re-couple the damaged private-owner wagon with a tail-rope, the express was leaving the Wath Road section at a speed of about 45 mph. Unfortunately, the driver of the express was not keeping a proper look-out, and as a consequence he overran the Manvers Main distant signal which had also been kept 'on'. The driver of this engine, No. 51, was occupied in teaching a young 'passed-cleaner' how to fire the engine and he was not aware of the danger until the signalman shouted to him as he steamed past Manvers Main 'box. When he realised his error he got his steam-brake fully on and managed to get the engine into reverse gear, but the train slid past Wath distant signals and it was now too late to prevent the collision. The engine smashed through the brake van and the last coal truck, before mounting the next two vehicles. The spectacular results of the collision are captured in the photograph, though in view of the speed of the light-weight express it is very fortunate that no-one was killed. The express driver was clearly at fault, but the guard of the freight train was censured for not shunting his train earlier. Meanwhile, the signalman and station-master at Wath were criticised for not sending the 'obstruction danger' signal when the train became divided. The signalman at Manvers Main was also reprimanded for accepting the express from Wath Road, when he could clearly see that the coal train was standing on the main line.

PHOTOGRAPH; NATIONAL RAILWAY MUSEUM

CHEVINGTON

North Eastern Railway
25th October 1887

The theme of drivers missing signals is continued in our next accident which occurred at Chevington, where we come across a classic case of self-delusion. On many occasions throughout railway history, accidents have occurred because drivers believed themselves to have a clear road even when they hadn't. The rules and regulations make no provision for passing a signal at danger, but what is the case if driver misses a signal or is unable to see it? Well, the rule book clearly states that if signal is not observed, it must be treat as though it were at danger! The incident we now discuss considers this very issue, in the case of an Amble Branch train which worked north along the ECML behind a new NER 2-4-2T, No.469. The last station on the main line before the Amble branch junction was Chevington, and the train had to pick up two cattle wagons for Amble which had just been dropped off a down goods train. This goods train was crossed to the up line to allow a down passenger to pass it, and then the branch train was set back through the cross-over to pick up the cattle vans. The procedure was carried out under signals set against other traffic on the main line, but a late-running Tweedmouth - Heaton goods behind 0-6-0 No.934 ran past all the signals and collided with the engine of the goods train, driving this back into the branch train and forcing its coaches to overturn against the platform. When interviewed, the driver of the offending freight train said he had expected to have a clear road through Chevington as he usually had!

PHOTOGRAPH; THE LATE KENNETH HOOLE COLLECTION

HAMPTON WICK

London & South Western Railway
6th August 1888

Another accident occurred the following August at Hampton Wick station, following a signalman's error. The scene was the Kingston Loop of the LSWR which runs from New Malden Junction to Twickenham and had two intermediate junctions, a double one at Strawberry Hill where the Shepperton branch diverged, and another at Kingston for the goods depot. Just to the west of Kingston Junction the line crosses over the River Thames, after which it shortly enters the station at Hampton Wick. Just before midnight, on 6th August 1888 the signalman sent a 'light' engine, No. 484, on the the wrong line from the junction to Twickenham. Meanwhile, running towards Kingston, bunker-first, was sister engine No. 486. Working the 10.50pm down passenger train from Waterloo, the 14-coach local was just slowing down in preparation for its penultimate stop at Hampton Wick when the two bogie tank engines collided head-on at the north end of the station. Both were badly damaged in the violent collision, the light engine being embedded under the bunker of the passenger train. The fireman of No. 486 was killed instantly and his driver was fatally injured, the passenger guard was seriously injured as was the driver of the light engine. The front five vehicles were badly damaged, claiming the lives of two passengers and seriously injuring 13 others. The leading coach, bird-cage brake van No. 96, mounted and telescoped into the following vehicle, Third-class coach No. 728. The next three, all composite carriages, Nos. 2, 269, and 509, were all extensively damaged.

The accident was attributed to four specific causes:

1. the primary cause was the signalman's error, which was then compounded by;
2. the lack of attention by the light engine crew who failed to notice they were on the wrong line;
3. poor signal installations at Kingston Junction; and finally,
4. the extreme length of time required to make the emergency bell-code as laid down in the L&SWR's signalling instruction.

Though I do not normally quote direct from newspapers of the day, I felt that the report in the *Surrey Comet* provided an adequate example of the more than graphic comments that have had to be read as part of the research for this book. 'When the collision occurred the lamps in most of the carriages were extinguished, and the groans of the dying and injured, the screams of the terrified imprisoned passengers, and the hissing noise of the escaping steam all combined to form a ghastly and heart-rendering scene.'

PHOTOGRAPH; BOROUGH OF RICHMOND ON THAMES LIBRARY SERVICE.

ARMAGH

Great Northern Railway of Ireland 12th June 1889

In our next incident we step outside mainland Britain to look at an odious series of events which led to a horrendous disaster. The fact that it happened in Northern Ireland is irrelevant, for it was born of a practice that was universal in its application throughout the British Isles; this was the division of trains when locomotives were unable to haul their loads up a gradient, a situation which usually led to half a train being left behind. It went on far more often than readers may realise in the early days of railways, but the dangerous practice was not quickly eradicated by any means. For example in 1850, a heavily loaded train run to celebrate the opening of the Huddersfield & Sheffield Junction Railway came to a halt midway through a tunnel and was unable to restart. The only option was to divide the train in half, so the front portion was taken on to Stocksmoor station with the intention that the engine would then return for the second half. One can only imagine the discomfort of those left behind in the tunnel for 25 minutes, but few would have realised that they had been left in a position which was far more dangerous than was immediately evident. As the coaches were left standing on a steep gradient the weak handbrakes had been supplemented by placing large stones across the rails in order to chock the wheels; if this sounds dangerous in theory it can be demonstrated that it was deadly in practice. Thirty nine years later another excursion train came to a stand on an incline at Armagh on the Great Northern Railway of Ireland.

The Newry & Armagh was a single track line worked by staff and ticket, but in common with many railways of the day, the absolute block system had not yet been introduced. Time-lapse working was in force and passenger trains were despatched at 10 minute intervals. It was not the most efficient of railways, and it had been repeatedly beset by financial problems. The line had opened as the independent Newry & Armagh Railway, and it was not absorbed in the GNoIR until 1879. It was also a steeply graded line with the route up to the summit at Dobbins Bridge as severe as 1:75 in places. On the day in question, the first excursion train which had to take this steep ascent was a 15-coach affair, with no less than 940 passengers. However, the driver who was sent from Dundalk arrived with only a four-coupled engine to pull this heavy load. The driver at once quarrelled with the station-master about this and said that he should have sent proper word to Dundalk so that they might have sent a six-coupled engine. The official in charge of running the train then intervened, and suggested that the engine of a second excursion be detached from its train and used to bank the first train up to Dobbins. In a temper because of the station-master's 'do it or else' attitude and snide comments, the driver declined the offer and stormed off back to his engine and began preparations for departure. All went well to start with and the engine had a good head of steam, but as it climbed the incline the load became insurmountable. Within sight of the summit, the train finally ground to a halt. Knowing that the second train was due from Armagh, the driver and the official finally decided to use this to assist them over the summit. The official ordered the guard to divide the train, but the handbrake was known to be very weak so stones were put behind the wheels to chock them. It should be stated at this time that the actual train brake worked considerably different to the 'fail-safe' way it has done throughout the 20th century, that is to say coming on automatically when the train-pipe was broken. In those days, when air was admitted to the pipe, it ceased to function completely. So, with only the handbrake in the rear guards van to hold them on the embankment, the front guard tried to lift the coupling between the the fifth and sixth coaches but the tension on this meant that he was unable to do so. To ease the pressure the driver let his train move back ever so slightly, but just as the guard lifted the coupling the train nudged the buffers of the stationary portion. It was only the slightest of bumps, but it was sufficient to set the rear portion rolling backwards. The rear guard tried screwing down the handbrake, whilst the front guard tried to re-couple the portions. The driver set back the front portion and the guard twice nearly succeeded in rejoining the train, but each time he tripped at the last minute. As the rear half of the train began to pick up speed re-coupling was no longer an option, so the front guard tried pushing stones under the wheels, but it was to no avail. No-one inside the train could help, as all the compartment doors had been locked at Armagh and the passengers were therefore imprisoned inside the runaway train. Some 1¼ miles further down the embankment the coaches met up with the second train from Armagh, and smashed violently in to it, hitting the engine with such force as to turn it over on to its right-hand side, whilst its rake of coaches broke into two. The rear portion of the second train now ran away, but prompt action by the crew prevented a tragedy of an even greater magnitude and the coaches were brought safely to a halt. The ten rear coaches of the first train were by no means anywhere near as fortunate, and they smashed up around the engine of the second train, or over-turned down the 40 foot high embankment. Eighty people died as a result, a number of which tragically included several young children who's day out had turned to disaster. Yet out of adversity is born improvement, and within a few months two fundamental railway safety practices, absolute block working and the continuous automatic brake, were made law. The victims of Armagh had not died in vain.

PHOTOGRAPH; THE LATE ARTHUR TREVENA COLLECTION

NORTON FITZWARREN

Great Western Railway 11th November 1890

In the course of this book we will come across many cases of signalmen forgetting trains which were standing in their section, and subsequently allowing another train on to the same piece of line. Such mistakes were more common than might be appreciated, particularly during the hours of darkness or fog. A classic example of this was witnessed on 11th November 1890 on the GWR's dual gauge main line at Norton Fitzwarren in Somerset. The day was just thirty minutes old when a narrow (standard) gauge down goods train arrived at Norton Fitzwarren with a broad gauge pilot locomotive, which was duly detached and stabled on the Devon & Somerset branch until the goods train was ready to go on. The shunting operation took nearly three-quarters of an hour, and when it was completed the goods train was shunted through a cross-over onto the up main line in order to allow a fast down goods go through at 1.17am. The driver of the stationary goods train decided to change his head lamp from red to green, as he assumed that the signalman would 'give him the road straight away.' However, some seven minutes later they were still standing on the wrong road with their headlamp showing green, when the crew heard a train coming down Wellington Bank.

Having completely forgotten that the goods train was on the up main, the signalman gave 'Line Clear' for a special fast passenger train from Plymouth to Paddington at 1.19am. Comprised of a broad gauge engine, a van and two 8-wheeled coaches, the train was conveying 50 passengers who had alighted from a mail ship which had just arrived from the Cape of Good Hope (South Africa), it was racing down the bank at 60 mph. It met the stationary engine head-on with an extraordinary force, and the body of the leading coach (No.302) was completely smashed in and torn from its frames. Only one compartment escaped unscathed and ten people were killed as a result. The crew of the express, although seriously injured, escaped alive as their engine remained upright on the rails; once again demonstrating the superiority of the broad gauge when it came to the prevention of overturning. The signalman openly admitted his fault, explaining that he had thought the goods train to be in a siding. It was further revealed that he suffered from bad headaches following an incident the previous January, when he had been knocked down by a light engine. On the evening in question he said that he was worse than usual! Could this have been a contributory cause to his lapse of memory? With the benefit of hindsight and with a greater medical understanding of similar head injury cases today, this would seem quite likely!

The driver of the goods engine was also to blame for changing his headlamp to green, and it was clearly evident that it was the responsibility of both driver and the signalman to ensure that an engine did not stand 'wrong road' on a main line for seven whole minutes. To prevent this problem Rule 55 had been devised, and as it has a direct bearing on many of the accidents which follow, it is worth recording the basic principles of this rule. *When a train has been brought to a stand owing to a stop signal being at Danger, the driver must sound the engine whistle, and, if still detained, the Guard, Shunter or Fireman must go to the signal box and remind the Signalman of the position of the train, and insert in the Train Register "Rule 55" the line on which his train is standing, and sign his name against the entry with the time it is made, which entry must be initialled by the signalman. He must then remain in that signal box until permission is obtained for that train to proceed. In clear weather a train must not stand for more than two minutes at a stop signal before the man goes to the signal box but during fog or falling snow the man must at once proceed to the signal box.* Subsequent additions were made to Rule 55 as the years passed, progressively refining the conditions by imposing additional regulations as accidents revealed new elements which required legislating upon. By the time that the British Railways Standard Rule Book was published in 1950, Rule 55 was to occupy some eleven pages and therefore became the largest of the rules contained therein. Sadly we shall meet many cases where it was either ignored or not applied, so in these cases the signalman needed something else remind him of a train's presence. The Inspector, Colonel Rich, recommended 'train waiting' reminders in the form of either collars, loops, slide bars or wedges which could be slipped over his levers to act as visible reminders. Although Norton Fitzwarren, brought about this new innovation which was both inexpensive and easily applied, it was one of those suggestions which many railway companies failed to adopt, notably the Midland, and they would pay the price for this at Hawes Junction in 1910. Interestingly, one very unusual piece of railway history emerges from the report into this accident; in as much as it is commonly believed that even where the GWR had a mixed gauge line, the trains which ran upon it were either broad or narrow gauge and were never mixed. Such a view is of course completely logical as there would have been severe problems, such as difficulties with the drawbar and buffer-locking, in the operation of mixed trains. Nevertheless, the official report into the accident shows that mixed trains were run, and in the absence of any adverse comment from Colonel Rich on this matter, we can surmise that this may have been a more widespread practice than previously believed.

PHOTOGRAPH; L&GRP COLLECTION, COURTESY DAVID & CHARLES LTD.

CAMBORNE

Great Western Railway
9th March 1891

As adverse weather seriously affects our roads today, so it has done with railways over the centuries. An fascinating example, which would probably have had serious ramifications for a standard gauge locomotive was the derailment of a GWR 4-4-0T in 1891. The first week of March that year offered a promise that winter was at last drawing to an end, particularly when a warm front brought in unseasonably hot weather from the Atlantic. Yet it was just a facade, for on Sunday 8th March one of the greatest blizzards of all time swept across the South-west of England. It snowed hard that Sabbath day, and it did not let up on the Monday, with the consequence that drifts up to 20 feet deep blocked the Devon lanes. In the rough seas off the Cornish coast, fishermen froze to death in their tiny open boats. By the evening of the second day hardly a train was moving, and very few had managed to get through to Plymouth. Two down express - the 'Zulu' and the 'Flying Dutchman' - were both seriously delayed. The trouble was that no-one knew what the exact situation was because the telegraph system was down at Tavistock due to the snow, whilst at Dawlish Warren rough seas had washed away all the poles. Now the progress of these trains was a matter of priority, as the Duke of Edinburgh was aboard the 'Dutchman' en-route for Devonport. To relieve pressures on the down services, a relief 'Dutchman' was formed up behind broad-gauge saddle tank *Leopard* and despatched westwards from Plymouth. It arrived 40 minutes late at Truro, but it had to wait there until 9pm while the branch train battled its way up from Falmouth. By this time the snow was much worse, and as the relief train crossed the exposed mining districts west of Truro the carriages swayed from side to side to the alarm of the passengers. It crossed the moorlands at Carn Brea in safety, but as it neared Camborne the engine became derailed close to Stray Park Level Crossing. The engine left the metals and ended up against a hedge, but thankfully no-one was hurt. Due to what we might term 'white-out' conditions the guard was unsure as to the position of the derailment, so he set off alone to fetch help. Fortunately they were just 200 yards from the safety of Camborne station, or the accident may well have claimed him as a victim - not from injury but from exposure to the blizzard. The passengers were duly led from the snow-bound train and by 11pm all were safely accommodated in Camborne. The only fatality on the GWR during these horrendous storms was at Ivybridge where a platelayer was run over whilst he was engaged in rerailing a goods locomotive. However, elsewhere over 200 people died in Devon and Cornwall, the majority being aboard the 63 ships that were known to have sunk in the first 24 hours of the storm.

PHOTOGRAPH; DEREK HUNTRISS COLLECTION.

NORWOOD JUNCTION

London, Brighton & South Coast Railway
1st May 1891

In our discussion of the Tay Bridge Disaster we have lightly touched upon the fact that there were growing suspicions in the efficacy of cast-iron for railway bridges. Poor castings and financial problems in the foundry at Wormit, led to the use of highly dubious components in the Tay Bridge, but evidently this problem was not unique. A spate of serious bridge failures throughout the 1870s and 80s had already led to questions about the use of cast-iron, but (excluding the Tay Bridge) there had been few serious accidents as a consequence and the matter was not given the prominence which should have been attached to it. A typical example of the innocuous nature of cast-iron bridge failures was demonstrated on 1st May 1891 when LBSCR No.175 *Hayling* was derailed whilst crossing Portland Road at Norwood Junction. The 12-coach train was brought safely to a halt and the passengers detrained without any ill-effect. However, as clearing-up took place later in the day, the damaged bridge girder suddenly gave way and the last vehicle in the train fell vertically into the roadway below. Although its severity was considerably less than an accident which would have befallen a moving train, this one incident did far more than any other to prompt a nationwide review into cast-iron bridges. It is very interesting to read contemporary reports into how many lines enjoyed bridge renewal programmes in the subsequent decade, whilst the order books of iron foundries specialising in railway work seem to have swelled dramatically during the same period.

PHOTOGRAPH; R. C. RILEY COLLECTION.

LAVENHAM BANK

Great Eastern Railway
17th October 1891

We now move to the rustic countryside of rural Suffolk and the secondary line which ran from Marks Tey, near Colchester, to Cambridge and Bury St. Edmunds. Part of the line still exists today, but north of Sudbury the branch to Cambridge closed in March 1967, whilst the section from Long Melford to Bury St. Edmunds lost its passenger services six years earlier. In Great Eastern days, life on this railway must have been quite idyllic as little 0-4-4Ts pulled trains of 6-wheeled coaches over the lengthy route. One such train left Bury St. Edmunds at 4.05pm on Saturday 17th October, with a guard's brake, five coaches and an empty horse-box. It set off from Northgate station a good three minutes late, but it was a journey which was going to end in disaster for just half an hour later the engine had left the rails as it was going down an incline known as Lavenham bank. As it did so the tank engine turned a complete somersault, then tipped over on to its side and slid down the embankment it was travelling on. Fortunately no-one was badly hurt, and the only ones to suffer harm were the driver, fireman and guard who's injuries ranged from concussion to deep lacerations to their head and legs. None of the eight passengers in the coaches suffered any harm but a local JP who was travelling first class told reporters that this was his second serious railway accident in five years. He had been looking at the latest copy of *The Field* at the time his carriage went down the embankment, and afterwards he said that he found himself sat among the reeds 'still reading and wondering what ever next.'

The serious consequences that could have come from such an accident were considerably reduced by the prompt action of the guard, who was writing up his journal when he felt a bump at the front of the train. Realising they had become derailed, he quickly applied the Westinghouse brake and thereby prevented telescoping taking place, however the three coaches immediately behind the engine followed it down the 12 foot embankment and overturned. Though the guard had suffered head wounds, he set off walking to Long Melford station where he had a carriage attached to a goods engine in order to form the relief train. He returned to the scene about 5.40pm acting as the relief train's guard, intent on seeing his passengers arrive safely at Sudbury. Some three hours after the accident he finally set off to walk home, a journey of two miles. When he arrived there he was suffering badly from the loss of blood, so his wife called a local doctor to attend to his wounds. Yet this conscientious man's thoughts were still for others, as he solicitously enquired from the doctor after his mate the driver, and wondered 'however he would manage until he worked again on account of him having nine children to feed.' Because of the fact that there was no serious injury there was no necessity for the Board of Trade to order an enquiry by the Railway Inspectorate, and we are left guessing as to the probable causes of the accident.

Whilst we can only speculate into the causes, we have many other precedents upon which to base our assumptions. It is significant that the locomotive was a tank engine, and in addition it was being run with a driving axle leading, which is a situation that we can prove caused numerous accidents elsewhere. In view of the fact that tank locomotives placed an undue strain on the track, it would seem that in this case they probably took advantage of irregularities in the track; indeed, on this line the permanent way was not kept in a condition which permitted high speed running. Therefore it would appear likely that it was the combination of these two elements which came together to form this accident and all things considered, we might safely assume that as the engine was being run at speed down the 1:110 gradient, it either began 'hunting' or 'nosing' as it went along the track, causing the water to surge around the side tanks. This would, in turn thrust extra force on to the leading axle, which would then begin to cause damage to the track. If so, it was exactly the same type of accident which occurred at Crowborough in 1916, and it also bears chilling similarities to the events which we will encounter under much more serious circumstances as we examine accidents like Sevenoaks and Ashton-under-Hill.

PHOTOGRAPH; SUFFOLK RECORD OFFICE

ESHOLT, BRADFORD

Midland Railway
9th June 1892

In the history railway accidents, a number of incidents are recorded when trains were signalled into a section under the clause 'section clear but junction blocked' or 'junction clear but station blocked'. This was a dangerous enough situation if a driver was not alert, but on a number of occasions this clause was used to allow two trains to make an approach to the same section at the same time. Although, in theory, this movement could be carried out in safety, in practice it was an arrangement fraught with danger. On 9th June 1892 it worked out to be a deadly arrangement when a train from Ilkley to Bradford was struck by another train running from Leeds to Ilkley at Esholt Junction near Bradford. As the Leeds train, headed by 2-4-0 No.179, approached the junction the driver was allowed to come forward under the aforementioned clause (No.16), but as it did so the fireman was distracted by a blocked lubricator and the driver failed to see the signal which was partially obstructed by a brush. As a consequence it overran the signals and collided with the 3.10pm from Ilkley which was being hauled by 0-4-4T No.1642. One passenger died instantly, and four others were fatally injured, whilst 26 others were 'more or less seriously injured'. Both footplatemen of the Leeds train and its two guards were criticised for not keeping a good look out, but the bush was cut back and the signal subsequently re-sited. The Inspector also decided that due to this incident and a similar one at Birmingham, the Railway Companies would not be complying with the Regulation of The Railways Act 1898 if they allowed trains to simultaneously approach a junction under Clause 16.

PHOTOGRAPH; THE LATE ARTHUR TREVENA COLLECTION

MANOR HOUSE SIGNAL BOX, THIRSK

North Eastern Railway
2nd November 1892

We now move to the North Riding of Yorkshire, where we find one of the most tragic accident reports that were ever written, and one which stands as a severe indictment against the manner in which railway servants were then regarded by their employers. I refer to the tragedy of a signalman who allowed the up Scotch Express to collide into the rear of a stationary goods train that was stopped in his section. Although eight passengers and a goods guard were killed and 39 others injured, anyone who has read the account of this accident will quickly realise that although he had committed an act of severe negligence, the man was a hapless victim rather than a culpable perpetrator. His full story is told in a past issue of Atlantic's historic railway magazine *BackTrack* (Vol.8 No. 2), but in essence the sad story begins on the night of 31st October when the signalman's child was taken ill. By the following morning its condition was so bad that the signalman set off to find a local doctor, but he had gone off on his rounds so the man tramped around the countryside in an effort to find him. When he finally returned home he found his child had died, and his wife was so greatly distressed that he could not leave her alone. He then had a telegram sent to his mother in York to come on the train to stay with her; he next reported to the Otterington station-master requesting that he contact headquarters at York to arrange a relief as he felt quite unfit to go on duty. The station-master could see the truth of this statement and he duly sent a telegram to the Signals Inspector stating 'Can you send relief to Manor House tonight? [signalman's] child dead.' The reply came back with the brutal clarity stating that as no relief could be found he would have to carry out his obligations. Yet, this was an illogical decision in

view of the fact that the man had clearly indicated that he was not fit for duty, and considering that the lives of others rested upon his fitness, the NER were acting not only insensitively but negligently also. Resigning himself to his duty, he asked his mate in the Otterington 'box to let him know over the telegraph when his mother arrived, and then he set off to walk to work. Yet as he left he said 'I am just about done to start duty. I haven't been off my legs since 12 o'clock.'

We now move into the small hours of the foggy morning of 2nd November, with the exertions of the day compounding the previous night without sleep. It was small wonder that he was having a job of keeping awake, let alone managing to keep his emotions under control. That night the up Scotch Express was running in two parts as it was extremely well-patronised, the first leaving Edinburgh at 10.30pm. The second part was held for late-arriving connections from the north and it left 32 minutes later. The first part passed Manor House 'box without incident, following which he accepted an up goods train from Middlesbrough. As this train progressed into his section, the unfortunate man fell asleep and the goods train came to a halt at his signals only a few yards from the 'box. Yet, despite what should have been learnt about Rule 55 after Norton Fitzwarren, the crew of the freight engine sat there for seven minutes without making effort to go and report as they ought to have done. After dozing for about 13 minutes the signalman awoke, and very soon after he was offered the second part of the Scotch express by the man at Otterington. Finding his instrument still showed 'Train on Line' he thought that he had not cleared it after the first part of the express and he then unpegged his block instrument and gave the all clear to Otterington. He had completely forgotten the goods train, and as the express rushed into the section at 60mph under clear signals its driver had no chance of avoiding it. He saw the red brake light of the stationary goods train, shining dully through the fog at a distance of just 40 yards. The express engine turned over on to its side, and the first three vehicles came up hard against it. The first two were completely demolished, but whilst the Pullman Sleeping Car *India* in third place came off its bogies, its superior construction saved its occupants from all but the lightest of injuries. After forty minutes a fire started and this then consumed much of the wreckage, but by this time all the survivors had been detrained. The signalman was charged with the manslaughter of the goods guard and brought before the York Assizes where he was found guilty, thankfully the judge discharged him and the case set a precedent in the betterment of conditions for signalmen throughout the land. In the Report into the accident, not only was the unfortunate man found negligent, but so too were the crew of the goods engine and the Otterington station-master who it was said was not explicit enough in the telegram that he sent. However, the guilty ones were surely the railway companies themselves who forced men to work in, and subserviently accept, such hard conditions of service!

PHOTOGRAPHS: THE LATE KENNETH HOOLE COLLECTION

YETMINSTER AND CREECH

Great Western Railway
12th November 1894

In our record of railway accidents we have already come across two of the major elements (fog and snow) which have had a part in railway accidents, and we now meet the third - rain. Whilst exceptionally heavy rain was not a new phenomenon, the way it affected railways certainly was. Normally the problem of heavy rain was associated with bridge failures, track-bed washouts and landslides, in themselves all serious causes of accidents, but to these might be added another danger - flooding. Normally when tracks became submerged, it was the usual practice to suspend traffic until the waters receded, as deep water could come up through the ashpan and cause the firebox to blow out its contents on to the footplate. There are few recorded cases of such incidents in the Railway Inspectorate records, but many incidents of this sort occurred in the early days of the railways prior to the 1840 Act authorising investigations into the causes of accidents. The fact that few such troubles are recorded after this date seems to demonstrate that the lessons were quickly learnt, even so in some areas it became practice not to stop the trains unless the flooding was exceptionally heavy. As might be imagined, places like East Anglia, Lincolnshire and the Somerset levels were among those parts of the country where flooding was more common and people had become adept at handling the problems it presented.

We therefore present two pictures of heavy rains affecting the South-west of England in November 1894, the upper view showing the flooded track in Creech Cutting. With a depth approaching four feet, the 2-4-0 tank engine heads a train of mixed stock on what looks more like a canal than a railway line. This train made it safely to its destination but at Yetminster, a few miles to the south, the situation was quite different. At 5.20pm on Monday 12th November, GWR 2-4-0 No.720 left Weymouth with an up boat train. As it was 'out of season' the demand for connections to the Channel Isles was not particularly heavy, and the train was comprised of just four coaches and a milk van which was coupled next to the engine. On arriving at Yetminster the signalman warned the footplatemen of severe flooding in the Dorset/Somerset border country ahead. Having been instructed to 'proceed with the utmost care', the driver eased forward at a scant five miles per hour. However, he had gone just three-quarters of a mile when he encountered flood water which averaged a depth of somewhere between four and five feet. The driver now slowed down to a snail's pace and began to negotiate the floods but, unbeknown to him, the swirling floodwater had broken up the permanent way beneath its surface. At 6.31pm precisely the 2-4-0 canted over to the right and left the line, the milk van and leading coach were also derailed but they remained upright. The surge of water which was caused by the derailment made the firebox blow back, resulting in hot coals and scalding steam spraying across the footplate, injuring the two crew members. Fortunately the train had two guards, and they both plunged into the waters to see what they could do to assist. The driver was badly hurt, and whilst the fireman was less severely scalded, he had also suffered bad cuts to his face and scalp. It was decided that one guard should return to Yetminster for help, whilst the other would wade through the floods and make for Beer Hacket to seek assistance. None of the six passengers travelling on the train were hurt in anyway, as all were in the rear coach which stayed on its rails. A relief train was sent out from Yeovill and it arrived on the scene at 7.05pm, whereupon railway employees affected the rescue of the passengers by carrying them through the swirling waters on their backs. The following day the waters had receded and breakdown crews from Yeovill, Weymouth and Swindon recovered the coaches, but left No.720 laying against the embankment for a week. It was eventually retrieved from this position on 18th November, whereupon it was taken back to Swindon for repair.

PHOTOGRAPHS; D. C. VOSPER COLLECTION (ABOVE), AND NATIONAL RAILWAY MUSEUM (BELOW)

DOUBLEBOIS and ST. NEOTS

Great Western/Great Northern railways 13th April and 10th November 1895

We have seen with the accidents at Penistone how faults developed with individual locomotives in service, and in Lavenham Bank we have briefly touched upon actual design faults which affected entire classes of engines. Whilst this is a subject that has a complicated history, it is worth looking at a couple of accidents which well illustrate the dangers associated with badly designed locomotives. Having made assertions that the GWR's broad gauge locomotives were far superior to their standard gauge counterparts when it came to stability, we might well look at a couple of rather poor examples which came out of the Swindon stable. We begin with a class of 30 engines to a design by William Dean which commenced manufacture as dual-gauge engines, but were completed as narrow (standard) gauge engines. With 7 foot diameter single driving wheels, the engines had a 2-2-2 arrangement and weighed in at 44 tons. This seems to be a considerably heavy loading for such a wheel arrangement, and it turned out to be a contributory cause in the accident which befell one of the class in Box Tunnel in the autumn of 1893. Following the derailment of *Wigmore Castle* the whole class were withdrawn and rebuilt as 4-2-2s with extended frames. Another of Dean's classes, a batch of 20 0-4-2 narrow (standard) gauge tank engines were built at Swindon in 1887-8, but immediately upon entering service they began to display the nasty habit of swaying violently at speed. It was decided to rebuild them as 0-4-4s and use them to replace the broad gauge engines that were being withdrawn in the West Country. It was two of these engines that were involved in the accident at Doublebois on 13th April 1895, where it became evident that the improvements to the class had not eliminated their defects. The design element in this accident is clearly demonstrated, and a glance at the upper picture of No. 3458 will reveal the odd proportions of the engine. Taking the 5pm from Plymouth the train was heading between Doublebois and Bodmin Road at 50 mph when pilot engine No.3521 left the track quickly followed by No. 3458. The pilot engine ran on for about 100 yards then overturned where it met the slope of a cutting, No.3458 ended up leaning over to its side and at right angles to the track. On investigation it was found that the track had been badly damaged by the passage of the preceding train, which was drawn by two more members of the same class. The Inspector felt that it was the speed and oscillation of the engines which had led to both the damage and the derailment, and he emphatically pronounced that the class was totally unsuited for working fast express trains. As a consequence they were completely rebuilt and emerged from the works in a substantially different form.

It would of course be unfair to point the finger of blame solely at the GWR, as numerous companies experienced similar problems. One such railway was the GNR who were having problems with the majestic looking Stirling Singles. With their graceful lines and 8 foot diameter driving wheels, there was little to choose between these engines and their GWR counterparts in aesthetic terms. Yet, like those GWR engines the Stirling singles had a hidden defect, but it was one which was to strike twice in rapid succession. First at St. Neots on 10th November 1895, and then again the following March at Little Bytham as we will show on page 27. Ironically the first of these accidents took place the day before Patrick Stirling passed away, and it is perhaps fortunate that the great man did not see the blacker side of his design. Whilst the St. Neots accident was undoubtedly caused by a fault in the permanent way, the design of the engine played an important role. When the Report into the accident was published, the Inspector commented adversely on the abnormally heavy axle loading which existed on the single driving wheel. The fact that the weight on this axle was nearly 20 tons did not immediately sway the GNR to institute improvements, as the doubts over the track were more than sufficient grounds for them to procrastinate. Yet when the derailment of No.1006 which claimed two lives was echoed by the derailment of No.1003 just 156 days later, rebuilding had to follow.

PHOTOGRAPH; ABOVE, THE LATE ARTHUR TREVENA COLLECTION; LEFT, ST. NEOTTS MUSEUM

CHELFORD

London & North Western Railway 22nd December 1895

Before we look at the continuing problems with the GNR's Stirling singles, we must briefly return to the subject of runaways and obstructions on the main line, and to do this we travel to the tiny Cheshire village of Chelford. Passengers who travel on the former-LNWR Manchester - Crewe line a century later, may notice the seemingly insignificant station which is located roughly halfway between Stockport and Sandbach. Yet, the relatively quiet station which is still open today conceals the awful tragedy which happened there just over a hundred years ago. On 22nd December 1895, the 4.15pm up express left Manchester and headed towards Crewe in the face of a raging gale. It was made up of some 16 coaches, a mixture of 4-, 6- and 8-wheeled vehicles, drawn by a 2-4-0 'Jumbo' No.418 *Zygia* and No. 520 Express, a Webb split drive compound 2-2-2-0. At the same time as the express approached Chelford, shunting operations were being carried out by a pick-up goods train on the down side. In the course of the shunting, an empty wagon had been 'knocked back' on the down main line, and this had come to halt some 162 yards away. Unfortunately, a sudden gust of wind started the wagon rolling back up the slight incline towards the point where the shunting was being carried out. The run-away then fouled a rake of wagons being pushed back into the siding, and was derailed on to the up line. Despite the efforts of station staff, they were unable to warn the express and it hit the wagon at full speed, with the result that both engines were derailed. Midway along the platform there was a small ramp, which gave access to the barrow crossing. The two year-old 'Jumbo' had the misfortune to run up it, and mounted the platform, where it smashed into the signal box before rolling over on to the up line - badly injuring the footplate crew. Number 520 *Express* and the first four coaches were also derailed, but fortunately they remained upright. The next six coaches were all badly damaged, and the smashed remains were mixed up with the debris of the derailed wagons. This tragic accident was one which can be attributed to a caprice of nature, but nevertheless that sudden surge of wind accounted for the death of 14 passengers and occasioned injuries to 79 more.

PHOTOGRAPHS; NATIONAL RAILWAY MUSEUM

LITTLE BYTHAM

Great Northern Railway 7th March 1896

There are a number of accidents in the annals of railway history which, at the time of investigation had one apparent cause, but in reality had a much different set of origins; the accident which occurred at Little Bytham at 7.38 pm on 7th March 1896 was one such example. The train concerned was the 5.30 pm express from Leeds to King's Cross, which was comprised of seven passenger vehicles and one of the Stirling singles, No.1003 which had been built just 18 months earlier. As it was running south between mile posts 93 and 92, it encountered some seriously disrupted track and the rear portion became derailed in the region of the fourth and fifth carriages. In view of this the last two coaches were completely derailed, and the first vehicle of this rear portion smashed into the parapet of an under-line road bridge; the second vehicle (the last coach in the train) was catapulted down an embankment and came to rest in the roadway below as our picture shows. Although the engine and leading coaches remained on the lines, two people were killed in the coach which struck the bridge and three more were injured when the last coach ran down the embankment. The permanent way on this portion of line had just been replaced with 85 lb. bull-headed steel rail, and work on this relaying had ceased just a few hours before the accident. It was therefore on this aspect of the disaster that the Inspector concentrated his examination, and where he determined that the fault lay with the permanent way department for withdrawing a speed restriction over this section of track when the ballast was not fully made up and the sleeper ends boxed in. There can be no doubt that he was aided in this determination in the way the track had become displaced, for after the accident it gave the impression of a corkscrew twisting first this way and then that. The official report said 'I attribute it [the accident] to the road being unfit for trains to run over at full speed, owing to the deficiency of ballast on the permanent way.'

From a detailed examination of the circumstances of Little Bytham, and a series of other accidents involving the Stirling singles, I think that the Inspector was wrong not to have shown that the engine more than likely contributed to its own demise. Its front bogie carried a weight of 20 tons 5 cwt., and its training axle had a load of 11 tons 19 cwt., but the single, 8 feet high driving wheel carried a massive 17 tons 1 cwt. on its axle. In a whole raft of minor derailments, this exceptional load strenuously tested out the permanent way, and in a significant number of instances it bodily displaced track as it passed along. In at least four derailments on the GNR in the mid-1890s a Stirling single had travelled on the same section of track just prior to an accident being sustained by a following train. A similar view was expressed by the permanent way men who had relaid the track, but one could expect such statements from the people involved in order to free themselves of any serious responsibility for the accident. Yet, it was a member of the GNR's locomotive department which made the assertion that he was of the opinion that the track had been displaced by a preceding train. In all probability that was sister engine No.1005 which had gone through at about noon on the 10am express from Leeds, and then stopped at Little Bytham to report that the new section of track was riding a bit rough. Each successive engine of the next 29 trains which traversed this section of track that Saturday afternoon reported that the track was riding badly, and these effects seemed to be getting worse with each report. Of these trains none were hauled by the Singles, and the next member of the class to come down this line was the ill-fated 5pm from Leeds. The excessive force which No.1003 applied to already distorted track would have been too much and it was this which displaced the track so badly that it presented a severe obstacle immediately in the path of the train it was pulling behind it. Even though the engines were not blamed in any way whatsoever in the official report, I do not think that the GNR could have failed to recognise the fact that they were part of the problem. The solution was a major rebuilding programme at Doncaster Works, in such a way as to reduce the severity of the axle-loading despite a relatively high cost for the six engines involved; it seems unlikely that the GNR would have under taken this solely because there was 'a deficiency of ballast on the permanent way.'

PHOTOGRAPH; THE LATE ARTHUR TREVENA COLLECTION

PRESTON JUNCTION

Lancashire & Yorkshire Railway
3rd August 1896

In a study of railway accidents, evidence is soon gathered that holiday periods suffered more than their fare share of troubles. The same is also true of special excursion trains run at other times, and in both instances less than adequate stock was often pressed into service for the occasion. Whether such accidents were caused by the sheer bulk of extra trains being run, or by the fact that many of these special passenger trains were worked by freight train crews or 'trainees' is not so readily determined, but both factors appear to have had some bearing on many of these incidents. A large number of the reports into 'holiday' period accidents shows them to have been crewed by passed firemen as drivers, passed cleaners as firemen and passed porters as guards. Similarly, the frequency with which we come across late-running and delays in such trains, is also another significant factor. The case at Preston Junction on Bank Holiday Monday, 3rd August 1896 is a notable example.

To ease pressures on the LNWR/L&YR joint station at Preston, the L&YR provided facilities for watering locomotives at Preston Junction some 2 miles to the south, where they also had a ticket platform. At 6.05am a special excursion of 14 six-wheeled, non-corridor coaches left Leeds for the Lancashire resort of Blackpool. The train engine was an Aspinall 0-6-0 No.1058, which was supposedly awaiting repair as it was running very poorly. The climb over the Pennines at Copy Pit had not been easy for this ailing engine, and by the time it reached Preston Junction it was 30 minutes late. It was supposed to stop there for 10 minutes, so the signalman moved it into a loop off the down main line in order to allow it to be overtaken by a scheduled West Lancashire Railway passenger train which was following. However, the crew of the excursion train quickly completed the watering of their engine and were anxiously wanting to move on; particularly the guard who had endured 'stinging criticism' from passengers over their lateness. Without looking at his signals he gave the 'right-away' to the driver at 8.45am. Whilst this was bad enough, the driver compounded the error by popping his whistle, opening his regulator and starting to move out of the loop. Obviously the driver had never checked the signals at all, for they were clearly set for the WLR train from Blackburn to Preston and Southport which was almost abreast of No.1058's tender as it began to move forward.

Though the signalman was alert to danger, he could do nothing to prevent the now inevitable collision. The near-side front of WLR locomotive No.2 struck the motion of the L&YR engine, causing No.1058 to derail to the left. The WLR engine remained upright and connected to its train, which it dragged through the wreckage. The first two coaches were not too badly damaged, but the next two (both saloons) were completely wrecked. Fortunately the Southport train was not heavily loaded, and of the 30 people on board only six were injured. However, one man suffered the cruelest of fates; having been thrown clear of the wrecked coach he landed on the ground, only to be killed instantly a few seconds later when the roof of his coach fell on him. The L&YR train was barely marked, and after a change of engine, the subdued excursionists continued on for their day's outing.

ABOVE *The scene at Preston Junction looking towards Blackburn shows the damaged WLR train and the signals which the excursion train driver must have been able to see. Whether he simply ignored them or at best misread them, the Inspector could not determine. But this error was so typical of many where drivers assumed they had a clear road, when they did not have.*
PHOTOGRAPH; B. C. LANE COLLECTION

BELOW *Looking towards Preston, this view shows No.1058 derailed to the left and part of the damaged WLR train beyond it. The ticket platform being located on the far left, with the lattice signal post opposite the end of the two carriages.*
PHOTOGRAPH; THE LATE ARTHUR TREVENA HOOLE COLLECTION

PRESTON

London & North Western Railway 15th August 1896

We remain in Lancashire for our next accident, which occurred just twelve days after the incident at Preston Junction. This time we move to the LNWR system where it passed through Preston station, and thus formed part of the West Coast Main Line. It was the improvement of, and acceleration to, the services along the WCML that led directly to the accident of 15th August 1896 which left one person dead and several more injured. The great competition which was developing between the West Coast and East Coast routes to Scotland, was having a profound effect on the development of locomotives, rolling stock and services. Such competition was generally leading to the overall betterment of railway travel, but there was an adverse side which had already been experienced by the very same working at Wigan on 2nd August 1873. Thirteen passengers lost their lives on that occasion and after the five week long enquiry that followed, the cause was attributed as being due to too high a speed been taken through Wigan. During 1895 'the races to the north' had led to the already tight schedules being pared even more, as crews and locomotives were pushed to their limit; on both routes it was evident that the margin of safety was being cut to the barest minimum. On the evening of 15th August, the Scottish Tourist Sleeping Car Express left London's Euston station at 8pm and began its northward race between Wigan and Carlisle where the schedule allowed just 112 minutes, for a 105 mile journey which included the severe banks at Grayrigg and Shap. This sort of working demanded men of the highest calibre, but sadly those who were assigned to duty on the double-headed express that night were not in the top link. Neither driver had worked the express before, nor had they worked non-stop through Preston station. Whilst they were probably adequate for other sections of the route they had to work, the short section through Preston was particularly difficult due to the awkward curves through the station.

To prevent problems with these curves a permanent speed restriction of 10mph had been applied some years previously, but the express raced through Preston at 45mph behind two Webb 2-4-0's, No. 2159 *Shark* and No. 275 *Vulcan*. The results were spectacular, as they both burst through the rails and ploughed into the ballast. Although both engines remained upright, the carriages behind piled up around the locomotives and then spread across the tracks. Fortunately the improvements in passenger comforts had already led to a strengthening of coaching stock designs, and this prevented the casualty list from being much higher than it actually was. However, the legacy of the tight schedules was a direct cause of the Preston accident, and it was seen by many as the inevitable result of unregulated competition. A great public outcry was caused, and questions asked in Parliament. Yet despite this, the problems of speeding were not eliminated, and almost seven years to the day, another accident was recorded at Preston station when high speeds and failure to observe signals led to a rear-end collision on 1st August 1903, but this time the injuries were of a much less serious nature despite the devastation to the coaching stock involved.

PHOTOGRAPHS; ABOVE, THE LATE ARTHUR TREVENA COLLECTION BELOW, BY PERMISSION OF THE LANCASHIRE COUNTY RECORD OFFICE.

WELSHAMPTON
Cambrian Railway
11th June 1897

Ten months after Preston, another railway was to suffer the effects of a derailment at high speed. This time it was the turn of the tiny Cambrian Railway, and the location was Welshampton on the Shropshire/Flintshire border. On 11th June 1897 a long excursion train had been run from Lancashire to Mid-Wales, and it was on the return leg of this journey that disaster struck the train which was drawn by two Cambrian 0-6-0s, Nos. 75 and 77. These engines were just three years old, having been built by Neilson & Co. in 1894, they were also running at a fairly high speed. Now, we have already mentioned that, more often than not, excursion trains of that era were made up from antiquated stock and this one was no different as it was comprised of mixed Cambrian and Lancashire & Yorkshire Railway stock. During the outward journey the Cambrian guard who taken over the train at Whitchurch, had complained strongly about a rough-riding 4-wheel L&YR brake coach in which he was positioned. Accordingly when the train was formed up for the return journey, this was placed at the front of the train. Cambrian officials maintained the view that it was the derailment of this vehicle which led to the disaster that evening, but investigation showed the cause to be something entirely different. At that time the Cambrian were busy relaying long sections of track, as the rails were far too light for the speeds of the trains being run upon them. Ironically, the section between Ellesmere and Whitchurch was one of the few parts of the system where such work had still to be undertaken. It would appear that whilst travelling at speed the two engines literally burst the track and caused the train following them to derail. Eleven passengers were killed in the pile-up which followed, as many of the coaches were completely wrecked. The damaged vehicles included 4-wheel, 6-wheel and 8-wheel coaches, and five of these were subsequently scrapped. The two engines were, however, only lightly damaged and they were repaired and quickly put back into service, eventually being absorbed into the GWR where they became Nos.878 and 880. The problem of high speed derailments was not eliminated however, and with Welshampton following sharp on the heels of Preston and Wennington the issues of high speed derailments was again coming to the fore. In the case of the Wennington Junction eight lives were lost when a Leeds - Lancaster passenger train took the junction at too fast a speed, this was compounded by the inadequacy of the train's brakes. The Midland Railway's failure to supply many of its trains with a continuous braking system was a contributory factor in Wennington Junction, and it was a case which the Railway Inspectorate used to force general improvements in this regard; even so the high speed derailments were set to continue as we will discuss later in this book!

PHOTOGRAPHS: THE LATE ARTHUR TREVENA COLLECTION

HEATHFIELD

London, Brighton & South Coast Railway 1st September 1897

On the anniversary of the opening of the London, Brighton & South Coast Railway a train running from Eastbourne to Tunbridge Wells suffered a spectacular derailment at a location known to railwaymen as Tooth's Bank not far from Heathfield station. In many ways this accident was similar to one which would follow in 1916 at Crowborough on a neighbouring LBSCR line. At this stage there was little inclination that much of the trouble with this type of derailment was associated with tank engines being run at high speeds which, in turn, could seriously combine with any defects found in the permanent way. Time after time, accidents would be noted with tank engines running at speed on poor track, but where these engines were travelling down an incline, the prospects of an accident increased dramatically; and there was an incline at Tooth's Bank. The gradient was 1:50 for a length of two miles, and this was followed by a similar incline heading up hill on the opposite side. It might well be appreciated that in view of the climb ahead, drivers would race down one side and charge up the other under full steam. There was no reason why this could not be done on a good road with a tender engine, but on a bad road, and with water slopping around in the side tanks, it was not such a good practice to try with a tank locomotive. Now, in the pages ahead I shall keep making reference to the problems that were manifest with tank engines in this way, and lest anyone thinks that I am against such types of motive power, let me say that I am not. Indeed, my childhood memories are of branch line tank engines and not tender engines, and my collection of model locomotives contains many examples of this type. However, it has to be said that tank engines were fine in their place, but that place was not at the head of fast trains. In the pages that follow we will see this in a variety of accidents, and despite the very clear evidence in this types of derailment it is an area which was not initially given a lot of importance by the various railway inspectors. It was not until incidents such as that which occurred near Tavistock in 1898 that the design element of certain tank engine types began to be questioned. Even then it was not until the accident on the L&YR near Hebden Bridge that we find really serious questions being asked about the use of tank engines for express work. Many years ago an old driver put the point to me that his father, a driver on the Midland 2000 Class 0-6-2Ts had warned him of the dangers of tank engines 'waltzing' at speed due to water-surging causing oscillation on bad sections of track. 'Mind you' he said 'it was never the fault of the chief mechanical engineer, it would always be the driver, the ganger, or the permanent way inspector; but,' he contended 'they must have known what the condition of the track was and yet they still designed engines that were born to derail.' In many ways what he said is a true reflection of the case of the River class locomotives designed by Maunsell for the Southern Railway which had a notorious existence until their conversion into tender engines. In my study of high speed derailments, I think that my late driver friend was far closer to the truth than he guessed. Whilst it is not an area where many of the writers on accident matters have concentrated, I think it is safe to say that tank engines derailed because of these circumstances far more often than has been acknowledged.

For example, on 1st September 1897 LBSCR 0-6-2T No.297 was running the 8.18am from Eastbourne with six coaches when it approached Tooth's Bank; then as it raced down the incline, the engine left the rails and overturned. Five of the six coaches were also derailed, many turning over on to their side. Sadly the driver was fatally injured and 30 passengers were in need of medical attention. In the investigation which followed the engine was thoroughly examined and despite rigorous tests no faults or weakness could be found when it was checked over at the LBSCR's Brighton Works. The state of the permanent way was another matter, and when it was examined the 78 lb. per yard rails were found to have worn down significantly. The cost of renewing the whole road had already been found to be cost prohibitive, but nothing had been done to address this problem by imposing a set of speed restrictions. Concerning this matter, the Inspector wrote "It would appear that, at different times, complaints have originated on one side from the drivers, of the state of the road, and, on the other side, from the permanent way gang of drivers running too fast. These complaints scarcely seem to me to have assumed a sufficiently definite form to necessitate special action being taken by the Officers of the Railway Company concerned, but it would evidently have been better had they been taken more serious note of!'

PHOTOGRAPH; THE LATE ARTHUR TREVENA COLLECTION

DUNBAR

North British Railway
3rd January 1898

We now turn to two strikingly similar accidents which took place in Scotland within a month of each other, where signalmen were negligent in carrying out their duties. The first was on the ECML at Dunbar at 6.51am on 3rd January 1898 and involved the East Coast Express which had left King's Cross at 11.30pm the previous evening. It was approaching Dunbar behind two NBR 4-4-0s, Nos. 642 and 492 which were running at a speed of around 60 to 70 mph when they collided with some wagons fouling the down fast line which had come from the 4.15am goods train from North Leith. This train had arrived at Dunbar 50 minutes early, and in view of this the signalman decided to shunt it ahead of the express. This movement involved taking the wagons through a crossover to the goods yard which was located on the opposite side of the down line and it would have begun about 6.35am. However, at 6.42am the signalman at Dunbar East was offered the express by his colleague at Cocksburnpath who sent the message 'is line clear'. There is some doubt in the evidence as to whether the Dunbar East man accepted the train at this time, but he certainly offered it on to Dunbar West three minutes later. Unfortunately, as some of the wagons were being put through the crossover they derailed and, as the goods train had not yet entered the sidings, the interlocking made it impossible to set the signals for the main line. The express driver believing he had a clear road raced on past the signals at danger and collided with the derailed vans; the front portion of the passenger train was entirely wrecked and one lady passenger died in the wreckage whilst the driver of the leading engine and 21 passengers were all injured. Although the driver was to blame for failing to observe the signals, the Inspector felt he had been misled by the signalman, commenting that the express should not have been allowed to leave Cocksburnpath if the section through Dunbar was not clear. He then drew a comparison with the fatal collision at Falkirk on 20th November 1897 and referred to a comment in his report into that disaster saying 'Collisions of this nature raise an uncomfortable suspicion that the rules for block working are not strictly followed during the night. This suggestion receives startling confirmation in the case now under review.'

PHOTOGRAPH; THE LATE ARTHUR TREVENA COLLECTION

BARASSIE

Glasgow & South Western Railway
4th February 1898

The second incident took place at Barassie, on a junction where the new line to Troon and Ayr diverged from the old route. Since its inception most passenger trains would follow the new loop, whilst goods traffic was concentrated on the original line. Two such trains were running on the morning of 4th February 1898, an Ayr to Glasgow goods behind G&SWR No.49 and the 7am Kilmarnock - Ayr passenger train behind No. 65. Both trains were approaching the junction around 7.12am, and the goods train should have been let across the junction first, however the signalman at Barassie decided to put the passenger train first even though it was crossing the path of the accepted freight working. Unfortunately the distant signal for the junction was not showing a correct indication, for its light was part red, part green due to the fact that the signal wire leading to the signal arm had contracted severely overnight. Now, although a doubtful signal should always be treated as a danger signal, the Inspector concluded that the goods driver might have thought that this was an 'all right signal'. Even so the home signal was at danger, but in those days many drivers tended to rely more on distant's and less on stop signals since the distant generally gave them an indication of what the home signals were saying; as railway union appointed solicitors frequently commented in such cases, this was not an unreasonable view, because if a distant showed clear, then the driver had every right to expect the road beyond to be clear as well. Unfortunately in this instance it was not clear and the two trains met in a violent collision which cost the lives of four passengers and killed the driver and fireman of the goods and the fireman of the passenger train. The signalman was duly dismissed from the railway service, and the Inspector commented 'Had the Lock & Block system been installed at Barassie it would have been impossible for the signalman to allow the passenger train to cross the path of the goods once it had been accepted.'

PHOTOGRAPH; THE LATE ARTHUR TREVENA COLLECTION

LONDON; ST. JOHN'S

South Eastern & Chatham Railway
21st March 1898

Another signalman's error occurred the month after Barassie when the 10-coach 7.45am from Tonbridge to London was struck in the rear by the 7am Parlour Car train from Hastings to London whilst it was standing in St. John's station on 21st March 1898. In thick fog the Tonbridge train was stopped at the up main home signal, and obscured from the view of the signalman in the busy St. John's 'box. The line was worked by the Sykes Lock & Block apparatus, which should have prevented the possibility of rear end collisions, but it reckoned without the human element. At 8.54am the signalman had accepted the Tonbridge train from Parks Bridge, and at 8.55am he offered it to New Cross who accepted it at once. All the signals were thus lowered, but when he turned to deal with an up train on the adjacent North Kent line he evidently threw the up main levers to danger by mistake. Anyway with that, the Tonbridge train came to a halt and sat waiting in the fog, but the signalman had firmly convinced himself it had gone on. His booking lad however warned him that it had not passed, and the station-master even came up to the 'box and told him that there was a train waiting at the up home signal and asked him to let it into the station.

When the signalman was offered the Hastings train the electro-mechanical system of the 'lock and block' did not allow him to put the advance starting signal to clear, and this should have served as yet another warning. However, he decided that the treadle must have failed (as it had done twice the previous Saturday) so he used the special key which was provided to release the electrical lock in cases of emergency. Having done this, the signalman then asked New Cross if the Tonbridge train had arrived there, and when he found it had not, he lowered the home signal to bring it into the station. Unfortunately this action was too little too late, for the accident occurred as just he did this. Three people were killed and 20 injured as the rear coaches of the Tonbridge trains telescoped then splintered open when hit by the pioneer Stirling Class F 4-4-0 No.205. The signalman immediately acknowledged his error, but the reckless way he had used his release key exposed an inherent weakness in the Sykes' system. Indeed, the occurrence at St. John's confirmed the view of the Inspecting Officers of the Board of Trade that the train itself should release the block instrument by depressing a treadle as it entered the next section. The Inspector wrote 'It should not be in the power of a signalman to use the key without permission from another box, and there are several plans which have been proposed, and tried, with this object in view; failing the adoption of one of these devices, the key should be so protected that it cannot be used without a record being left. The Company should take the necessary steps to improve upon the present arrangements, in respect of these deficiencies.' However, as later events would show, the misuse of the Sykes' equipment release key was to continue to have catastrophic consequences and the deficiencies were not satisfactorily resolved for well over half a century. Whilst we will learn that it was signalmen's errors which caused those future disasters, we might well keep in mind the question, were these men wholly to blame, or did the railway company bear some responsibility for failing to fully act on the words of Lieutenant Colonel Addison following the St. John's accident?

Regretfully the St. John's accident was not the last incident on the South Eastern & Chatham Railway involving telescoping in 1898, as the lower picture taken at Deal on 6th July reveals. At 5pm that day three 3rd class coaches and 2 loaded trucks ran away following a shunting procedure at Walmer Station and set off down the incline leading towards Deal. The guard chased after them trying to pin down the brakes, and the shunting engine also set off in hot pursuit. However, the runaways escaped capture and ran on to Deal where they struck an empty train which was in the process of being shunted after dropping its passengers. The picture below graphically portrays the extent of the damage, and it is very fortunate that no-one was in either train when they collided.

PHOTOGRAPHS: THE LATE ARTHUR TREVENA COLLECTION

WELLINGBOROUGH

Midland Railway
2nd September 1898

The incident which took place at Wellingborough station on the evening of 2nd September 1898 was a tragedy borne out of one of the simplest of mistakes possible. A postman had arrived at the station with a consignment of mail which had to be transmitted on by rail and, having left his cart outside the station, he went inside to find a luggage barrow on which he could bring it to the platform. On seeking out a suitable truck, he drew it along the platform towards a gate which had been let into the wall to allow an exit to the outside. As he went along the platform a group of boys waiting to collect newspapers from a later train ran alongside the barrow jumping on and off it, until the postman turned the corner into a narrow alley leading to the barred gate. Leaving the barrow unattended for a moment, he reached up to take down the key for the gate which was kept on a nail in the alleyway wall. However, in parking up the trolley it seems likely that he forgot to turn the handle right round until the wheels locked. What started the barrow rolling backwards is not known, but due to an inclination in the platform level, a downward slope existed from the buildings to the platform edges. On this inclined slope the trolley picked up speed and finally dropped over the edge on to the down platform road. The postman gave chase to the barrow and he tried hauling it back on to the platform, but it was too heavy for him to manage on his own. A station inspector had seen the events and he rushed to help, knowing that the 7.15pm from London, St. Pancras was due any minute, he jumped down on to the rails to try and help drag the runaway trolley from the running lines. However, before they could get it moved, the driver of an up passenger train which was standing in the adjoining platform began sounding his whistle to warn them that express was upon them. The postman managed to jump back on to the platform, but the station inspector had to dive under the stationary train to get clear. At the head of the express 4-4-0 No.1743 struck the trolley smashing it to pieces, but simultaneously suffering a partial derailment as its wheels mounted the track. It ran on for some distance in this condition, but when it reached a diamond crossover at the north end of the station, its derailment was completed. The engine was thrown over on to its side and the coaches behind squeezed past the wrecked engine, the second one being completely wrecked. Seven people (five passengers and the express's footplate crew) were killed in the accident and another 65 were injured. Surely few accidents have had such a simple cause, but the lessons were not learned that quickly as we will see at Wembley Central Station in 1940. However, one of the recommendations of the investing officer's report led to a general improvement in platform design, and as the century neared its end, most railway companies took advantage of platform heightening and improvement programmes to give the surfaces a slope which inclined away from the platform edge.

PHOTOGRAPHS: THE LATE ARTHUR TREVENA COLLECTION

PENMAENMAWR

London & North Western Railway
12th January 1899

On a dark stormy night in January 1849, the crew of a South Eastern Railway goods train was running through the Kent countryside between Tonbridge and Penshurst. Unbeknown to the crew, however, the River Medway was in full spate and all its backwaters were filled to a much higher level than normal. One of these was spanned by a wooden trestle bridge carrying the SER line, and around midnight the force of the water undermined the trestle and it was washed away. Into the void left by the bridge failure, the night goods engine and the leading wagons of its train were precipitated. The fireman managed to find his mate in the swirling waters which surrounded the wrecked train, but despite these heroic efforts the driver died shortly afterwards. Some fifty years later (almost to the day), another goods train was to suffer a similar fate. This time the accident occurred in North Wales, where the LNWR line hugged the Carnarvonshire coast. During the dark stormy night high tides and storm force winds were lashing the coast, and as a result watchmen were recruited from the ranks of the permanent way department in order to keep an eye open for any possible breach caused by the sea. As the sea reached its maximum height waves swept over a low retaining wall near Penmaenmawr, and the back-wash began breaking up the ballast beneath the track. Three more high waves crashed in quick succession and within minutes a long section of track was left suspended in mid air. With several hundreds of yards of track badly damaged, the two platelayers who witnessed the events set off running in opposite directions to warn the oncoming traffic. The man who headed in the Chester direction very soon saw the headlamps of a down goods heading towards him through a tunnel just 150 yards from the breach. He gave a warning as best he could, but he had no way of knowing whether the crew had seen it; in all probability, it seems likely that they had not, for they failed to slow down. The Crewe-built 0-6-0 DX Goods No.1418 had not slackened its pace in any appreciable way when it reached the chasm, and the next minute their train had turned over to its right and disappeared into the broiling seas below. Sadly both enginemen were drowned as nature once again showed its capriciousness towards the operation of railways.

PHOTOGRAPHS: THE LATE ARTHUR TREVENA COLLECTION

COUPAR ANGUS

Caledonian Railway
23rd October 1899

Our examination of railway accidents now comes to the end of the 19th century with yet another atrocious accident caused by a lack of diligence on the part of experienced railwaymen. On 23rd October 1899 the 6.55pm express train from Perth was heading north towards Forfar behind 4-4-0 No.13. As it was passing through Coupar Angus, another Caley engine, 2-4-0 No.431 began pulling out of a siding with a cattle train behind it. The sidelong condition which resulted was of such a violent nature that the driver of the Aberdeen-based goods engine was killed on his footplate, and the engine completely wrecked. A view of that engine was shown on page 16 of *Trains In Trouble* Volume 2, and from this picture we are left in doubt as to why the engine was duly scrapped. Number 13 was subsequently repaired, but as will be seen from this picture of the wrecked engine on a Caledonian low-loader wagon (No.41), the damage to the express locomotive was substantial enough in its own right.

PHOTOGRAPH; THE LATE ARTHUR TREVENA COLLECTION

SLOUGH

Great Western Railway 16th June 1900

Our first accident of the 20th century is one of the most notable railway disasters in history; not for its cause but for its effect. Yet the incident which took place at Slough Station on 16th June 1900 has been given scant coverage in books on railway disasters, and was completely omitted from *Red For Danger* and *Disasters Down The Line*. Yet both these books readily point to the Great Western Railway/Western Region as a shining example of a railway company/region that was relatively accident free. In no small way this excellent record was thanks to its Automatic Train Control system which was progressively introduced after the Slough disaster of 1900, so it prompts us to look at this accident which claimed five lives and injured 35 others on Windsor Race Day 1900. The 1.05pm Paddington - Windsor train had left London on time but its heavy load resulted in it progressively dropping behind schedule, so by the time it arrived at Slough it was some 10 minutes down. Whilst it was protected in the rear by a seemingly adequate signalling system, it was being closely followed by the Paddington - Falmouth express which had left London at 1.15pm. By now the 10 minute margin between the two trains had now been eroded to nothing, but the Falmouth train was still running at around 60 miles per hour. On the footplate of No.3015 *Kennet*, one of the GWR's 7'8" singles, the crew were working hard all the way between Langley and Dolphinton Junction. This may have accounted for the driver of the Falmouth train's omission to see the Slough East distant signals as he sped through the junction, but why he also missed the Slough East home signal set at danger remains a mystery. He was probably expecting a clear road through the station as his train was not booked to stop there, so he was quite surprised when his fireman shouted 'whoa' after seeing the home signal set against them. The driver made a full brake application, put his engine into reverse gear, threw open his blast valves and dropped sand on the rails. But it was all to no avail, and No.3015 slid onwards into the rear of the stationary train, ripping into its rear coaches as though they were boxes of tissue paper. It was just a simple error, and one we will meet time and time again as we progress through our story of British railway accidents, yet it was one which need not have occurred had there been a system of making sure that drivers were alert to any signals which may be placed at danger in front of them. What was needed was either a physical, or audible means of conveying to a driver the state of the signals! Such a system was brought about by the Slough disaster, as the GWR devised equipment to prevent a repetition of this type of accident. This was to become known as Automatic Train Control (ATC), and was based on Kemp & Rowell's patent device; it would also allow for the discontinuance of a need for fog signalmen in times of bad weather, as it could make an indication in the cab of a locomotive to show the state of the signals they were passing. The GWR apparatus included a fixed ramp located between the rails at a distant signal and a contact shoe on the locomotive; when the distant signal was 'clear' an electric current passed through the ramp and the shoe, sounding a bell in the cab. However, when the signal was at danger, no electric current passed through the ramp, but the ramp still raised the shoe, and this caused a warning device to go off in the cab. Then, if the driver failed to correctly react to adverse signals, the device would make an automatic application of a locomotive brake. After initial trials on one of the pre-grouped GWR's branch lines, ATC was introduced to the main line between Paddington and Reading from 1908 onwards. The widespread application of the system on the GWR, and (by comparison) the far slower progress on the other lines was, in part, due to the fact that the company's policy was relatively unaffected by the 1923 Grouping. Regrettably, ATC systems being experimented with elsewhere (such as the NER, LNWR, GCR GER and LBSCR), were to founder in the quagmire of post 1923 reorganisation. Yet as we will see, the issue of ATC/AWS is one to which we will return again and again and again!

PHOTOGRAPHS: THE LATE ARTHUR TREVENA COLLECTION

PECKWASH

Midland Railway
21st October 1900

Our second 20th century accident under consideration was that which occurred at Peckwash Sidings between Ambergate Junction and Derby on 21st October 1900, and it is another of those mysterious incidents that has never been satisfactorily explained. On this occasion a Johnson 0-6-0 No.1433 was running from Shirland Colliery to Derby with a train of 44 empty and loaded wagons and a 10-ton brake van when it failed to come to a stop at the home signal on the up goods loop. By this time in railway history, many loops and sidings were provided with a head shunt, sand drag or trap points, which served as a means of stopping trains or runaway vehicles overrunning signals protecting the main line. At Peckwash the up goods line terminated in catch points, but these were lengthened by 3 or 4 additional rails and terminated in a stop block 45 yards on from the catch points. Some 50 yards on, another stop block faced in the opposite direction at the end of Peckwash Mills Siding, but the tracks did not continue across the intervening gap. We have no way of knowing why the Midland crew failed to come to a stop at the signals, but the Inspector concluded that one of three specific reasons would be the most likely cause; these being either, the falling gradient, greasy rails, or the 0-6-0 approaching the junction at a much faster speed than it ought to have done. Any way No.1433 collided with the buffer stop and along with six wagons it rolled down an embankment to the side as our picture clearly shows. Unfortunately its tender was thrown across the up passenger line and into the path of a Rowsley - London express goods train. Although the signals for this train were still set to danger, a piece of debris from one of the wrecked wagons had landed on the signal wires and forced the semaphore arm to show a false clear. The driver and fireman of the mineral train were both killed, having been buried by the contents of the wagons which cascaded down on to the footplate when the truck followed the engine down the embankment. Typical of many of the railway accidents of that era, colleagues rallied round to help raise money for the dependants of the two dead men, and a poem was written by a local signalman and published at a price of one penny by Simpsons Printers of Derby. Whilst I have tried to avoid (wherever possible) the use of the names of individuals involved in accidents throughout this book, I thought it worth reproducing this sheet in facsimile even though it identifies the names of those killed.

PHOTOGRAPH; THE LATE ARTHUR TREVENA COLLECTION

. . THE . .

Peckwash Disaster

IN WHICH

Driver Hitchcock & Fireman Teagle

Met with their Death, Dec. 1st, 1900.

Driver Hitchcock.

Fireman Teagle.

A train left Derby Midland Station,
Shirland was its destination;
Progress was slow, relief required
For driver and the man who fired.

I telephoned for the relief
For the train which came to grief,
To be relieved at Ambergate,
Little thinking of the fate.

That on returning to their home,
To which, alas! they never come,
Through accident their life was took,
Perhaps caused by a mistaken look.

But, be that as it may, we'll try
To help, and dry the mourner's eye;
They need our sympathy and aid,
As no more wages will be paid

To those who toiled for daily bread,
And shared the table's daily spread;
Father, mother, children three,
Who prattled round poor Hitchcock's knee.

Teagle was his mother's joy,
A dutiful and loving boy.
She'll miss his bright and sunny face,
Alas! there's none can take his place.

They are now gone, but not forgotten,
If we do our duty well,
Surely all can do a little,
For the bereaved a sum to swell.

I pen these lines by a request
From mates who want to do their best
To help them in their hour of need,
The widows and the children feed.

I gladly would have shirked the task,
'Twas love impulsed the hearts who asked;
We all are Brothers, or should be;
But do not always seem to be.

The fatal spot was Peckwash Mill,
Where paper is made, with care and skill.
The buffer stop was struck with force,
Although the Engine was reversed.

Their best was done, but on they went
Till all their energy was spent;
Bravely to their post they stuck,
And thus the thread of life was cut.

Engine Fourteen-thirty-three
When over-hauled, again you'll see;
But the faces of the men
On earth we'll never see again.

To one and all we now appeal,
The leaflet price is not a deal,
Augment it more if 'tis your will,
I write no more, my pen is still.

Signalman Passey.

PRICE ONE PENNY

The Proceeds to be devoted to the Widow and Children of the late Driver Hitchcock and the Widowed Mother of the late Fireman Teagle.

PRINTER, DERBY.

GRETNA JUNCTION

Caledonian and Glasgow & South Western railways 14th May 1901

Our next accident is another of those instances where an engine rolled down an embankment, but this time we move from Derbyshire to Gretna Junction where the Glasgow & South Western Railway diverged from the Caledonian's main line. The participants in this accident were the 8.20pm Caledonian goods from Gushetfaulds (Glasgow) to Carlisle, and the G&SWR's 1.15am goods service from Carlisle to Dumfries and Glasgow behind pilot locomotive No.57 and train engine No.364. The origins of the incident are to be attributed to the derailment of a wagon in the Caledonian train which occurred just over a mile to the north of Gretna Junction. This was witnessed by an alert signalman who saw sparks coming from this wagon (probably the 18th) as it passed his box and he gave seven beats to the next box, meaning 'stop and examine'. However, as the train crossed the junction the wheels of this derailed wagon struck the outer rail of the G&SWR line and several more wagons were derailed. As the train was running down a gradient at a speed of 40 mph it dragged the vehicles behind it as far as the viaduct carrying the railway over the River Sark, where many of these piled up around (and subsequently destroyed) the parapet. The train then divided behind the 17th wagon, but the engine, tender and partially derailed front portion continued south for a distance. The bridge over the Longtown Road some 90 yards south of the viaduct was also badly damaged, as were 90 feet of platform coping at Gretna Junction station. Whilst all this was happening the double-headed goods from Carlisle was approaching the scene at a speed of 28 mph under clear signals. At the north end of the station it came into collision with the wreckage of the derailed train which had fouled the down line and this resulted in the pilot engine being turned over on to its left-hand side. It was then pushed along the tracks by the train engine as far as the Longtown Road under-line bridge, where it demolished the parapet before plunging down the embankment on the northern side. The train engine pushed passed it before it came to a halt some 90 feet further on, but miraculously no-one was seriously hurt.

This time no blame could be attached to drivers or signalmen, nor to anyone concerned with the running of the train, rather the fault lay with the person (or persons) who loaded one of the wagons (probably the 18th) near the middle of the Caledonian train. In this was placed four round forgings, each with a diameter of either 9 or 10 inches, and lengths of 16' 2", 16', 15' 10" and 13' 6" along with a pair of angle irons both 12' 9" long. The total weight of these castings was 7 tons 3 cwt. 3 qtrs. whilst the wagon in which these were located was an ordinary 8-ton truck with a tare of 5 tons 6 cwt. Not only was it inadequate in that way, but it was only 15 feet in length and thus too short to accommodate three of the forgings in a lateral position. Therefore they were arranged each with one end on the floor of the wagon, the other projecting at an angle beyond the top of the planking at the other end. There does not seem to have been any method employed to secure these in place and being round, they would have easily rolled and moved from the position they were stowed. Then, at some stage as the train journeyed southwards, these seem to have shifted to such an extent as to cause an uneven distribution of weight. It is quite probable that they were thrown to one corner of the wagon at its raised end, and this 'overhang' would have then caused the wagon to lift at the end where the castings were resting on the floor. Little wonder then, that such a derailment took place, but great wonder indeed that no-one was killed or seriously injured.

PHOTOGRAPHS; DAVID JENKINSON COLLECTION

LIVERPOOL, WATERLOO

Lancashire & Yorkshire Railway 15th July 1903

The derailment which took place two years on from Gretna Junction was a much more complex affair, and one which was attended by a significant loss of life and personal injury. Yet this is also one which was never fully understood at the time and where the Inspector had to make an educated guess as to the reasons behind the events. The Liverpool suburban station of Waterloo is located on the line to Southport which opened in 1848, though there had been a proposal for a coastal line from Liverpool to Preston as early as 1838. Such a through route offered considerable promise, but initially there seemed little likelihood of generating much local traffic particularly north of Southport as most of the communities which the railway would serve were little more than small villages. However, the promoters were pressed into building a railway, and the single track line opened from Southport that July. It did not initially reach Liverpool however, as the branch had to be content with a terminus at Waterloo until such time as a junction could be made with joint L&YR/ELR line at Sandhills in October 1850. Passengers heading for the city were served by a horse-bus service, but the popularity of Waterloo as a residential area was already beginning to grow. As the Victorian era progressed, the prosperity which was attached to Liverpool and its docks became reflected in the living standards of many people who desired to escape from the mean back-to-back terrace houses that crowded round the docks and industrial districts. A slow migration took place to the healthier countryside to the north and Waterloo (six stops out from Liverpool), was one of first stations in the commuter belt. It therefore enjoyed an early boom in commuter traffic, which was accentuated greatly as the L&YR improved its services.

Unfortunately, confidence in those services took a severe battering on 15th July 1903 when an express from Liverpool Exchange station to Southport became derailed as it entered the station at speed. The train, behind 2-4-2T No.670 was running at an estimated speed of around 50 mph when it suddenly jumped the rails just below an over-line bridge which spanned the tracks at this point. It then ran up the ramp of the island platform smashing the coping stones and disturbing the surface as our pictures show. Next it ripped through one of the supports for the bridge and caused severe damage to this structure as our illustration also reveals. Having hit this obstruction, the 2-4-2T was spun round to such an extent that it came to rest with its chimney facing the opposite direction to which it it had been travelling. Its right-hand trailing end overhung the platform, and it smashed in the sides of the bogie coaches as they tried to run on past under their own impetus. Six passengers and the fireman were either killed on the spot or died of their injuries shortly afterwards and 112 passengers, the driver and 3 other railway employees were injured, 30 of them seriously so. The Inspector concluded that the accident was due to a number of factors, primarily the speed of the engine, the curvature of the approach to the station as the lines turned to pass round the island platform, and (most probably) the dropping of the right hand trailing driving wheel. It was concluded that a restriction of 35 mph was highly desirable as the curves started at 40 chains radius for 80 yards and then changed to a radius of 23 chains where there was a maximum super elevation of 2½ inches. With the benefit of hindsight, we can also add another factor, which may have contributed to this accident, the problem of the instability evidenced in tank engines when running at high speeds. I have already mentioned these types of incidents on other lines, but on page 61 we will come across a very similar accident involving an engine of the same class which left the rails on a section of curved track where there was a super elevation of five inches and a radius of 30 chains.

PHOTOGRAPH; THE LATE ARTHUR TREVENA COLLECTION

LOUGHOR BRIDGE, NR. LLANELLY

Great Western Railway
3rd October 1904

Following the Slough disaster the GWR began to build for itself an enviable safety record, a policy which boldly led where other railway companies struggled to follow. Yet on Monday 3rd October 1904 a serious derailment in Carmarthenshire, witnessed the wreck of an express passenger train from New Milford to London (Paddington). The train was drawn by Bulldog Class 4-4-0 No.3460 *Montreal* from Neyland engine shed, and comprised of eight 8-wheel bogie coaches and a 6-wheeled milk van. All went well for the first part of the journey and on reaching Carmarthen a new driver and fireman came on for the section to Landore. The driver was a man with a good record who was later well spoken of by G. J. Churchward, who said he was due to be promoted on to Class A work.
Shortly the train reached Llanelly where No.3460 took on water whilst a pilot engine, 1661 class 0-6-0ST No.1674, was added for the section ahead. It left Llanelly seven minutes late at 1.15pm, but as it was proceeding to Loughor, reputedly at a speed of 25 mph, it became derailed and ploughed down a small embankment. The tank engine and the tender of *Montreal* were both over-turned, and though the damage to the engines was not as serious as might be expected, the train was another matter. The first coach was entirely wrecked, with the steel underframe breaking up and separating from the body; this ended up lying at the foot of the embankment which was around 6 feet high on the down side. The second coach had its steel underframe buckled and its side smashed in, whilst the third and fourth coaches each suffered heavy damage at one end. Tragically there was quite a high toll in human casualties with the driver and firemen of the tank engine being killed outright and the fireman of the 4-4-0 receiving fatal injuries. Two passengers also died, whilst 18 people were seriously hurt. There was some considerable debate as to whether the derailment was due to the failure of a connecting rod, or undue oscillation. Churchward being adamant it was the former, the Inspector opting for the latter. Whatever the case, the fault evidently lay in the tank engine, and in all probability was caused by its running at a far higher speed than that which it had been designed for.
The practice of using tank engines on the long section from Llanelly to the bottom of Cockett Bank came in for strong criticism from the Inspector, and he recommended that only tender engines should be used for this purpose in future. If tank engines were to be used as pilot locomotives, he suggested that they ought to be attached at Gowerton; adding the comment, 'It does not commend itself as good practice to attach an engine designed for moderate speeds to a train timed to run at high speed over a straight level road. When this is done, one of two things must happen; either the slower engine will cause delay to the train, or will itself be run at a speed which is unsuitable and may become dangerous.'

In conclusion he recommended that the Associated Railway Companies appoint an expert Committee for the purpose of enquiring into, and reporting on, a type of classification by which tank engines might be made according to the work they were suitable for. Like Colonel Pringle's similar recommendations into a committee for evaluating train control systems, Lt. Colonel Yorke's suggestion was one of great foresight because, despite the great number and diversity of tank engines then running, designs still left a lot to be desired.

PHOTOGRAPHS: THE LATE ARTHUR TREVENA COLLECTION

AYLESBURY

Great Central & Metropolitan Joint Railway 23rd December 1904

Whilst the derailment at Llanelly was surrounded by controversy and mystery, we can recognise an element that relates to the design of engines which, in turn, gives the probable cause of the derailment. However, just two months after Llanelly, began a series of almost inexplicable high speed derailments that were experienced over a three year period. Of these, perhaps those at Salisbury, Grantham and Shrewsbury are best known, but that which occurred at Aylesbury on 23rd December 1904 is equally shrouded in mystery. More importantly, it is an accident which has never been satisfactorily explained, and one in which even the official report had difficulties in determining the reasons. It was an awful foggy night which began to worsen in Buckinghamshire just before midnight on the 22nd. Into these conditions a Robinson 4-4-0, No.1040, set out with the 2.45am night express from London, Marylebone. The train was not well patronised, for its formation included only four coaches, and the occupants of these were mostly Great Central Railway employees. The rest of the train was made up of three fish vans (bound for Grimsby), a meat van, a parcels van and a full brake. The train maintained a high speed as it raced north on the joint GCR/Metropolitan line towards Aylesbury, but in its path a speed restriction of 15 mph was in force. Why the crew failed to slow down for the station is a matter of conjecture, perhaps they were lost in the fog, maybe they were affected by the same sort of malaise we will encounter in the other mysterious derailments. Whatever the case, No.1040 was derailed to the left, and it then began to mount the ramp of the down platform, followed by the tender and the four coaches. These then turned over to the right and the engine ended up almost at right-angles across the platform, with its smoke box, buffer beam and leading bogie wheels resting on the down line. The remainder of the train piled up around the wreckage, and debris from this was scattered for 50 yards along both running lines. The danger was not over yet, for bearing down on the scene was the 10.20pm Manchester - Marylebone express, which ran into the wreckage strewn across its path. Fortunately the driver had already made a brake application and as the up train screeched to a halt, it escaped serious damage. However, the footplatemen on the down train were both killed in the collision, as were two passengers. Why the driver had precipitated an action which led to his own demise is hard to determine, but the official view was that he had failed to see the 15mph warning board which was situated just 200 yards from the commencement of the speed restriction. Whilst this speed restriction was necessary, the reasons for it (the severe curves through Aylesbury station) were not. Accordingly, Sam Fay of the GCR managed to persuade the Metropolitan to ease these in order to permit high-speed running through the station. He is reputed to have later commented that 'it was a shame that it took an accident to achieve a quick road through Aylesbury.'

PHOTOGRAPHS: THE LATE ARTHUR TREVENA COLLECTION

CUDWORTH

Midland Railway
19th January 1905

Whilst the lapse of the driver at Aylesbury is hard to explain, what occurred at Cudworth near Barnsley just four weeks later is almost beyond comprehension. Most readers will agree that it would hardly seem possible that an experienced driver could run past no less than eight distant and five stop signals when they were all 'on', yet this is exactly what happened with a double-headed express train in the early hours of 19th January 1905. From this summary of events, we can only conclude that this was driver error of the greatest magnitude. The consequences of this action were extremely serious, for in the resulting collision, the mass of tangled steel and splintered wood claimed the lives of six passengers and the fireman of the leading engine. Though it was very foggy at the time, drivers of previous trains had all been able to see the signals, but they had been running very slowly. The general rule book of the day made provision for the fact that signals may be obscured in bad weather, yet it made absolutely no allowance for drivers running past them at danger. Under no circumstances should the driver have tried to run past them at 50mph as happened in this case. Taking into account the fact that the driver was entirely to blame, the Midland Railway's duty of protecting signals in time of fog (or falling snow) also comes into question in this incident. In adverse conditions fog-men were stationed at various signals, where they would be used to provide a supplementary warning to train crews at signals which were showing stop or caution. Being equipped with detonators and hand-lamps (Rule 80), they should be able to halt any train which looked likely to overrun a signal set at danger. At Cudworth, however, it would appear that the Midland Railway's abilities to comply with this rule were not all that they might have been. The fog-signalmen in this area all lived some distance from their places of duty, and to compound this the regular call-out man was sick. What is more he had not reported this fact and his deputy did not know where some of the men lived; furthermore, detonators were not even supplied to some of the fog-men. The BoT report was as critical of this aspect as it was of the driver, and suggested that the company should make provision for line-side housing for men employed in such duties, and the installation of telephone equipment in their cottages to facilitate a prompt call out. This was particularly essential in areas where fog was known to be common, such as at Cudworth. When I was writing volume seven of *Trains In Trouble* I decided to go and do some local research into the accident at Cudworth and, by strange coincidence, I found myself driving through the town on 19th January 1990 when exactly the same sort of conditions prevailed. Even though I know the area well, I succeeded in driving past a Stop sign in the fog. Fortunately I was only going a few miles an hour and had ample time to avoid the other traffic, and was thus quite unlike the driver of the express which had come to disaster just a few hundred yards away some 85 years previously.

PHOTOGRAPHS; NATIONAL RAILWAY MUSEUM

HUDDERSFIELD

London & North Western and Lancashire & Yorkshire railways 21st April 1905

Over the years Huddersfield's joint station suffered a number of serious accidents and its layout was criticised on a number of occasions in official reports from the Railway Inspectorate but, perversely, it was long after the required improvements were made that the area's most serious accident occurred. Due to staff shortages on Good Friday, 21st April 1905, a driver who was getting ready to 'knock-off' was asked to do one small job before he finished. It was the relatively simple task of taking a 4-6-0 tender locomotive, No.610, to be turned at the station as it was too large for the 42ft diameter turntable at the Hillhouse shed. As the driver approached Huddersfield No. 2 'box at the end of the viaduct, a shunter directed him to No.1. platform because the approach to the turntable was blocked by three coaches. He drew this rake out of the dock road, and placed the coaches on the 'up-main' line inside the station. As soon as the empty coaches were uncoupled, the engine ran through the station and onto the turntable. At the same time as this was happening, the signalman allowed the 2.15pm train depart for Halifax, before setting the roads for No.610 to back into the station. However, the signalman had no intention of letting No.610 return to Hillhouse, because he had just accepted the 2.33pm L&YR train from Mirfield. Before the signals cleared for the approaching train to go into No.2 platform, a disc signal covering No.610 had to be set at danger. For some reason the LNWR driver failed to see this change, and he slowly backed out of the station running tender first. Even though a stack of coal impaired his visibility, he should have seen he was running in a 'facing' direction on the up-main. Not only was this against all the rules, but it also put him on the same set of rails as the approaching Aspinall 2-4-2T No.664. Though the driver of this engine blew his whistle and applied the brakes, he was still travelling at about 15mph when the engines collided buffer to buffer. The 4-6-0 was doing just a third of that speed, yet the force of the impact was horrendous; all seven coaches in the L&YR train were damaged to some extent, but the first three telescoped and the second completely disintegrated.

The sound of the crash was heard throughout the town and twelve local doctors rushed to the scene. The majority of passengers emerged with little more than shock and bruising, but rescue operations were hampered by the precarious condition of the first three coaches, which were piled one on top of the other. Shortly after 3pm the body of the first victim was recovered, but it was too dangerous to enter the wrecked coaches until the breakdown crane arrived. About 4pm the crane eased the wreckage just enough for men to climb into the first class coach. Inside they found the wife of an army surgeon, trapped below a wooden beam who, despite being fatally injured, insisted that she was in no pain, and chatted cheerfully with the rescuers and urged them to help the others. Despite the two fatalities, there were some lucky escapes, including a businessman who was flung from his seat in the first class coach through a hole in the floor. When he picked himself up, he found that his hat, coat and boots had been torn off him. Another lady was found suspended (by her cloak) from the roof of the same carriage, having been pinned there by a piece of timber. We must now consider what was said earlier about holiday workings, because this accident would, almost certainly, have not occurred if this hadn't been a Bank Holiday, because there would have been sufficient staff to have the engine turned and thus no need to use a driver who had been on duty over ten hours. On the other hand, the fact that it was a holiday resulted in fewer passengers using the local train than would usually have been the case. Ironically, though things were back to normal by midnight, the following morning a shunting accident occurred at the west-end of the station blocking Huddersfield Tunnel for several hours. The *Huddersfield Examiner* had much to report on that weekend, for in addition to the train accidents, there was also a tram accident and a minor earthquake! Eighty-three and a half years later, another accident occurred in exactly the same place, when a class 141 DMU collided with a class 150 Sprinter DMU, thus making Huddersfield Viaduct another of those locations to suffer two or more accidents at the same place.

PHOTOGRAPHS; ALL AUTHOR'S COLLECTION

HALL ROAD, LIVERPOOL

Lancashire & Yorkshire Railway
27th July 1905

Our next accident also involves the Lancashire & Yorkshire Railway, but this time we move from the woollen textile manufacturing districts of Yorkshire's West Riding, back to the commuter belt on the Lancashire coast between Liverpool and Southport. In October 1904 the L&YR introduced a full electric service over this route to accommodate the growing traffic, and as such it became the first main-line in Britain to convert from steam to electric traction. This also allowed the withdrawal of the 2-4-2T's from express work over the route, thus resolving the possible threat of high-speed derailments of the type experienced at Waterloo. However, in view of the high acceleration that these electric trains attained, the *Railway Magazine* of September 1905 noted, 'High acceleration is far from an unmixed blessing'. This comment was brought about by an unusual accident that occurred at Hall Road, which was the terminal station for Liverpool suburban traffic. Once the last passengers had alighted from trains which terminated there, the empty multiple units would pull out of the down platform and run into a long carriage siding situated between the two running lines. In due course it would run through another set of points into the up platform. Though this arrangement was quite ingenious, it was flawed with having a set of facing-points on the Down main line. Therefore, in order to ensure that through trains could not run into the siding, the point's switch-blades were inter-locked with the inner-home signal and, whilst ever the points were set for the siding, an electrical detector insured that this signal could not be lowered for through traffic. Unfortunately, the points were some 200 yards from the box and it required a strong pull to move them.

On 27th July 1905, the 6.20pm from Liverpool - Hall Road service had just run into the siding, but the signalman was momentarily distracted and forgot to reset the points. So, when he tried to set the road for the 6.30pm express to Southport, the inner-home and the two distant signals remained at danger. Thinking there had been an equipment failure, and being anxious not to be reported for unnecessarily delaying an express he waved a green flag to the now near-stationary train. Now the correct procedure, according to the rule book, was to send some competent person to the signal with a hand signal and detonators, and then let them flag the train past the signal if the road beyond this point was clear. Unfortunately the points were set towards the centre siding, and this could not be seen from the signal box. The motorman also knew that to accept a signal in such a manner was completely without authorisation, nevertheless he put on power and accelerated away; later claiming that he had seen the signals set at clear for the Southport road, which was completely impossible in view of the interlocking. In the 350 yards from the signal to the toe of the facing point, the express got up to over 40 mph. When it was evident that the road was still set for the siding the motorman made a full brake application, but he skidded into the empty train some 50 yards further on. An eye witness stated that the rear coach of the local became detached from its trailing bogie (which was forced under the express) and its body shot into the air with the force of the impact. This then dropped onto the leading coach of the express causing the deaths of 21 passengers, and serious injuries to many others including the motorman. The damage was entirely contained to the leading coach of the express and the trailing coach of the 6.20pm, and not a pane of glass was broken in any of the other vehicles. Naturally all the deaths and injuries were confined to those travelling in the leading coach, but here the injuries were quite horrific. According to the local newspaper, it would seem that many suffered serious head wounds. Almost half of those who died were women passengers, mostly secretaries and clerical workers who were returning home after their day's work in the city. Both the express motorman and the signalman were found censurable by the Coroner's Court, but they were not subjected to criminal proceedings. Meanwhile much criticism was made of the L&YR's new electrified system by the press, notably the *Liverpool Echo* who also had much to say about the issue of facing points on main lines. Yet the electrified line to Southport is still extant today (although few services now terminate at Hall Road), even though the Beeching Report saw no future for a commuter service outside London and scheduled the line for closure. Fortunately Beeching was strongly opposed, and after protest letters filled 14 oil drums on the platform at Liverpool's Exchange station his proposal was over-ruled and the Southport line lived on.

PHOTOGRAPHS; B.C. LANE COLLECTION

WITHAM

Great Eastern Railway
1st September 1905

The bad year of 1905 continued with another high-speed derailment on the Great Eastern's main line between London and Colchester, when the 14-coach 9.27am from Liverpool Street to Cromer came off the rails at a 'V' crossing in Witham Station. The train was running at nearly 70 mph when the derailment took place, and as a consequence its coaches were scattered around the station. The first three were thrown beyond the platform and one of these then caught fire, the next five fouled the platform and demolished the station buildings, whilst the ninth was turned over on to its roof and was completely destroyed. Sadly, nine people lost their lives, including a station porter.

Two platelayers and a foreman platelayer had been working on the track immediately before

the accident, but they emphatically assured the inspector that they were merely clearing ballast prior to re-packing the timbers, and nothing they had done could have affected the running of the express. With this the Inspector, Colonel Von Donop was faced with another inexplicable high-speed derailment but, just six weeks later, evidence was presented which caused him to reopen the case. This curious state of affairs began when a railwayman went into the District Locomotive Superintendent's Office in Ipswich, and made a statement concerning a friend of his who was employed as a shunter at Witham. This man was working in the Witham goods yard on 1st September and, at the time of the accident he had been standing directly opposite the crossing. As he was waiting for the express to pass before he could report to the signal box, he watched the engine go by at very close quarters. As it did so he saw a rail jump, which was quickly followed by the leading coach wheel ploughing into the ballast. The shunter was soon preoccupied by the rescue work at hand, during which he sustained some injuries to himself. Yet later that afternoon, and much to his surprise, he found himself being suspended for being drunk on duty, although he adamantly insisted he'd had just a single glass of beer and some biscuits at lunch

On reaching home the dejected shunter took himself to bed, and the doctor was called to attend to his injuries. Six weeks later his friend visited him, and upon hearing the shunter's account of what happened, this man duly made his report to the officials in Ipswich. With this matter now being formally recorded, the GER had to call the Inspector back to examine the extraordinary story. The three Witham platelayers were still emphatic in their assertion that they had not done anything untoward, and it appeared that this was the word of just one man against three, and a suspended man at that; Colonel Von Donop had to determine whether there was any merit in his story or if it was a case of 'sour grapes'. He therefore recalled the train crew who's evidence was quite significant. The driver said that as he approached Witham he noticed the three platelayers working intently on one spot ahead of him, and he felt very alarmed that they were not getting out of the way as they should have done. Were these men busily engaged on trying to complete repairs? The question seems to have been placed beyond doubt, when the train's front guard was recalled, for he confirmed that the wheels of his van had certainly seemed to strike something very solid as it ran through the crossing. In view of this the Inspector decided that, despite their statements to the contrary, the platelayers had erroneously loosened the fastening at the 'V' crossing and been unable to rectify their mistake in time; this had allowed the wing rail of the crossing to jump under the weight of the engine, in turn this had struck the wheels of the front van and derailed the whole train. Whilst the question of why the shunter was suspended from duty after the accident was not raised by the Inspector's report, one can but wonder whether this action was done in order to cover up the foreman platelayer's error. If so, we can only conclude that there was a complicated cover-up to avoid the true facts of the accident from emerging!

PHOTOGRAPHS: THE LATE ARTHUR TREVENA COLLECTION

SALISBURY
London & South Western Railway
1st July 1906

Having eliminated the 'mystery' element from the accident at Witham, we now turn to the terrible destruction of the weekly boat train from Plymouth to London's Waterloo station which was one of the LSWR's most valuable workings. This was back in the days before Southampton had fully developed as a trans-Atlantic terminal, and when many ships still used Plymouth. It would seem that the railwaymen took great pride in the service, and it was always worked very smartly. Signalmen would give it preference over almost every other type of traffic, and there can be no doubt that the boat trains raced up to London as fast as they could. To this end the LSWR had been forced to issue orders that the boat trains had to run to schedule, and if any driver failed to comply with this order he would face the penalty of being taken off his engine. Every effort was made to provide passenger comforts, and to this end several bogie coaches were converted into elegant open-first saloons offering every possible luxury. On 1st July 1906, three such coaches were formed into a five coach train with a baggage van and a kitchen-brake, which was drawn by a T9 class locomotive as far as Templecombe. The passengers who had disembarked from the liner *New York* had enjoyed a good run to Templecombe, and the change of engines went smoothly so the replacement Class L12, No.421, set out on time for the 112 miles to London. This part of the journey was scheduled to take just 116 minutes, and it obviously called for some smart working and average speeds of 60 mph. However, although it was an experienced crew on the footplate of No.421 that night, they had neither done this trip before nor worked non-stop through Salisbury. Twenty miles out from Templecombe the train had dropped four minutes behind schedule, but they made a good speed on the long falling gradients which lead down to Salisbury, where they averaged around 70mph. Whilst this was by no means exceptional for this stretch, a 30mph limit was in force through Salisbury station due to the curves which existed there. As No.421 came towards the station, the signalman gave it a clear road, but the driver failed to slacken his speed. The guard, sensing something was wrong made a gentle application of the brake, but did not dare to fully apply it for fear of splitting the train.

At the up distant signal the driver opened his whistle and kept it open as he steamed hard past Salisbury West 'box. Had something gone wrong on the footplate, was the driver trying to sound a warning, we will never know! In any case of taking sharp curves at high speed there is a theoretical point where an engine will overturn; however, before the 'point of no return is reached' there are increasingly significant warnings of danger. Surely the driver must have experienced this as he passed through Salisbury, his speed still an estimated 70 mph. As it roared through the curve on the station's western approach, No. 421 remarkably kept to the rails at first and they incredibly made it to the east end of the station, but a 10-chain radius curve then proved to be their undoing. Between the east end of the platform and the over-line bridge carrying Fisherton Street, No.421 came off the track and it smashed into the rear of a down milk train which was passing just at that very moment. The time was put at 1.57am, and if this is correct, it sets the boat train's average speed as having been 72mph since it left Dinton. The rear vans in the milk train were smashed to pieces and its guard was killed instantly, meanwhile the first three coaches overturned killing half their complement of passengers and seriously injuring seven more. The driver and fireman of the express also succumbed, as did the fireman of a light engine which was standing in the nearby bay platform. In all 28 people died in a mystery which has never been truly understood. Speculation was rife, had the LSWR train been trying to beat the GWR times, had the driver been tipped by a wealthy American passenger to get him up to London in good time, had the crew been drinking? None of these questions could be answered with any degree of certainty for the only men who knew were dead, and dead men can tell no tales. It certainly did not seem as though the driver had been under the influence of drink, and a comment he had made before Templecombe showed that he knew exactly what would happen if he arrived at Waterloo ahead of schedule. The fact that such an action would lead to a heavy fine seems, therefore, to preclude the other two popular suggestions. The Inspector, Major Pringle, could shed no light on the mystery that would explain such a serious error, and could merely make the suggestion that the speed restriction through Salisbury should be tightened to 15 mph. After a very detailed study of the accident, my personal theory is that something went badly wrong on the footplate or at least distracted the driver and his mate to such an extent that they miscalculated their approach to Salisbury, but that too is just speculation; and speculate is what we must now do with the case at Grantham which occurred three months later.

PHOTOGRAPHS: WILTSHIRE LIBRARY & MUSEUM SERVICE

GRANTHAM

Great Northern Railway
19th September 1906

A little after 11pm on 19th September 1906, the small town of Grantham was awakened by the sound of a terrible crash. Looking out of their windows local residents could see a vivid orange glow lighting the night sky. Combined with a loud noise and curiosity, this sent many householders rushing to the junction of the Harlaxton and Old Wharf roads, which were spanned by the Great Northern Railway. The scene which met people's eyes was awful in the extreme, for strewn around the bridge and down the embankment to its side lay the remains of what had been the 8.45pm Scots Express from London, King's Cross. The locomotive, Ivatt Atlantic 4-4-2 No.276 lay on its side, whilst its tender and five of the vehicles in the train had run down the side of the embankment, four more were wrecked behind the engine; only the last three vehicles were still standing upright. Eye witnesses who actually saw the train said it had raced through Grantham Station at speeds of around 40 mph, when it was supposed to stop. Indeed this train had been driven on many occasions by the

same driver including the two previous nights, so there is no reason why he should have forgotten he was booked to stop at Grantham. But fail to stop he did, and as he raced through the station there is conflicting evidence as to whether the brakes were applied or not. Beyond Grantham the Nottingham branch diverged to the left of the track, and on this line was the GNR engine shed. As many trains exchanged engines at Grantham, a practice of leaving points set for the branch had developed. Though there is no reason why this should not have been done, it remains a fact that, had the points been set for the main line (as they were elsewhere), the disaster would have been averted. But, with them set for the branch, No.276 was in effect being sent through a double reverse curve at speed and derailment was inevitable. The driver and fireman were killed instantly, as were eleven passengers and a postal sorter.

Yet why should an extremely experienced driver fail to stop and, in effect, drive his personal locomotive in such a reckless fashion. There are no end of ideas and suggestions, all of them plausible, all of them with adequate reason to be discounted. There has been no end of speculation on the matter, and each writer on railway disasters has their own personal theories. Signal failure was an immediate suspect, but examination found no such defects at Grantham. Next we might consider poor visibility, but even though it was drizzling slightly all the signals could be clearly seen by other trains passing through prior to the accident. Next comes the suggestion of brake failure, yet it looks as though this can be discounted as the evidence tends to indicate that they were used by the driver at the last minute as he went through Grantham station. If not brakes, then what about mechanical failure? It seemed unlikely as No.276 was a nearly new engine, which had been in the charge of the same driver since being built. It was regularly maintained and a trouble- free member of her class. It was also inspected by no lesser person than its designer, H.A. Ivatt, just hours after the accident and he found no fault at all. The unions felt the presence of a 'Premium Apprentice' from Doncaster Works as a fireman was the root cause, as this person was an educated gentleman who could not fairly pull his weight on a heavy duty such as firing on the ECML. Yet the apprentice was already an experienced fireman, having done numerous trips on the main line. Other suggestions were put that the driver did not get on with his relief fireman, and they had been fighting on the footplate, yet the only man to see the crew as the train raced through Grantham said each man was standing stock still and looking ahead through their respective spectacle plates. No the driver was drunk, claimed some, but in all the testimony given about the man, it was emphatically stated that he rarely took any alcohol, even though he was not a total abstainer. People who saw the driver at Peterborough before he coupled on to the express say both footplatemen were quite sober. Was the driver suddenly taken mad? Whilst there are one or two well-documented examples of this happening abroad, very few cases were ever reported in Britain and such an event does not fit the character of the man in question. Neither does the suggestion that this was nothing more than sheer reckless driving. Similarly a suggestion that he was struck by an agonising bout of sciatica does not hold much water; as debilitating an illness as this is, it would not cause a man to let his engine race on out of control. Indeed, when the driver had suffered a previous bout of sciatica on an earlier date whilst passing Corby, he managed to go on to King's Cross completely unaided, although he then declared himself unfit for duty and returned home to Doncaster by passenger train. Possibly it was the conditions under which locomotive crews were then expected to work, with days in excess of 10 or 12 hours being the norm; for example, when the accident occurred, the driver had already been on duty for over eight hours. Then there was the possibility that he was racing down from Stoke Summit to make up time, as they were already down on the scheduled time. He had been eight minutes late the previous night, and in those days drivers could be fined for such actions. All or non of these theories could have had a bearing on the matter, any one may have been an ingredient in the disaster, perhaps it was a combination. The simple truth is, that for all our speculation, we will never know what went wrong on the footplate that night!

PHOTOGRAPHS; ABOVE, AUTHOR'S COLLECTION
CENTRE LEFT, THE LATE ARTHUR TREVENA COLLECTION

KIRTLEBRIDGE

Caledonian Railway
6th April 1906

Leaving aside the mysterious high speed derailments of 1906, we now move on to two examples from a series of major collisions which were noted that year. We begin just north of the English/Scottish border, in an area which seems to be prone to disaster. Inside a very short distance the Caledonian Railway and its successors endured a catalogue of serious accidents which would include Beattock, Dinwoodie, Ecclefechan, Gretna Junction, Kirtlebridge, Lockerbie and Quintinshill. Of these Kirtlebridge was the scene of two accidents, the first of which occurred in October 1872 when a goods train collided with a passenger train and claimed 12 lives; on 6th April 1906 history was destined to repeat itself. At 7pm that evening a 15 vehicle express goods left Glasgow's Buchanan Street for London, calling at Carstairs Junction where two more vans were added. Around 20 miles north of Carlisle, and not far from the point at which the Solway Junction Railway diverged, the third vehicle in the train suffered a sudden and catastrophic mechanical failure. The vehicle was an 8-ton West Coast Joint Stock meat van, and its wheel had become detached from the axle boss causing a partial derailment. It ran in this condition for around a mile, the wheel sliding back and forth along the axle. Two miles south of Kirtlebridge the coupling behind the meat van finally broke under the strain and the front section of the divided train came to a halt upright, as did the first four trucks in the divided portion. However, the nine vehicles behind these all left the track and tipped over, fouling the down line in the process. Before any remedial action could be aken by the train crew, an 11-coach express to Glasgow was on the scene. Despite frantic efforts the crew were unable to turn the engine lamps to red, and in the absence of any other means of warning the express crew, the passenger train sped through the darkness and on to the wreckage in its path. One passenger was killed and several more seriously injured, but little could have been done to prevent this type of accident when trains were so close together; or could it? In the USA and certain other countries quick-igniting warning flares were supplied to train crews for just such an emergency. The Inspector recommended trials into this type of system in Britain, but no action appears to have been taken. Yet as we will discover on page 130, such a provision could have prevented at least one similar accident.

PHOTOGRAPH; JOHN HUGGON COLLECTION

ULLESKELF

North Eastern Railway
24th November 1906

Six months on from Kirtlebridge we move from the West coast route to the NER's line from York to Leeds, and an accident of undeterminable cause. The engine involved in the incident near Ulleskelf was NER Class F1 4-4-0 No.85, which was crewed by men from Hull, working a Hull - Scarborough - York - Leeds - Hull diagram. It was the type of working much favoured by crews in the era of the 10-hour day, but it was one which would lead to their untimely deaths that day. At Bolton Percy, the signalman had arranged to turn the F1 off the up Leeds line and put it on to the up Normanton line which ran parallel with the Leeds line as far as the large junction at Church Fenton. He had done this to the Leeds train because an empty goods train was occupying the Leeds up line at Ulleskelf. Now on an adjacent track an L&YR train was running from York to Normanton and Manchester, and it had been more or less side by side with the NER train since leaving York. There was the suggestion that the two trains were 'racing' each other, and this was not an uncommon event by any means. In view of the occupation of the various tracks, the Bolton Percy signalman set his signals against the NER train, intending to switch the 4-4-0 on to the Normanton line as soon as the L&YR train had cleared the section. For whatever reason, the crew of the NER engine failed to observe these signals and they ran into the section on which the 60-wagon goods train was standing. Having passed all means of protection, the NER train slammed into the rear of the goods train. Fortunately the guard of this engine was not in his van at the time, for in compliance with Rule 55, he had gone back to the 'box in order to remind the signalman that they were still standing on the main line. The badly damaged engine was photographed at York a few days later, prior to being taken back to Darlington for repairs.

PHOTOGRAPH; THE LATE KENNETH HOOLE COLLECTION

ELLIOT JUNCTION

Dundee & Arbroath Railway 28th December 1906

It has to be said that some railways had developed a markedly polished safety record by the start of the 20th century. However, there were examples on other lines where working practices were so remarkably lax, that the slackness was tantamount to danger. On the 27th anniversary of the Tay Bridge Disaster another example of inefficiency led to the disastrous year of 1906 being rounded out in fiendish circumstances. Ironically it was just 20 miles north of where NBR No.224 plunged beneath the waters of the Tay, that the company suffered another disaster once again in fierce storm conditions. The Dundee & Arbroath Railway was in the joint ownership of the North British and Caledonian railways and each company ran its own trains along the route, but for all other operations it was basically run as a separate concern. It was a far from well-managed line, funding was limited, and the Caledonian and North British were the most acrimonious of partners.

In foul, snowy weather, a south-bound goods train became divided into three parts at Downie Sidings, about a mile south of Elliot Junction. This somehow or another went unnoticed as far as Easthaven, a good two miles further on. The driver of this train then had the bright idea of running back for the derailed trucks, and then propelling these down to Easthaven where his train would be reformed. This was the first mistake in a day of serious errors, for as he began to push the trucks ahead of him, they derailed due to the heavy snow. The up line was blocked, and single line working had to be instituted between Elliot Junction and Easthaven; mind you, it would appear that no-one took the trouble to inform Arbroath of this situation! Similarly, the pilotman appointed to take trains through the three mile section was not given an engine, and because there were not always counter-balancing workings, he sometimes had to make the return journey on foot through the deep snow. As I have said, it was a slack set up! At 10.31am the 7.35am Edinburgh Waverley - Aberdeen express, drawn by Holmes NBR 4-4-0 No.324, arrived in Arbroath just one hour late. In view of the conditions it was quite a remarkable timing, but its progress northwards was prevented by deep drifts in which it was reported that no less than six trains were already stuck. The express hung round Arbroath for four hours, and by then the passengers were getting restless; wanting to either press on or return to Edinburgh. A decision was taken to do the latter, and at 3.26pm No.324 set off back for Edinburgh.

Some 16 minutes earlier a Caledonian local train had set off for Dundee, and a decent interval had to be allowed for this train to get away due to the fact that the trains had been forced to work to the old time-lapse principle following the failure of the telegraph system. Unfortunately No.324 was still facing north and, as it had not been turned, the crew had to work their engine tender first. Whilst such operation was not uncommon on the D&A Joint line, it was not the most conducive of conditions to drive an engine through the teeth of a raging blizzard without any protection. Perhaps this is why the driver missed seeing the home signal at Elliot Junction which was set at danger to protect the stationary Dundee train. The driver protested it was showing clear, but it was discovered that whilst it was not fully in the 'on' position, it had only drooped by 10 degrees. More reasonably he claimed that a fog man should have been placed at the distant signal to give him a caution, but fogmen were barely used on that slack railway. The fireman could not give any evidence as he, along with 21 passengers perished on that snowy day at Elliot Junction. Afterwards the driver was clearly in shock and greatly affected by what had happened, his speech was slurred and he was shaking. As a consequence it was automatically concluded that he was drunk and he was brought up on charges of 'Culpably and recklessly driving his train while under the influence of drink.' He did admit to having a 'nip' of whisky with one of his passengers before leaving Arbroath, but came out of the bar straight after; refusing a double as he did so. Nevertheless he had run at speed in adverse conditions when he had been warned to proceed with caution, and this was enough for the Inspector, Major Pringle, to comment; 'The lack of intelligence, or of caution and alertness, displayed by [the driver] were, in part at all events, induced by drink, the effects of which may have been accentuated after he left Arbroath by exposure to the weather.' The rail unions fought the driver's case and he was released from the cells in Dundee on £300 bail - a sad end for a man who had twice been chosen to drive Royal trains. None of those who supported the driver's case thought he was drunk, and fewer still thought it was a lack of intelligence on his part; that, they contended, was demonstrated by none other than the managers of the slackly set up joint railway.
PHOTOGRAPH: AUTHOR'S COLLECTION

FELLING, NEAR GATESHEAD

North Eastern Railway
26th March 1907

The night of 25th March 1907 suffered a very sharp frost, with ice forming well before midnight. A clear, cloudless night followed, but a warm sun quickly dispelled any vestiges of the frost that remained by mid-morning. As the day progressed it grew hotter and hotter, but down in a cutting on the East Coast Main Line, something strange was happening to the tracks. With the cutting acting as a sun trap (and with the rail gaps still set to winter expansion clearances), the track began to buckle. In the early part of the afternoon a man who was deaf and dumb was proceeding on his business on the east side of Felling when he chanced to look at the railway and saw what was happening, but how could he convey this alarming intelligence? Crossing the bridge he hurried to a man operating a steam roller nearby, and with some difficulty he managed to get him to come and view the scene. On seeing the rails 'in a shape like an elongated letter S', the driver ran to Heworth signal box a short distance away. There he mounted the steps and told the signalman to put his signals to danger, to which he received the reply 'Who are you and what has twisted the rails?' instead of promptly setting his signals to danger. Moments later the 8.35am express from Liverpool arrived on the scene behind NER Class R 4-4-0 No.725. The engine hit the twisted rails, derailed and canted over to the left before coming to rest against the cutting's sloping side. Seven LNWR vehicles in the train were badly damaged and eight passengers were seriously injured, two fatally so.

PHOTOGRAPH: THE LATE KENNETH HOOLE COLLECTION

BROCKLESBY

Great Central Railway
27th March 1907

The tiny Lincolnshire village of Brocklesby formed the south-east corner of a busy triangular junction, where the incoming route from Wraton Junction (where lines from Doncaster, Gainsborough and Lincoln merged) split to serve the Great Central branches to Grimsby, Immingham and New Holland. As may be imagined, it was an extremely busy location, alive with traffic to and from the south Humber ports; particularly coal and fish. The day after the accident at Felling, another incident was noted at Brocklesby as two goods trains collided in the station. The wooden bodied vehicles were literally ripped apart by the force of the collision and their contents were scattered all across the tiny station. One of these trains was loaded with wet fish (packed in boxes) and brined fish (packed in casks of salt water). As our pictures show the fish were literally sprayed around the accident scene, and were later picked up and deposited in piles on the platform. Whilst these goods legally remained the property of the consignees, there can be little doubt that the good folk of Brocklesby enjoyed a few fish suppers that night - no questions asked!

PHOTOGRAPHS: THE LATE ARTHUR TREVENA COLLECTION

SHREWSBURY

London & North Western Railway
15th October 1907

Just thirteen months after Grantham, we come to the final instalment in what have become known as the *Mysterious Midnight Derailments*. This time the scene shifts to the 32½ mile long line from Crewe to Shrewsbury and the West of England Mail which left Crewe at 1.20am. This service was formed up at Crewe from trains which had arrived from Scotland, Yorkshire and Merseyside and on 15th October 1907 it included 15 vehicles, of which only five were passenger coaches. At its head was LNWR Experiment class No.2052 *Stephenson*, on the footplate a pair of men from Crewe who had begun their turn at 7.30pm the previous evening, having had over twelve hours rest since they last booked off duty. Through no fault of their own they did not get away from Crewe until eight minutes after their scheduled time, but they made good time on the run and had clawed back all but three minutes of the arrears as they began the long descent down to Shrewsbury. As they came down the Crewe Bank, the signalman in the 'box at the incline foot offered the train to Crewe Junction 'box. The man there accepted the train under the condition 'Section Clear but Station Blocked', which obliged him to stop the train and caution the driver. The signals were therefore kept in the stop position, but regardless of this No.2052 raced past the box at a speed of around 75mph. Just 600 yards beyond the Junction 'box, the LNWR converged with the GWR line from Chester just before the platforms. The resulting curve of this junction was at a radius of about nine chains, and a 10 mph speed limit existed for trains crossing this. At 75mph the Experiment class loco had no chance and it turned over on to its right and skidded on for about 75 yards, only stopping about 20 yards short of the platform end. The first two vehicles were totally wrecked, the third was thrown to the right, but the next six piled up in a tangled heap behind the engine. Both footplatemen, two guards, three postal workers and eleven passengers were lost.

With this accident rumours were once again rife, and the same sort of stories which were being promulgated after Grantham quickly reappeared. The resulting investigation was an exhaustive one, and this time it even included the forensic examination of the dead driver's vital organs. This ruled out seizure, sudden illness and drink, but it did not elaborate on the questions that were on everyone's mind. It was half felt that the driver must have fallen asleep on his footplate, but his duty was not an exhausting one. Yet, in fairness to those who held this view, it must be pointed out that the driver had been out of bed for four out of the past six nights and at that time railway drivers, like doctors today, were being called upon to work exceptionally unreasonable hours. I am in no position to disagree with this theory, but a glance at the driver's disciplinary record card might just suggest another cause. On this there are thirteen entries, five for missing his train and being absent without leave, four more for running past stations where he was due to stop, one for dropping 17 minutes without good cause, one for emitting black smoke in a station and, most significantly, two for overrunning signals set at danger. The driver was a man who obviously took chances or, at best, suffered from lack of attention. To my mind he was aiming to get right back up to time and miscalculated his approach down into Shrewsbury. But, my theory is just as questionable as the other ideas which have been put forward into the mysterious midnight derailments, for we have no way of knowing the true facts. All we know is that Shrewsbury was, thankfully, the last of these inexplicable accidents.

PHOTOGRAPH; LENS OF SUTTON

HINDLEY & BLACKROD JUNCTION

Lancashire & Yorkshire Railway
22nd January 1909

Following an overhaul at Horwich Works, two L&YR engines were being despatched back to their home sheds in Liverpool when they found themselves being shunted into a siding at Hindley & Blackrod Junction in order to let a Chorley - Wigan passenger train pass. It was a fairly typical winter's day in Lancashire, and fog mixed with smoke from mill chimneys and household fires combining to create 'a real pea-souper'. The leading engine was No.8 an 0-4-4T Sharp Stewart of 1885 vintage, but there seems to have been some confusion on the footplates of the two engines. Whatever went wrong during the setting back of the two engines was never satisfactorily explained, but whatever it was, No.8 was left fouling the running line. The passenger train, under clear signals came upon the scene, but the smog prevented the crew having any advance warning of the danger which lay ahead. They thus smashed into No.8, killing its driver and severely injuring the fireman. On board the Chorley train 32 passengers suffered injury, though none were of a serious nature. Number 8 was taken back to Horwich, where it is pictured next to the L&YR compound 0-8-0, No.1476, which is fitted here with an indicator shelter on the smokebox platform. The wrecked engine stood at the works for over a year before it was confined to the scrap, presumably because the management were reluctant to dispose of such a recently refurbished engine.

PHOTOGRAPH; B. C. LANE COLLECTION

TONBRIDGE

South Eastern & Chatham Railway
5th March 1909

If we are honest, most of us will admit that we hate being watched-over while we do our work - particularly so if the person watching is in a position of superiority. The feelings this can engender are often worsened if that person is younger than us, for such is human nature! But did such feelings lead to a collision at Tonbridge Junction on 5th March 1909? This particular day the Royal Train was conveying King George VII to Dover, and such a train had to be very precise in its timing. In the case of Tonbridge, its time was scheduled as 10.24½ am, and to ensure no delays were occasioned, the Locomotive Superintendent ordered that any train which preceded the Royal special should carry an inspector to ensure punctuality. Two trains were scheduled to pass through Tonbridge Junction before the 'Royal', these being the 'Continental Mail' which left Cannon St. at 9.05am, and an 8.30am fast train from Charing Cross to Dover. The booked times at Tonbridge being 9.50am and 9.55am respectively, but these trains were running slightly behind schedule and both approached the junction about 9.59am. The road was cleared for the mail train, but when the fast-train passed Penshurst it was only allowed to

work forward under Rule 5, 'section clear but junction blocked'.

However, all was not well aboard the footplate of 4-4-0 No. 497 as it made its way down to the junction. The right-hand feed pipe (situated under the foot-plate) was frozen and the fireman was trying to thaw it with burning tow; meanwhile, steam from the chimney was beating down on the boiler-casing obscuring the driver's view. But further problems were being experienced between the 45-year old driver and the assistant locomotive inspector who was only 24. Regretfully, neither the fireman nor the inspector survived the crash, so only the driver's testimony remains as to what actually happened. He claimed that he was worried and over-anxious to make up time due to adverse comments which the younger man had sniped continuously after leaving London. Whatever the case, it remained the driver's responsibility for observing signals, and he ran straight through the junction and smashed into the side of the 9-coach mail train drawn by 4-4-0 No. 165. Even though the consequences were not as severe as they might have been, the incident does bring into question the need for the presence of premium apprentices on the footplate. Some may even ask did the incident at Tonbridge answer the mystery of Grantham?

PHOTOGRAPH; SOUTHERN RAILWAY COURTESY KENT COUNTY LIBRARY SERVICE

CRAWFORD

Caledonian Railway
2nd April 1909

Another recently refurbished engine was involved in a spectacular, but thankfully innocuous, accident on 2nd April 1909. The engine in question was 4-6-0 No.903 *Cardean* which had just passed through Crawford Station having climbed over Beattock Summit from Carlisle with the down 'Corridor' express. As it was descending the 1:240 incline the drawbar between the engine and tender suddenly failed. The Westinghouse brake came on automatically, but when the driver tried to get the engine into reverse gear he was unable to do so, and as a result No.903 ran on for three-quarters of a miles before coming to rest. The train it left behind was derailed completely, but all the vehicles remained upright. On investigation it was discovered that one of the front driving wheels was missing, and the main frames were twisted and bent. Furthermore the reversing gear and engine brakes were badly damaged, thus explaining the inability of the crew when they had tried to stop the engine. The missing wheel, complete with a piece of coupling rod still attached was found later against an embankment some 150 yards from where it had parted company with the engine. Microscopic examination of the fracture revealed that the crank-axle had been made from inferior metal, which at some stage in the manufacturing process had been left in an overheated condition. Thankfully no-one was seriously hurt in this incident, but it forms an important part of railway history like the two accidents at Penistone where similar defects claimed lives. How could such a failure have occurred so quickly, and was the BoT report correct in its findings. On this point there was much informed debate. Metallurgists considered the issues and many asked searching questions. Given that the axle had a serious fault, could it have failed so quickly or was there some other cause (such as a locomotive design fault) which speeded up the failure?

PHOTOGRAPH; NATIONAL RAILWAY MUSEUM

FRIEZLAND

London & North Western Railway
10th August 1909

We have already met an errant driver from the LNWR's Huddersfield Hillhouse Shed, and it is the crew of another engine from that shed that we now discuss. However, in this instance the two footplatemen on 0-6-2T, No.1608, were considerably more diligent in their duties than the driver who made the fatal error in 1905, yet both these men were killed outright when their train was involved in an accident near Friezland station on 10th August 1909. The train in question was the 9.20am Huddersfield - Stockport express which was usually comprised of just three coaches and a Webb Coal Tank engine, with perhaps around thirty or forty passengers on board. This day it was no different, but it is easy to reflect how serious this accident could have been had the train been fully loaded. Indeed such a situation had been witnessed the day before, as the same train had been a heavily laden eight coach affair due to the fact that it was the first day of the Huddersfield holiday fortnight. As it was not booked to stop at local stations it was run along the Micklehurst loop, a diversionary route built by the LNWR in the mid-1880s to relieve traffic congestion on their line from Stalybridge to Diggle. Passenger trains had been running on this line since 3rd May 1886, and it was used by many of the LNWR trains destined for Stockport. For some reason, as the train reached Friezland that Tuesday morning, the leading bogie of the front coach became derailed. It ran for some distance in this condition, possibly for half a mile, at a speed of 40 to 50 mph. The driver made no immediate effort to stop, and it was later assumed that he must have guessed the terrible consequences which might come from trying to make an emergency stop with a derailed coach on Friezland Viaduct. Despite what was going on behind him, he bravely kept on the steam and thus had sufficient momentum to reach safety on the Manchester side. Unfortunately, as he began to brake, the derailed coaches caught on a trailing siding, which acted as a fierce brake to the train. The engine, which was still on the rails, was flung violently to one side, so much so that it spun completely around and smashed into the train. Both the driver and his mate were killed instantly and several passengers were injured, but none seriously. Local station staff from Friezland station, were the first on the scene, but within a short period of time, special 'rescue' trains had arrived from Stalybridge and Huddersfield. Medical aid was soon at hand, with the arrival of local doctors, who were reinforced by surgeons from the infirmaries at Oldham and Huddersfield.

PHOTOGRAPHS; BOTH AUTHOR'S COLLECTION.

ROWLEY

North Eastern Railway
29th January 1910

The problem of snow is one we have already discussed, but as will be imagined such problems were considerably exacerbated on moorland and mountain railways. The highest standard gauge railway system in Britain once ran over the Pennine fells in County Durham. The backbone of this system was the Stanhope & Tyne Railroad which opened as early as 1834, and pioneered a remarkable railway over this wild and desolate countryside. The majority of the train services on the western section of the S&T were mineral, though passenger services were attempted in the early days. Unfortunately, the problems with this pioneering attempt was the number of inclines, in which passengers had to be raised or lowered in open trucks. The dangers in this were evidenced on the very first day of operation, when four trucks being lowered down the 1 mile 128 yard long Weatherhill Incline broke free. A total of between 40 and 50 people were in the trucks, and of these two men and a boy were killed outright with many other suffering horrendous injuries. Though this type of service was thankfully short-lived, it is interesting to note that they were the highest standard gauge passenger workings ever operated in this country. However, the high rental which the company had agreed to pay for the land it used was already creating serious problems, and in an attempt go get out of trouble they borrowed no less than £290,000 and agreed to an interest on 11% per annum. When the problems continued, the creditors began to demand settlement, and on 29th December 1840 the railway was wound up. It was reopened by the Derwent Iron Company as a purely mineral line and, along with an extension to Tow Law, it eventually passed into the hands of the Stockton & Darlington Railway who looked at ways to improve the route. It was decided that this would best be achieved by deviating two of the worst inclines, Nanny Mayers and Hownes Gill, by a route along Whitehall Moss. Once this deviation had opened, a Consett - Darlington passenger service was introduced and this lasted until 1939. However, in view of the line's isolated position it was one which frequently suffered blockage by snow. The tiny engine sheds at Waskerley even had the luxury (or was it the necessity) of two snow ploughs. On 28th January 1910 the 6.26pm for Darlington left Consett behind 0-6-0 No.910. By 6.53pm it was stuck in deep snow at Rowley, but with the snow ploughs already busy on the upper reaches of the S&T, sister engine No.915 was detached from its moorland shed down to Rowley. Unfortunately as the engine made it's way down Whitehall Moss, the snow filled into the cuttings behind it and both engines were trapped. There they remained for two days, until an engine and plough from Consett battled its way through to free them. During this time the passengers were accommodated in the few local houses and the station buildings, the same buildings which now attract thousands of visitors in their rebuilt form at Beamish Museum.

PHOTOGRAPHS; BEAMISH, THE NORTH OF ENGLAND OPEN AIR MUSEUM.

STOATS NEST

London, Brighton & South Coast Railway 29th January 1910

Whilst passengers were stranded up in County Durham, their contemporaries on the the 3.40pm up express from Brighton that same afternoon were experiencing even more hazardous conditions. As their train approached Stoats Nest station, it suffered a serious mechanical defect which in turn caused a spectacular derailment and led to the death of five passengers, two people standing on the platform, and injured a further 65. The train was drawn by a 4-4-2 locomotive, with brake third No.1325 behind the tender. Behind that came the Pullman cars *Albert Victor, Princess Patricia* and *Prince,* a composite and another bogie third brake. At Earlswood it took the 6 mile long short-cut route to London which had been built at the end of the 19th century, but as the train approached Stoat's Nest station the automatic brake was suddenly applied whilst the express was travelling at 45mph. In an attempt to reach East Croydon the driver made a

serious error of judgement by applying full pressure to the train pipe, without first looking back to see what had actually happened. Unable to keep the brakes off, he finally turned round and saw the train had divided behind the fourth coach. The signalman at Stoat's Nest saw sparks emerging from below the train, and he at once prepared to send the message 'stop and examine train' to the next box. Unfortunately, before he could do this the situation had passed beyond salvation. The leading bogie of the fifth vehicle (54ft. third-class carriage No.1325) had, however, derailed on a diamond crossover south of the station and caused it to take the down local line. Spread across the tracks, the coach ran broadside up the ramp leading to the station platform and demolished the starting signal and water column located there. The damage to rolling stock and infrastructure was extremely severe as our pictures show. To investigate the reasons for this spectacular but deadly incident, a detailed mechanical inspection was undertaken. The axle-box was examined first, but this bore no signs of being run 'hot'. The wheel was therefore immediately suspect, so it was completely removed from its axle under pressure; this was achieved when a pressure of just 11 tons was applied, and when they tried to re-fit the wheel it only took two tons to force it home. It was then found that the axle's wheel seat was slightly ovaloid, and the tight grip of the usual press fitting had not therefore been fully achieved. It should have taken a pressure of 62½ tons to move this wheel from its seat, but in its defective condition it required just a fraction of this pressure. Indeed it would seem as though the axle could have gone out of gauge at any time since it was built in 1902, because it looked as though it had never made a complete fit with the wheel. It is so unfortunate that it took a knock on the approach to Stoat's Nest which meant that the axle went out of gauge at one of the worst possible points. Officially the Railway Inspectorate stated that only two such incidents of wheels slipping on their axles had been recorded, both on the GWR (at Maidenhead in 1895 and at Exeter in 1898). A similar view was expressed in *The Railway Engineer,* which said 'the shifting of a wheel on its axle is fortunately a very unusual occurrence', but as we have already seen such an incident had taken place at Kirtlebridge just four years prior to the incident at Stoat's Nest, and I have also come across other references to the movement of wheels on their axles, particularly on goods vehicles of older (pre-1895) origin. The railway companies were struck by this event, and from then on most of them followed the GWR's example of applying a back test pressure of 50 tons to a wheel when it was fitted to the axle. Once again the GWR led, and others followed.

PHOTOGRAPHS; ABOVE AND CENTRE, NATIONAL RAILWAY MUSEUM. BELOW, AUTHOR'S COLLECTION

DARLINGTON

North Eastern Railway
15th November 1910

In the case of the collision at Elliot Junction we came across a case where a driver, suffering shock after an accident was thought to have been drunk on duty. Whilst this man admitted having had a single nip of whisky before taking his train out, he vehemently denied having taken anything more. That case well illustrates the difficulties faced by the Inspecting Officers, and indeed other railway officials, for there was no way of being medically certain whether a man was under the influence of drink or not, that is other than the the usual signs such as slurred speech, blood-shot eyes, illogical behaviour and so on. Whilst these characteristics are plainly evident in some drunks, we all know that it is possible for others to act perfectly rational even after heavy drinking. Yet, even so, such a person would have very slow reactions to fast-developing situations, such as driving a car (or a railway engine). Whilst Breathalysers are well known to motorists of today, and the railways have their screening arrangements under the 'Alcohol & Drug Policy' rules, in past times there was no way to safeguard against a railwayman who put himself 'over the limit'. There are many recorded instances where drink and drugs have contributed to railway accidents, but in the days prior to scientific test, the Inspectors often had to make their conclusions on circumstantial evidence. In a number of cases which I have studied, I believe that they were somewhat wide of the mark, and one particular Inspector (who was a complete abstainer) seems to have 'uncovered' quite a few offences. However, I think that the scenario which Lieutenant-Colonel von Donop hinted at, after the Darlington collision on 15th November 1910, was undoubtedly the correct one.

When the day was but 50 minutes old, the back portion of the 11.01pm Gateshead (Parkgate) - Hull goods train was struck in the rear as it was waiting at signals on the up main line. This main line provided a route round the back of the station, and was used by many fast trains not booked to stop in Darlington (including that which we will meet in the accident of 1928). As it waited for the off, it was hit by NER Class S1 4-6-0 No.2115 from Tweedmouth shed which was on a Newcastle - Leeds express goods. Although there was some irregularity on the part of the signalman, the Leeds train was running at a speed of 35 mph against the signals which were at danger. The Tweedmouth crew were killed outright, and for a while it seemed as though this would become another of the 'Midnight Mysteries' because the Inspector simply concluded that the driver had fallen asleep. However, evidence was subsequently given by the station-master at Tweedmouth which caused the investigation to be re-opened on 14th December. In a statement to the NER, the station-master said he had known the driver for three years, and twice during that time he had seen the man worse for drink; once on 11th May 1909 when his engine was involved in a slight accident. The Inspector thus began an detailed investigation at Tweedmouth, where it emerged that the driver's drinking habits and insobriety were well-known. As his drunkenness was always evidenced when he was off duty, no-one felt it was their business to report him. Firemen were reluctant to work with him, and the one killed at Darlington had put in a request for a change of duty just before the accident! A friend of the driver who had tried to talk to him about his dangerous habit had received the reply 'that he was impelled by a power he could not resist.' Whilst there was no firm evidence to suggest that the man had reported for duty under the influence, we are all aware of the cumulative affect it has and how long alcohol lingers in the blood stream. If the Inspector's suspicions were correct, such a condition may well have been more than enough to induce drowsiness as No.2115 raced down to Darlington that cold winter's night.

PHOTOGRAPH; THE LATE KENNETH HOOLE COLLECTION

WILLESDEN

London & North Western Railway
5th December 1910

Though it is essential to examine the cause of serious accidents, it is also often very interesting to look at the speed with which rescue work was effected and normal services resumed. Accordingly I now concentrate on the events which took place at Willesden Junction on 5th December 1910 after a terrible rear-end collision occurred between two trains running from Watford to London. This accident was almost a direct copy of that at Darlington, and human error resulted in the 8.30am train to Broad Street dashing into the back of the crowded 8.16am to Euston as it was standing in the station. The rear carriage of the stationary train was hit with considerable force and splinters of glass and wood showered platforms three and four. The carriage roof was detached and fell down on top of the next coach into which the body had been telescoped. Both these coaches then tipped over sideways against the the platform, but were prevented from falling right over by the stone edges. The next two coaches were also badly damaged, but all the passengers managed to get out through the doors.

Three people were killed and over forty others were injured - some quite seriously. However, the toll may have been even higher had it not been for the superb efforts of the rescuers. Railwaymen have had a long tradition in first-aid, and at Willesden Junction their skills were fully utilised. Pieces of shattered woodwork were used as splints, whilst carriage seats were torn out and improvised as stretchers. A lady who assisted in the station buffet managed to extract a large bottle of brandy from the bar, and passed among the injured asking them 'if they would like a little something to steady their nerves!' Men from the nearby engine shed quickly arrived on the scene with heavier tools, whilst a breakdown train was quickly made ready. The manager at the nearby Bedford Motor Company's works sent a fleet of vehicles to help convey the wounded to hospital, whilst several local doctors made their way to render assistance on the scene. One of the curious things about the accident, is the number of people who climbed onto the top of the carriages to render assistance; one man even made his way onto the damaged roof of the rear coach, but fellow rescuers urged him to get down quickly when they saw how precariously balanced it was. Because Willesden was such a major junction, it was essential that the running lines be cleared at the earliest opportunity. The breakdown gang arrived about 10am, just over an hour after the crash, and by 3pm almost all traces of the disaster (apart from the broken platform edges) had been completely removed. Therefore it is little wonder that photographs of this accident have been very hard to come by.

PHOTOGRAPH; LONDON BOROUGH OF BRENT

HAWES JUNCTION

Midland Railway
24th December 1910

Living right next to the Settle & Carlisle Railway I am daily able to witness modern day operations on this magnificent line which straddles the very backbone of England. It was one of the last great main lines to be built in Britain, and its course was one which was designed as an express trunk route, rather than one particularly aimed at providing a local service. The expresses which ran over it were fast, light trains, pulled by relatively lightweight locomotives. For years the Midland's locomotive policy provided nothing more powerful than 60-ton 4-4-0s for its passenger work, whilst its goods locomotives were 50-ton 0-6-0s. Due to this, rigid load limits were laid down for each class of engine and, if these loads were exceeded, a pilot engine had to be attached. With the Settle & Carlisle cresting at Ais Gill (1,169 feet above sea level), the use of pilot locomotives was extensive. In 1910, many of the locomotives used on this work were 4-4-0s of 1877 vintage, with large numbers based at Hellifield, Leeds (Holbeck) and Carlisle (Durran Hill) engine sheds. Other engines used on this work were rebuilt Class 2 4-4-0s, and it was two of these which were involved in the accident we now discuss. Whilst this incident was a direct result of a signalman's error, its indirect cause lay in the locomotive design policy of the Midland Railway which necessitated the use of so many pilot engines up to Ais Gill. In turn these engines had to be despatched down to Hawes Junction where they could be turned on the (now preserved) turntable built by the Carlisle engineers, Cowans, Sheldon & Co. There were obviously an awful number of light engine movements, and it is not difficult to see how easy it would be for a busy signalman to overlook an engine. The problem had happened before on numerous occasions, but these incidents had never led to disaster. However, it was just a matter of time before the Midland's methods of working would catch them out, unfortunately when it did there would be an errant signalman upon whom most of the blame could be conveniently placed.

The man in question had just forty minutes of his 10-hour night time shift to complete when he made his fateful mistake, and the length of that shift is a factor which will be found in many of the accidents in railway history prior to the implementation of the 8-hour day. Night shift at Hawes Junction, now known as Garsdale, might seem a cushy number today, but back in 1910 it was no easy duty. In the hour proceeding his mistake the signalman had handled no less than nine light engines which had come down from Ais Gill for turning. Two of these had come up from Carlisle with south-bound trains, and having been turned they were sent on to the back platform, normally used by NER trains to Hawes and Northallerton in order that a down express could go past. It was not unusual for the drivers of pilot engines to be held thus, and all drivers engaged in these duties knew that they could only be slotted into gaps in the busy traffic. Indeed, waiting was so familiar to these men, that they might only do one or two pilot trips in an entire shift at times; unfortunately, familiarity breeds contempt. As soon as the down train had gone the signalman moved the two Carlisle-based pilot engines, Nos. 448 and 548 from the back platform road to the down main, bringing them to a halt by the down starting signal. He then became preoccupied with the busy up line, where he handled two goods trains (at 5.20am and 5.43am respectively) before he dispatched two pilot engines back to Leeds. With only a few minutes to go before his shift ended, it is obvious that the signalman's mind was beginning to relax and he forgot all about the two light engines on the down line. Whilst this was bad enough, it was by no means a fatal error, as the previously described Rule 55 covered for just such an occasion. Remember its provisions required that a train must not stand for more than two minutes at a stop signal before the man goes to the signal box but during fog or falling snow the man must at once proceed to the signal box.

As I mentioned earlier, familiarity breeds contempt, and those pilot engine drivers were familiar with delays. However, having once been sent on to the main line, they had never had to wait for more than 4 to 6 minutes - the time it took for the express to clear Ais Gill. So, in view of this they sat there waiting far longer than they ought to have done; when questioned later both crews admitted that Rule 55 was rarely applied at this location. At 5.39am Dent signalbox offered the midnight express from St. Pancras to Hawes Junction, and with the two light engines still being overlooked, the signalman offered the approaching train to Ais Gill. It was accepted at once and, in the absence of Rule 55 or lever collars to remind him, the Hawes Junction man pulled off his signals so that the late-running express could have a quick passage through his section. At 5.44am the two light engines saw the down starter clear, and they applied power and moved out into the night. In the stormy conditions the signalman would have been hard pressed to hear them move off, even though they 'popped' their whistles before doing so. However, the driver of another pilot engine waiting to go back to Hellifield had seen it all, and having then watched the express race through he ran to the 'box to tell the signalman. The information was received with incredulity, as the signalman really believed that he had already sent the two engines on their journey to Carlisle; a look at his train register and a call to Ais Gill box confirmed his terrible error. It was too late to do anything now, and as they watched the sky to the north turned an angry reddish orange colour; the worst had happened. Running at 65mph the express (behind Class 2 4-4-0 No.549 and pilot engine Kirtley 4-4-0 No.48) had charged through Moorcock Tunnel and on emerging they smashed straight into the back of the rearmost of the two engines which were travelling at just 25mph. The impetus drove the two engines forward for 200 yards before they turned over, the two express locomotives followed suit and they came to rest on to their left hand sides in the cutting near Lunds Viaduct. The front two coaches of the express were completely telescoped, and in these twelve passengers were killed. The high pressure gas-lighting pipe on this coach was shattered and the escaping contents were immediately ignited by sparks, a blinding flash followed and the underbellies of the storm clouds above glowed an angry red. A Johnson 2-4-0 which was running past on the up line immediately stopped and dumped the contents of its tender on the fire, but with the gas still escaping and the wind fanning the fire through the smashed wooden coach bodies, all but the rear two coaches were consumed. In his report the Inspector, Major Pringle, came out with some scathing criticism of pressurised gas for train lighting, but his recommendation for electric lighting incurred the wrath of the *Journal of Gas Lighting* which asserted that the alternatives were just as dangerous. However, less than three years later the issue would be forcibly raised on the other side of Ais Gill when fire consumed yet another express.

PHOTOGRAPHS; AUTHOR'S COLLECTION

PONTYPRIDD

Taff Vale Railway
23rd January 1911

We have already seen a number of accidents which occurred when a signalman forgot about a train in his section, and then allowed another one to enter it. Though there are many reasons for such aberrations, Rule No.55 of the Associated Railway Companies Rule Book, had a very good safeguard to ensure these mistakes did not lead to an accident. Furthermore, in view of the national publicity which had been given to the Hawes Junction disaster, it is hard to comprehend how an almost identical accident could occur just one month later. Yet this is exactly what happened in South Wales on 23rd January 1911, after an 0-6-2T, No.121, working a Hafod - Barry coal train came to a halt at the outer-home signal of Rhondda Cutting Box near Pontypridd Coke Ovens. The signalman was preoccupied in a conversation with his Inspector regarding train delays, and it may have been this matter which caused him to have the unexplained lapse of concentration which led him to forget the presence of the coke train. Instead of applying the fundamental Rule No.55, the driver whistled for a signal, and then sent his mate to fill the engine's lubricators. How such a casual course could have been adopted after Hawes Junction is absolutely beyond belief, but it demonstrates more than any other case how railway companies (and those who worked upon them) failed to appreciate the significance of railway accidents on other systems. In many ways it was a question of

them not us, and the need to heed the warnings when they were presented (regardless of where they happened) was a lesson which had still to be learnt. Yet, this insular attitude was not unique to the smaller pre-Grouped companies

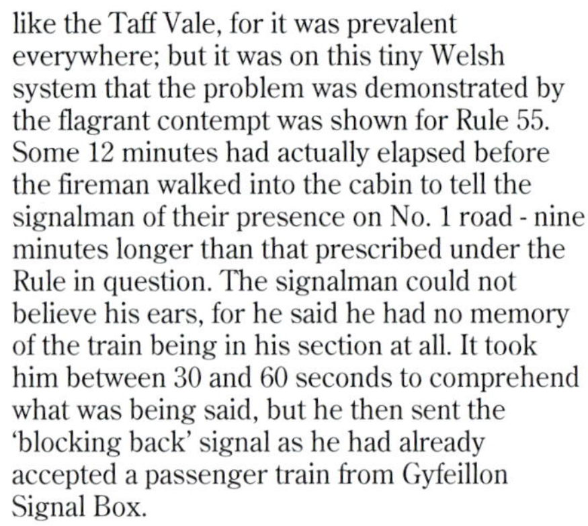

like the Taff Vale, for it was prevalent everywhere; but it was on this tiny Welsh system that the problem was demonstrated by the flagrant contempt was shown for Rule 55. Some 12 minutes had actually elapsed before the fireman walked into the cabin to tell the signalman of their presence on No. 1 road - nine minutes longer than that prescribed under the Rule in question. The signalman could not believe his ears, for he said he had no memory of the train being in his section at all. It took him between 30 and 60 seconds to comprehend what was being said, but he then sent the 'blocking back' signal as he had already accepted a passenger train from Gyfeillon Signal Box.

The Inspector concluded it was hard to understand how two experienced signalmen had made the mistake of 'losing' the freight train, but put it down to their irregular working of the Tyer's two-position single wire block telegraph instruments. Whatever the case, they had barely begun to take action when the 9.15am passenger train from Treherbert to Cardiff, headed by 0-6-2T No. 193 ran into the back of the standing train at a speed between 25 and 30 mph. The coal train's brake van, No.6361, was completely demolished and the guard was fatally injured, dying in Cardiff Infirmary some weeks later. Serious telescoping to the local train resulted in heavy damage to the first and second coaches as the pictures graphically show; eleven passengers were killed and four more were seriously injured. In this accident Pontypridd was yet another to become part of the infamous list of railway locations which have had the misfortune to suffer two or more railway accidents, the other occurring on this section of the Taff Vale back in 1878.

PHOTOGRAPH; ABOVE, TOPHAM PICTURE LIBRARY
LEFT, R. C. RILEY COLLECTION.

CHARLESTOWN CURVE

Lancashire & Yorkshire Railway

21st June 1912

With the accidents at Doublebois, Wellington, Llanelly and so on, we have already raised the question concerning the suitability of tank engines to handle fast passenger trains. Certain elements of those early accidents left the matter open to speculation, but an event which took place on Friday 21st June 1912 was to resolve the issue once and for all; thus demonstrating the undesirability of the use of these types of locomotives for fast working. The L&YR's 2-4-2 radial tank engines were an extremely numerous class in fact, with a maximum of 330 in service at one time, the L&YR had more of this type of engine than any other British railway company. For example, the LNWR and GER only had 487 2-4-2Ts between them. The first L&YR radial tank engine was built to the design of J.A.F. Aspinall at Horwich Works in 1889 and this engine, No.1008, has survived into preservation. With a variety of modifications, long and short bunkers, super-heating, thermal storage heaters, and so on, the 2-4-2Ts worked every kind of service from lowly shunting to express traffic.

The L&YR, with its many branches and intensified suburban routes, viewed them literally as being a 'Jack of all trades'. With the exception of Aintree shed at Liverpool, every L&YR depot had some, and Manchester Newton Heath shed were allocated Nos. 111-2, 230, 253, 275-6, 285 and 480. Numbers 111-2 were used almost exclusively for the Oldham branch and No.480 was the reserve, but the remainder were all regularly employed on express duties which had previously been the sole domain of the L&YR Atlantics. They ran express trains to Leeds, Blackpool, Southport and Colne, as indeed they had to because there were only two express tender engines based at Newton Heath in the summer of 1912; and, of these, No.1412 was kept almost exclusively for the Windermere train, whilst No.1417 worked the Liverpool expresses. Accordingly, the train which left Manchester Victoria at 2.25pm for Bradford and Leeds was hauled by 2-4-2T No.276.

Between Eastwood and Hebden Bridge, the L&YR main line had a sharp curve near Dover Bridge. This was a legacy of the difficult construction of this line, which meant an 'S' shaped cutting with embankments at either end had been erected in place of the tunnel which was originally envisaged at this location. Known as the Charlestown Curve, it had caused havoc for years and there had been repeated discussions about straightening the line. Generally express drivers were well aware of the problems this curve presented, and it was usual practice to brake hard as they approached the cutting at speeds of between 50 and 60mph. Slowing down to 30-40mph, the engines would then glide through the cutting at a controlled speed before putting steam back on. It usually worked well, but on this June day the use of a tank engine on this working led to disaster. Because the bulk of No.276's weight was on just two driving axles, an immeasurable strain was being placed on the permanent way. This was undoubtedly compounded with water surging back and forth in the side tanks, which would shift the weight on an axle by several tons; on tanks with four driving wheels the effects were more noticeable than those with six. This was probably an important factor in Charlestown and it bears out the damage to the permanent way, which was forced out of alignment for 175 yards before the engine actually derailed. With a super elevation of five inches and a radius of 30 chains, it is little wonder that the track's weaknesses were thus exposed.

According to *The Halifax Courier* 'the front two coaches were smashed to atoms, with the second being completely telescoped.' Four passengers in this coach were killed instantly and eleven more were seriously injured. All the Leeds coaches were either wrecked or badly damaged, but the three rear coaches suffered surprisingly little damage. The Inspector was extremely critical of the use of tank engines for express work and as a result Aspinall's 2-4-2Ts were rapidly transferred to other work, sadly other companies did not appreciate the significance of this and they continued to use tank engines for fast work as we shall see later on.

PHOTOGRAPHS COURTESY; G. GREENWOOD

EAST ANGLIA

Great Eastern/Midland & Great Northern railways 25/6th August 1912

Severe floods are nothing new in the history of mankind, from the global deluge encountered in the days of Noah, to the major inundations which affected most of western Europe at the start of 1995. Those floods swept through the low countries, and when the rivers Maas and Rhine rose to exceptionally high levels, it was thought that Holland's sea defences would be irreparably breached. However such floods have not been confined to other countries and as page 24 demonstrates, Britain has had its own fare share of such problems. One area which has particularly suffered is East Anglia, and in 1607 great floods covered the area around Norfolk. When a cloud burst was centred on countryside just to the east of the city in August 1912, 8" of rain (around 1,000 millions of tons of water) fell in just under 20 hours. The outer ring of the cloud burst spread from Hunstanton to Kings Lynn, Bury St. Edmunds and Aldeburgh, all of which recorded at least 3" of rain. Fen country as far back as Spalding and Peterborough was also affected, and no less than 52 road bridges were swept away in Norfolk alone. In Norwich 15,000 people were affected by water damage to their homes, but the railways also suffered in one of the busiest holiday periods of the year. As an example, our picture shows the extent of the problems as it portrays the conditions at the Midland & Great Northern Railway's Norwich City station. Railways were covered by impassable floods in no less than 36 places, stretching from Amsey in the west to the Southwold Railway in the east, Melton in the south and Helpringham in the north. Serious underline damage was sustained when culverts, embankments and bridges were washed away which, in scores of places, left the track suspended in mid air. Due to flooding to a depth of 16 feet 6 inches in parts of the city, rail communications with Norwich were completely cut off for 62 hours, in spite of the fact that the city had then no less than six separate routes to London. The GER even brought into use a rake of passenger coaches which could be used as a dormitory for stranded passengers and staff. As the flood waters receded, the clear-up work began and trains were started up again even though it was impossible to reach many of their destinations. Motor buses were introduced to span the gaps, where they could, and services were greatly modified or rerouted over less affected lines; for example many GER trains were diverted via Gorlestone to Yarmouth Beach and North Walsham in order to reach London. The worst affected lines were Fakenham to Wells, which did not reopen until 10th September, and the Brundall to Cantley and the Forncett to Norwich sections which were closed until the autumn. A major slip which occurred at Hall Bank Road Cromer required the establishment of a contractor's tramway which was laid on 17th September, whilst major works were still under way in Holt Road Cutting. At least 121 new signal posts and 487 telegraph posts had to be erected, as did miles of lineside fencing.

PHOTOGRAPH; COURTESY NATIONAL RAILWAY MUSEUM

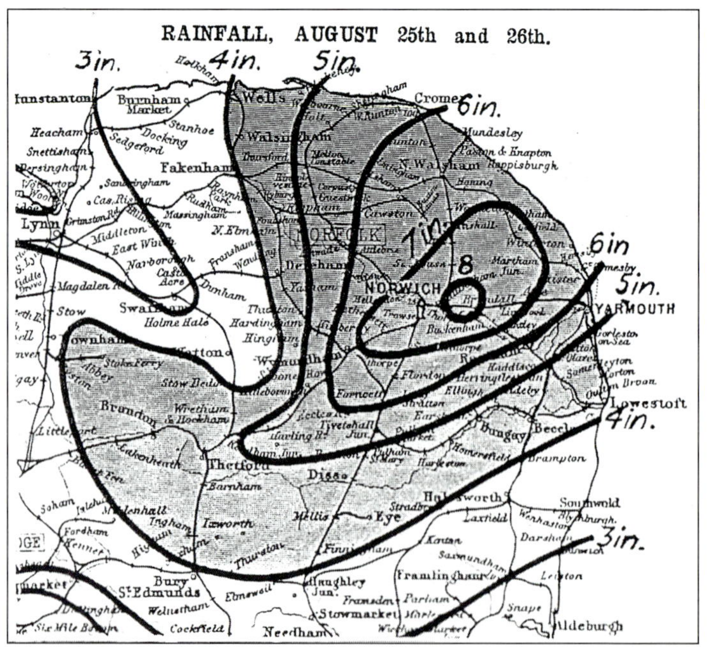

DITTON JUNCTION

London & North Western Railway
17th September 1912

As we have already learnt, a railway locomotive was a potent instrument of destruction, particularly when it ripped through wooden-bodied rolling stock. Due to the massive construction of even the smallest engines, it was rare for a locomotive to be completely destroyed in an accident. The damage might look bad, particularly when cabs and boiler cladding were ripped away, but rarely was an engine so substantially damaged that it had to be scrapped. In the coming pages we will see examples of engines that were destroyed, but one of the first express locomotives to be completely demolished occurred in an accident at Ditton Junction on 17th September 1912 when a Ramsbottom 2-4-0, No.1529 *Cook,* literally broke its back as it rammed into a brick-built bridge after derailing at 60mph. The coaches were thrown over the wrecked engine and then piled up in a confused and splintered mess beyond the bridge. To add to this, gas-lighting systems ruptured and the wreckage turned into a raging inferno. Thirteen passengers and the footplatemen died in the ugly, drab Cheshire countryside that September evening.

Our story begins at Chester station when the 5.30pm summer only service was made up for Liverpool. It was a motley selection of coaching stock, formed of a relatively antiquated Precedent Class 2-4-0, two GWR horse-boxes, three 6-wheel coaches and four 8-wheeled bogie coaches (in that order). In many ways it was typical of the aforementioned practice for 'specials' and 'seasonals' to be made up of second class stock. The age of *Cook* did not have a bearing in the matter, but its condition did. Unfortunately the front bogie wheels had no side play and this, in effect, gave the engine a rigid 15 foot wheelbase. As we have noted, the stock was all provided with the old gas lighting and this played another contributory part in what followed. However, the single biggest ingredient in this recipe for disaster was the inexperience of the locomotive crew and those who arranged their employment on the ill-fated express. They all came from Llandudno Junction Shed, which seems to have suffered a certain degree of laxity; the arranger of engines there was only a driver, and as the Inspector called him, 'a man of no authority'; the driver whom he appointed was the shed's 'spare man' who, although he claimed to know the Liverpool road, was sadly lacking in experience having only been along it 10 times in four years, and then never on an express; his fireman was merely a passed cleaner who had never been across the fast junction at Ditton. There was nothing wrong with their route knowledge as far as Chester, and here they could have requested a pilotman who knew the road to Liverpool Lime Street. Sadly they did nothing of the kind and went on trusting in their own inadequate skills.

From Runcorn Bridge a 1:114 gradient ran down to Ditton Junction where, to say the least, the track layout was quite unusual. At the incline foot the Chester line came in between two lines from Warrington which we will call Warrington North and Warrington South. The north line does not really affect our story, unless we accept that its presence may have helped confuse the crew of the Chester train. As for the south line, beyond Ditton it continued towards Liverpool as a slow line, whilst the Chester line became the fast line. Now to facilitate the many movements that were required between these two sets of line, two crossovers had been installed; the first of these was designed for freight trains, the second being the actual point where the Warrington South and Chester lines transformed into slow and fast lines. It would seem, from his actions, that the inexperienced man driving *Cook* was not aware that there were two separate crossovers, and he was therefore probably misled by the signals. With three sets of signals it would be easy for a driver who did not know the junction to convince himself that the centre signals applied to the centre (Chester) road; in fact they were nothing of the sort, for this was the fast to slow line signal! Alternatively the driver may have thought that he would have been given the straight (fast) road, as ordinarily he would have; however, on this occasion this had been given to a London express which was due to reach Liverpool ahead of the Chester train, even though the latter reached the junction first. The Chester train was thus put through the crossover. Had the engine not been so 'stiff' it would have probably negotiated the crossover in safety, even though this had a 15mph speed limit. Unfortunately the rigidity of the 2-4-0s wheelbase caused the engine to turn on to its side and thus the disaster was complete.

PHOTOGRAPHS: ABOVE, AUTHOR'S COLLECTION
BELOW, THE LATE ARTHUR TREVENA COLLECTION

TORSIDE, CROWDEN

Great Central Railway c1913

Although we have no date for this picture, it can be identified as one of three accidents which occurred on the descent from Woodhead Tunnel during the period 1910-1914. All of these resulted from crews being overcome by smoke fumes as they passed through the 3 mile long subterranean passage. It was often so bad within the tunnel bore that crews had to lie down on the footplate and cover their faces with handkerchiefs. If they subsequently passed out, there was then no hand on the controls and the heavily loaded west-bound trains would run-away as far as Torside. Alerted to the fact by the Woodhead signal man who would send the bell code 4-5-5, 'Train Running Away on Right Line', the runaway would be put into a head-shunt near Crowden which had a very substantial stop block at the end. To date I have discovered no less than 54 such instances and, as our one of rear cover pictures show, such runaways did not end the instant the line was electrified.

PHOTOGRAPH; D. L. FRANKS COLLECTION

NEWCASTLE, MANORS STATION

North Eastern Railway 3rd March 1913

The mention of driverless trains will undoubtedly bring to mind the incident recorded at Newcastle's Manors station in August 1926. This famous incident is discussed on page 86, but how many readers know that at least five accidents involving the Tyneside Electric sets occurred at this station including the one pictured here on 3rd March 1913. This shows the 9.58am from Monkseaton to Newcastle which was leaving Manors East station at 10.35am when it was run into by an empty stock train from Heaton to York. The loco-hauled train hit the wooden bodied 4-car set at a speed of about 10 mph, pushing the bodies of the rear two cars along the metal under-frame, causing injuries to 49 passengers, some seriously. Following a mistake in the nearby Argyle Street signal box, a signalman had passed the electric train intending to put back the No.5 lever which worked the Tynemouth line home signal. Unfortunately, due to the pressure of work he mistakenly set back No.9 lever which worked a ground disc signal and misled the driver of an empty stock train into thinking he had a clear road through Manors East. At this time he was going about 30 mph, but when he saw that an electric train was standing at the platform he immediately applied the brake and put the engine into reverse gear. This made all the difference to the outcome of the accident, for even if the stock train had been only doing 15mph, it is almost certain that lives would have been claimed otherwise. The signalman clearly admitted his error, but the Inspector considered it a boné fide mistake and did not criticise the man too harshly.

PHOTOGRAPH; BEAMISH, THE NORTH OF ENGLAND OPEN AIR MUSEUM

RAMSGATE TOWN

South Eastern & Chatham Railway
11th March 1913

If the error of the signalman at Argyle Street is open to criticism, what happened in Kent eight days later makes his actions pall into insignificance, for a catalogue of errors were noted in the build-up to an accident at Ramsgate Town. Whilst the consequences of these events were not particularly serious, it could have been a particularly catastrophic accident. For years the Railway Inspectorate had battled for the introduction of a continuous braking system on trains, indeed it was one of the three principle elements in the 'Lock, Block and Brake' campaign. The regulation of the Railways Act of 1873 required the railways to show the progress they were making with signal interlocking, block working and continuous braking systems, but these last two requirements did not become law until 1889. However, once these systems were introduced, it did not mean that they were always brought in to use as the unusual occurrence of 11th March 1913 revealed, after a run-away train collided with a brake van standing at the buffer stops in Ramsgate Town station. The train was the 1.55pm up passenger train from Margate to Ashford, which reversed at Ramsgate. The engine, a Wainwright H class 0-4-4T, No. 324, worked into Margate Sands station at 1.02pm with a three-coach train of bogie stock from Canterbury. On arriving here, the driver was informed that a 6-wheeled brake-van, No.681, was to be attached for through-working to London. The three coaches were detached, and the van marshalled in behind the engine before the train was coupled up by the duty carriage-shunter.

It was normal practice to first attend to the screw-link coupling, then join up the vacuum brake-pipes, followed by the steam-heating pipes. But, on this occasion, the shunter found the steam-heating pipe was burning his leg as he dealt with the coupling, so he attended to this next. Having taken this task out of sequence, his attention was diverted and he routinely climbed back on to the platform, leaving the brake-pipes unconnected. Though the train stood at the platform for about 20 minutes, the omission was not only missed by the shunter, but also the driver, guard and station inspector. The train duly set out on time for the 3 mile run to Ramsgate; unknown to all, the only operative brakes were those on the engine. As per local practice, the guard was riding in the brake van behind the engine, and not in the rear coach as prescribed in the rule book. On approaching Ramsgate the driver tried to apply his brakes, but the combined weight of the train, some 98 tons 15 cwt., pushed him into No. 1 platform at about 8mph. The van at the end of this road was knocked through the buffer stops, onto the platform and, as the lower picture shows, through the entrance doors. Nine passengers were slightly injured, and a young girl entering the station was badly bruised by falling bricks. The report noted that the locomotive collided with the van, because the percentage of unbraked to total rolling weight was as high as 72%. The final words on this accident should rightly go to Major J.W. Pringle, the investigating officer, who said: 'It seems hardly possible that a case of this sort should happen, where four men are responsible for the proper connection of brake pipes.' Indeed it does not, but this is yet another of those cases where slack practice had set in, and the duty of double checking had not been carried out. As many railway operations relied upon such diligence in cases where an operation could not be made 'fail safe', then it was the responsibility of those entrusted with safety duties to see that they were carried out in the prescribed manner.

PHOTOGRAPHS: KENT COUNTY LIBRARY SERVICE

COLCHESTER

Great Eastern Railway

12th July 1913

On 12th July 1913 the 1pm Cromer - London express was travelling towards Colchester behind No.1506 at a speed of around 40mph when it struck E4 Class 2-4-0 No.471 with such ferocity as to completely destroy the express engine. The crew of No.1506 were both killed instantly, as was the front guard of the train, but a locomotive inspector travelling on the footplate had a miraculous escape, even though he was amongst the 21 people injured. The light engine which it struck was being shunted after arriving with a passenger train from Harwich, but it was forgotten by the signalman after it had run past the starting signal, even though it was standing just 50 yards from his box. This signal was then put to danger, and the signalman should have placed a collar over its lever to prevent him pulling it off for any other traffic. However, having busied himself with a down goods he forgot about No. 471 completely, and he was not reminded of its presence by the fireman who should have carried out Rule 55. When the crew of the light engine had stood on the main line for about three minutes the driver saw the signals go clear for the express, and he at once sounded his whistle and shouted up to the signalman, but simultaneously sent his fireman to the 'box to ask the man if he knew what he was doing. As the fireman left the engine, the driver reversed his engine and put on full steam to try and get away from the express which was now fast approaching him. He had managed to move about 25 yards when No.1506 was on top of him, and with the impact he was suddenly propelled forward for some 283 yards. The driver's prompt action calls for special remark, as his decision to try and move the engine away undoubtedly lessened the severity of the crash. The cause of this accident was the serious lapse of the signalman in forgetting the light engine, but as the Inspector remarked, he was not alone in this. 'This accident is the third which has taken place in the last three years in which a serious collision has occurred owing to light engines being forgotten on running line, the two previous ones being at Ormskirk and Hawes Junction......It is clear that there is an undoubted liability of the presence of a light engine being overlooked by a signalman. The inquiries held into these accidents seem, however, to show that there is a tendency on the part of some signalmen and drivers not to adhere strictly to Rules and Regulations when light engines are being dealt with.'

PHOTOGRAPH: THE LATE ARTHUR TREVENA COLLECTION

YEOVIL

Great Western Railway

8th August 1913

At Yeovil Pen Mill Station the following month, it was another confusion between a driver and a signalman which led to a disaster in which 2 people died and one passenger was fatally injured whilst 9 others were also hurt. At 6.12pm a down excursion from Paddington was standing in the platform when it was struck in the rear by GWR 4-4-0 No.3710 *City of Bath* which was running a scheduled passenger express. It had been the intention of the signalmen at Yeovill to shunt the excursion order to let the express pass it, but as No.3710 approached the north box, it overran a signal at danger. This was the third of three stop signals controlling the approach to the station, and it was once again irregular working by a signalman which contributed towards the driver's error that summer evening. On approaching the outer home the train should have been brought to a definite halt, after which it would have been drawn up first to the inner home and then the starting signal. Regretfully the signalman considered that because his track indicator for the outer home had shown occupied for around 20 seconds, it was alright to bring the train on. Thus, without properly stopping the train, it ran on through the section past the inner home at clear, and then the starting signal which was at danger. A simple error where a few more seconds wait would have made all the difference, but that is the sort of timing which accidents are born of.

PHOTOGRAPH: R. C. RILEY COLLECTION

AIS GILL

Midland Railway
2nd September 1913

In the Hawes Junction accident the Midland Railway's locomotive policy had played a part in the disaster, and this same policy had its role in the accident which happened at nearby Ais Gill on 2nd September 1913. The sequence of events begins at Carlisle on the evening of the first, where two Midland 4-4-0 locomotives were being prepared to take over trains that were working from Scotland to London. The first of these, Class 4 No.993 was due to work the night sleeper from Glasgow and Stranraer; the other was Class 2 No.446 which was scheduled to take an express from Edinburgh. Both engines were loaded with supplies of coal that had been purchased locally, but this was full of shale and slack which made it very difficult for crews to maintain steam and there had been many informal complaints about it. When the first train came into Carlisle, the driver found it was 13 tons above its maximum capacity and he asked for a pilot. One was available but the Locomotive Superintendent refused to provide one, considering that it would take more time to attach it than the train would drop by not having a pilot. Unassisted, and with its fire burning sullenly in the grate, No.993 had difficulty in maintaining steam after it started to climb at Appleby. By Mallerstang the problems were acute and the combination of a heavy load and poor coal took its toll, eventually causing the train to stall just half a mile from the summit. To protect the stalled train, which would have to sit on the main line for several minutes before steam could be raised, a series of detonators should have been laid on the track to the rear in accordance with Rule 179. However, the driver told the front guard 'we'll be a few minutes', but the message passed to the rear guard was 'only a minute', so he did not bother to put down detonators. All of them should have known better, as the protection of a stranded train was paramount; a fact that would be demonstrated at almost the same spot 82 years later when a south-bound Sprinter collided with a northbound one which had become derailed due to a landslide. Even so, the absence of detonators would not have mattered had the Edinburgh express been observing the signals, but sadly it wasn't.

In those days drivers were in the habit of leaving their cabs and walking round the running boards to touch up the axle-boxes, even though the introduction of wick-type lubricators on the Class 4s had completely done away with the necessity for such a practice. Indeed, with an engine steaming badly and a novice fireman left in sole charge of the footplate, things were bound to go wrong. The driver returned after several minutes, to find his fireman struggling with the injector and the water almost down to the bottom of the glass. As the train approached Mallerstang 'box, the driver was preoccupied with the problems, after all a 'hot boiler' was such a serious offence that he might face dismissal. As it climbed the bank its speed had dropped by a good third and No.446 was barely making more than 20mph. The Mallerstang signalman witnessed the engine's slow progress and believed it was slowing down in accord with his distant signals, so he lowered his home signal with a view to bringing the train to a stop at his starter until he received the accepting signal from Ais Gill. Unfortunately the green light of this home signal was the only one which the driver of the Edinburgh train saw, and he took it as giving him a clear road. When the signalman saw that he had not slowed down at all, but was steaming hard he quickly dropped his home signal to danger and waved a red hand lamp out of his window at the train. The driver never saw this final warning and the train stormed off up the gradient, the crew working hard to keep up the momentum in spite of the poor coal loaded at Carlisle a few hours earlier. As the driver kept an eye on his new fireman's performance, he failed to see the obstruction standing on the road ahead. Then, in the absence of detonators to warn him, he crashed into the rear of the stationary express which had left Carlisle 15 minutes earlier. Number 446 smashed through the rear van and buried itself into the next coach and fire broke out at once. With the aid of extinguishers it seemed to have been brought under control, unfortunately the flames burst out again 15 minutes later and with the fire-fighting appliances exhausted, the three rear vehicles in the Glasgow train burnt out. The fire was less destructive than the one three years earlier, but 16 people were killed as a result of the crash and the Midland's reputation was dinted even further.

PHOTOGRAPHS: AUTHOR'S COLLECTION

BURNTISLAND
North British Railway
14th April 1914

Human error is all too often a major component in the accidents featured in this book, but determining precisely where the blame should be attributed was another matter, as we will see in our account of the derailment of a Scottish express train. It happened at 4.51am on 14th April 1914 at the busy Fifeshire station of Burntisland on the North British Railway, where important goods traffic was generated by docks on the Firth of Forth. Just before dawn broke on that spring morning the Carlisle - Dundee goods train was being shunted to allow the 3.55am Edinburgh - Dundee/Aberdeen express pass it. The goods had left Carlisle at 9.45pm the previous night and after its trip up the Waverley line, the crews had changed at Edinburgh. When it arrived at Burntisland, there had been a slight misunderstanding and a pilot engine had been allowed to come up on to the road intended for the 47 wagon goods train. This required a shunting operation to rectify, and the goods was being set back through a cross-over onto the up line when the express collided with it.

There is quite a degree of contradiction in the evidence heard at the enquiry for, whilst the signalman at the junction box admitted being at error by lowering his down starting signal, he was emphatic that he kept his distant at danger. His record was a good one and, if this is what happened, such a mistake appears completely out of character. Like the signalman at Hawes Junction, the man at Burntisland had a complicated job, because during the night he was expected to deal with a large volume of telegraph messages. It added confusion and was a practice which was thereafter discontinued as a result of union pressure; but was it sufficient to distract the man from correctly dealing with trains? I am personally unsure whether the investigating officer was correct in deciding that the signalman had lowered both signals, or if it was the engine driver of the express who was to blame; indeed, there are several facts which could suggest that, on seeing the starting signal, the express driver ignored the distant expecting the road to be clear. Whatever, the end result was the same and the North British Atlantic, No.872, hit the 0-6-0's tender and was derailed to the left. It ended up leaving the track, coming to rest on the local golf links, where it lay on its side partly buried in the ground. The driver and fireman of the express were both killed, and twelve passengers in the first coach received minor injuries. However, the situation could have been much worse if a gas-fed fire that started after the accident had caught hold. Fortunately that was prevented by the prompt action of railway staff, who rushed to the scene from the nearby engine shed.

PHOTOGRAPHS: ABOVE; THE LATE ARTHUR TREVENA COLLECTION; BELOW, W. LYNN COLLECTION

CARR BRIDGE

Highland Railway 15th June 1914

Two months later, on 15th June, disaster struck the Scottish rail scene once again, this time way up in the Highlands near Carr Bridge on the line from Aviemore to Inverness. Those who have travelled this way will tell of the striking scenic beauty which enfolds the former Highland Railway's main line, but in the area's rugged grandeur lurk hidden dangers. This is a remote and inhospitable area, and having walked many miles through the desolate hills I can personally testify to their fickle, volatile nature. It will surprise few, when I say that these hills can change from a place of beauty to a very inhospitable environment as the weather changes suddenly and dramatically. Some years ago I was on a mountain rescue exercise on the lofty heights of General Wade's military road, when we suddenly found ourselves in a savage cloud burst which smashed our camping equipment flat to the ground inside a few minutes. The date was not mid-winter as some may assume, but a previously fine Saturday in July; the conditions were probably not unlike those which had affected the area on a June day some seven decades earlier. On the night of 13th June a torrential downpour had descended on the Grampian mountains, with storms raging all through the night. As dawn broke, water was flooding down the steeply sided burns, tearing away earth, rocks, trees and heather. In the Baddengorm Burn, this debris built up around the road bridge where it blocked the culvert and turned the bridge into the retaining wall of a rapidly growing dam. When the stones and mortar could stand the pressure no longer, the bridge was swept aside, and thousands of gallons of water cascaded down the hill taking with it boulders weighing two tons or more. Just as fate would have it, the torrent arrived at the railway bridge at exactly the same time as the 10am Glasgow - Inverness express ran on to it. The track buckled, causing the derailment of the tender and the two leading coaches. Even so, the driver managed to bring his engine to a halt on the north bank of the burn. The first two coaches of his train had also crossed safely, but three coaches still stood on the bridge and the last coach had yet to leave the south bank. The driver ran back to warn the guard, but before any evacuation of the train could be organised, the weakened structure collapsed under the strain and the fourth coach was catapulted into the raging torrent where it was instantly demolished and all inside were swept away. Based on the number of bodies recovered the official death-toll was recorded as five, but no-one will ever be certain.

PHOTOGRAPHS: THE LATE ARTHUR TREVENA COLLECTION

ILFORD
Great Eastern Railway
1st January 1915

There are many historians who have looked at the significant changes in society which followed the outbreak of World War on 5th August 1914, indeed the *London Evening Star* wrote 'It [World War One] tore the whole world's political setup apart. Nothing could ever be the same again....some historian in the next century may well conclude the day the world went mad was August 4, 1914'. Indeed the year 1914 did mark a significant change in world history, and as such it was as though a demonic force had influenced mankind's thinking as nation took up arms against nation in a mighty conflict such as had never been seen before. If things were bad in general, the war years were to be an atrocious period for British railways, particularly in 1915. Such a sequence of events was experienced that it beggars the imagination, as the following pages show. Ironically it all began on 1st January 1915 when an accident took place at Ilford station. In terms of sheer numbers of injuries sustained by passengers, the collision which occurred there has to rank as one of the most serious ever experienced in Britain. Fortunately only ten people lost their lives, but no less than 500 passengers notified the Great Eastern Railway of injuries or shock sustained when an express passenger train ran into the side of a local train.

New Year's Day was just an ordinary working day, and in common with many other services on the GER during the first winter of World War One, it was very much business as usual at Ilford station. About 8.40am a local train from Gidea Park to Liverpool Street station, which ran non-stop after Seven Kings, was allowed on to the up through line in precedence to the 7.06am express passenger train from Clacton to London. The 2-4-2T was just drawing its train of 18 4-wheeled carriage across from the up local line, when 4-4-0 No.1813 overran the signals and ploughed into the side of the seventh coach practically destroying it. The cause was in part attributed to smoke hanging round the express engine's boiler obscuring the signals, but it is primarily attributed to the driver completely missing the home signal. Though he claims to have seen it at the last minute, and made an emergency brake application, the Inspector concluded it had only been the explosion of two fog detonators that had alerted him to the fact that he had passed the signal at danger. As a consequence he had less than 120 yards to bring his train to a halt, whereas if the emergency-detonator placing equipment had been installed at the distant signal, he would have had some 770 yards in which to stop.

Though the driver was clearly at fault, the omission of providing an audible warning when a distant signal was passed at danger was once again brought into question. By this time the GWR's system was being rapidly extended, even though the war years were placing radical demands on the company's resources. Regretfully, the same was not true elsewhere, and many of the companies who had begun train control experiments rapidly abandoned them at the outbreak of hostilities. In a way it was understandable that they should do this, *but this was exactly the time to press ahead with improved safety measures.* Traffic was growing substantially by the end of 1914, and the railways were to play a supreme part in the war effort - a story more fully told in my book *Britain's Railways At War* published by Atlantic Transport publishers. Without wishing to overtly push my own work, I would recommend those interested in this fascinating period to study this book because it shows the phenomenal levels of traffic being handled at this time, and sets this in context with the world scene. Yet the repeated urging of the need for train control and train warning systems was not only demonstrated in the accident at Ilford, but in those at Smithy Bridge and Quintinshill which follow.

PHOTOGRAPH; TOPHAM PICTURE LIBRARY

SMITHY BRIDGE

Lancashire & Yorkshire Railway 18th March 1915

As if to demonstrate the very accuracy of the Railway Inspectorate's repeated comments on the need for ATC/AWS, the accident which occurred at Smithy Bridge on 18th March 1915 showed the desirability of its wide-spread implementation for yet another reason. In discussing Cudworth, we have already touched on the rule concerning the observance of signals in poor visibility, especially during fog or falling snow and revealed the sort of consequences which could be encountered when drivers failed to treat unseen signals as though they were standing at danger. Such an occurrence took place on the L&YR's trans-Pennine route, a few miles south of Summit Tunnel, when the experienced driver of a Leeds/Bradford - Fleetwood express ran into the back of a stationary train. By this time the express traffic between Yorkshire and Lancashire had been taken away from the 2-4-2 tank engines and given back to the magnificent 4-4-0 Atlantics designed by J.A.F. Aspinall. It was one of these superb engines, No.1394, which was working the Fleetwood train on that snowy March evening.

Typical to form, the fickle Pennine weather was once again playing havoc with the trans-Pennine routes, a problem still experienced today with the M62 motorway which crosses the same sort of terrain. With the snow creating difficulties like frozen points and minor derailments, traffic had been building up all evening on the west side of the Pennines. So, when the 4.49pm empty stock train from Normanton to Manchester's Red Bank Carriage Sidings arrived at Smithy Bridge station at 8.25pm, the signalman had to hold it on the main line as all the available siding accommodation was fully occupied. According to Rule 55, the fireman went at once to inform the signalman of their presence, but he had already carried out his duties exactly to the book, by setting all his signals to danger behind the standing train. That should have prevented any further difficulties, even though it would have caused an even greater disruption to the traffic schedules. Quite why the driver of No. 1394, did not respect the commands he was given is something of a mystery but he ran past all the signals at danger. It is possible that the falling snow may have obscured his view, for it had 'blanked out' the spectacle plates at the front of the locomotive. The alternative was for the driver to put his head round the side of the cab to watch for the signals, which would have been both a difficult and unpleasant task. It is inconceivable that a man with the character and experience of this driver would have deliberately overrun signals at a speed of 40 to 45mph, so we must conclude that he had either not seen them or that he deluded himself into thinking that he had a clear road because he always had one. If it was the latter cause, the same comment applies here as it did at Cudworth, in that the driver should not have taken it for granted that even a principle express train would have an unrestricted passage. We can never be sure as to the real reasons for his error, because the driver was killed in the collision which also claimed three passengers and injured 33 others. Once again the need for an ATC/AWS system was raised in the report, which said: 'This unfortunate collision is another case which points to the desirability of the provision of some arrangement for giving the driver an unmistakable warning as to the position of the Distant signal when he passes it.'

The L&YR's main line is still in operation today, but it has seen its fare share of troubles over the years, beginning with the difficult construction period at Summit when nine lives were lost. The last brick was put in place on 11th December 1840, when its engineer Barnard Dickinson said that the tunnel "would defy the ravages of tempest, fire or war, or wasting of age". It was no idle boast, for Summit has defied the atrocious Pennine weather for over 150 years and safely passed through two world wars. More importantly, as far as this book is concerned, it is notable in the fact that the tunnel withstood one of the world's worst subterranean railway fires which began on 20th December 1984, after a train of oil tankers became derailed and then caught fire inside the bore. The blaze raged for several days, and despite determined efforts by the West Yorkshire Fire Service, flames roared out of the tunnel portals and belched skywards from the ventilation shafts. When the flames were eventually extinguished, and fire-brigade officials allowed BR engineers inside, it was feared that the tunnel would be irreparably damaged - but it was not. The subsequent inspection proved George Stephenson right, for on its opening he said that "he would stake his head and character upon it". His reputation unsullied, the tunnel re-opened on Monday 19th August 1985 when a Class 142 DMU, 142-001, was the 'first' train through. However, some may ask what this has to do with Smithy Bridge, well the fire has an interesting role in what happened to the small station which had closed in 1960; for support from the local passenger transport authority led to its reinstatement and the station came back into service when the Summit Tunnel re-opening took place. However, the new station no longer straddled the level crossing as before, but had both timber-built platforms on the Manchester side.

PHOTOGRAPH: METRO ROCHDALE, ROCHDALE CENTRAL LIBRARY

QUINTINSHILL

Caledonian Railway
22nd May 1915

Of all the accidents recorded in this book, that at Quintinshill, is the most horrific of all. It was set in some of the most romantic countryside in Western Europe, for Quintinshill is but a stone's throw from the famous Gretna Green where eloping couples could legally marry over the blacksmith's anvil despite their parent's wishes. Today countless thousands of visitors come to Gretna, and a few of these may notice a small memorial in the corner of the Visitor Centre car park which was erected to Britain's worst railway disaster in May 1995 - eighty years after the event. Whilst that plaque serves as a remembrance of those who died, it does not tell of the folly and lax working which led to their deaths. That story commences at 6am on 22nd May 1915, when a signalman was due to book on for duty at Quintinshill 'box, which protected a couple of refuge loops on the Caledonian main line from Carlisle to Glasgow. During World War One these loops were exceptionally busy, particularly in connection with the heavy war-time traffic then being run by the Railway Executive. At Quintinshill that bright spring morning the night signalman was having a busy time, for his down loop was filled by the 4.50am goods train from Carlisle, whilst he accepted an empty Royal Navy special coal train which was returning from the North of Scotland for his up loop. The next train to arrive, at 6.30am, was a local which had left Carlisle 20 minutes earlier behind 4-6-0 No.907. On this train the day signalman arrived for his shift from Gretna at 6.30am, a mere half an hour late. However, this was a regular practice worked out by the men concerned so that they would not have to walk to work. Now, the train register would have given this practice away should any inspector look at the book, so the night man would write down the train movements on slips of paper, and the day man would then enter them up when he arrived. That work was waiting for the signalman when he arrived, as his mate shunted the local across to the up main in order to allow the 6.27am from Carlisle to pass it. However, the night man failed to adequately protect the local, which could have been simply achieved by slipping a collar over the lever which controlled the up main signals. He also failed to send the 'Blocking Back Within Home Signal' bell- code to Kirkpatrick box to the north, which would have prevented them offering any more southbound trains.

Now, with the 6.27am express having passed the local, the fireman of No.907 went into the 'box to carry out Rule 55, but he also failed to ensure that his train was properly protected by the signalman as the rule demanded. As another late-running express from Euston was due to pass any time, the local was left standing on the up main, but now things started to go badly awry. At 6.43am the Kirkpatrick 'box offered a troop train conveying the 1/7 Royal Scots en-route from Larbert (near Edinburgh) to Liverpool where

they would embark for the Dardanelles on the *Empress of Britain*. Preoccupied with getting his train register up to date, the day signalman accepted it, then offered it to Gretna 'box which accepted it as well. At 6.47am he cleared his signals, with No.907 and her train still sat on the up line.

Now, and this is most remarkable, there were three footplate crews, three guards and two signalmen on the scene all of whom were trained in the observance of signals, and yet not one of them witnessed what had happened! The troop train was travelling fast down a 1:200 gradient towards Quintinshill under clear signals, and the Carlisle-based crew of 4-4-0 No.121 had little opportunity to take avoiding action. The force of the collision pushed the local train back 40 yards and knocked its tender across the down line. The ancient stock, mostly gas-lit GCR 6-wheel coaches, which formed the 639 ft. long troop train telescoped and was compressed into a distance of just over 200 feet. Wrecked coaches were littered across the tracks and one was catapulted over the troop train engine which was spread over both tracks. The errant signalmen, realising that the second northbound express was due any minute dropped the signals to danger, but it was too late. Fifty-three seconds after the first collision the second one occurred as pilot engine No.48 and train engine, No.140 sped into the wreckage at 60mph. The pilot engine struck the tender of No.121 and drove it forwards 90 feet into the goods train standing in the down loop, whilst its own tender overrode the front end of the train engine behind. The first three coaches were completely telescoped, and the mountain of wreckage outside Quintinshill 'box grew even higher. Once again gas cylinders ruptured and were ignited by coals from the troop train engine, and the resulting fire soon engulfed the wreckage. The lucky ones died outright, but many were trapped inside the burning train; injured men with no hope of escape begged their rescuers to shoot them, whilst gunfire added an eerie effect to the scene as small arms and rifle shells in the luggage vans began exploding with the intense heat.

The true death toll of Quintinshill was never fully confirmed, although it was officially put at 227; 215 soldiers, two passengers in the local train, seven in the express, the two footplatemen of the troop train and a sleeping car attendant. Few escaped uninjured from the troop train and when roll-call was taken in a nearby field at 4pm only 54 men were able to parade, the rest were either injured or dead. The survivors were eventually reunited with their fellow soldiers in the second troop train, and sent out to fight the Turks. In this campaign they fared no better than they had done at the hands of the Caledonian Railway, for few of those who went to the Dardanelles ever returned back home to Scotland. The two signalmen and the fireman of the local were all arrested and taken to Carlisle where they were sent to the Assizes, although this was technically illegal since their alleged crimes had taken place north of the border and were subject to Scottish law. Since they had already been arrested by Dumfries-shire police, they also stood trial in Scotland and thus became the first men ever to be indicted for the same crime in two British countries. Both signalmen were found guilty and each served a term of one year's imprisonment before they were released on compassionate grounds. The memory of their errors that were caused over an extra half-hour in bed was more than enough punishment to last a life-time.

PHOTOGRAPHS; ALL THE LATE ARTHUR TREVENA COLLECTION

WEEDON

London & North Western Railway

14th August 1915

Our selection of serious accidents during 1915 continues with an unfortunate incident that led to the derailment of the Irish Mail, which in turn caused the deaths of 10 passengers and injuries to 64 other persons. This unusual accident was due to the failure of a split-pin on a George V Class 4-4-0, which was working the 8.45am up express from Birmingham New Street to Euston. On Saturday 14th August 1915, No. 1489 *Wolfhound* left Monument Lane shed at 8.10am in readiness for its run to the capital. The trip was uneventful as far as Rugby station where the train had a brief wait during which the crew took the opportunity to attend to their engine. As the driver oiled round the locomotive, he noticed that a split-pin was missing from the right-hand driving crank-pin washer. A fitter was summoned to assist, and rather than delay the train by fetching a new pin, he removed a similar one from engine No. 665 standing in the station nearby. However, to open the ends of a split pin fitters usually used a hammer and cold chisel, but on this occasion he did not have these tools to hand. He therefore borrowed a hammer and used the jaws of an open-ended ⅝" spanner. The exchange took about four minutes, and the Euston train left on time but we must ask whether or not the job was adequately done. Somewhere after leaving Rugby the pin became detached, and the washer subsequently fell off as the train passed through Weedon Station at about 60mph. The loss of the pin and washer allowed the locking collar to unscrew itself causing the coupling rod to come off the driving crank-pin. However as the rod was still attached to the trailing crank-pin, it flailed round and round destroying the down track. The Euston train was brought to a halt near Stowe Hill tunnel, and the crew followed correct procedures for protecting the standing train. Unfortunately, it had not occurred to the driver that his broken coupling rod had damaged the other track, so he gave no thought to the danger which lay in wait for the down mail train. Headed by a 2-4-0 Precedent Class, No. 1189 *Stewart* (a sister engine of the one destroyed at Ditton Junction) and a Renown Class 4-4-0, No 1971 *Euryalus,* the 15-coach Irish Mail hit the damaged track and was derailed at high speed. The circumstances of this accident were of an unusual character, but it caused the deaths of ten people. Tragically, Weedon was attended by a further unusual mechanical failure on 21st September 1951 when No. 46207 *Princess Arthur of Connaught* was derailed at high speed due to incorrect maintenance just half a mile away from the scene of the first derailment.

PHOTOGRAPH; TOPHAM PICTURE LIBRARY

ST. BEDE'S JUNCTION, JARROW

North Eastern Railway

17th December 1915

Coupled with events at Ilford, Smithy Bridge and Quintinshill, Weedon had already done enough to make 1915 the worst year in the history of British railways, but the spiteful year was to conclude with yet another awful tragedy. This time our attention is focused on the North Eastern Railway, at the junction of the Tyne Dock Bottom branch with the Newcastle - South Shields main line. The branch leading down to the quayside was steeply graded and ranged from 1:100 to 1:600, but in places it was as steep as 1:49. This necessitated the provision of banking engines for many of the freight trains, and on 17th December 0-6-0T No.2182 was assisting the 6.50am departure. The banking

PENISTONE

Lancashire & Yorkshire Railway
2nd February 1916

The failure of railway structures, like for example the Tay Bridge, is usually quite spectacular, but it is not always particularly serious. Such an example is found in an incident at Penistone (yes we return there once again) when the scouring action of the River Don led to the collapse of a viaduct pier. Remedial action had supposedly been instituted years before to prevent such an 'accident', but these works were either inadequate or the strength of the river had been seriously underestimated. So, a potential death-trap awaited the crew of a freight train when it arrived from Huddersfield on 2nd February 1916. The train was drawn by another of Aspinall's 2-4-2Ts, No.661, from Mirfield shed. As the engine was standing on the viaduct, the crew felt it begin to shake so the fireman got down from the footplate and ran to fetch the station-master. As they went back to the engine, the station lengthsman followed behind. Fortunately, from his vantage point he could see the viaduct begin to move and shouted out a warning. The men started to run back towards the platforms, but as they did so the track began to bend and No. 661 began rocking on the rails. Then, as masonry fell from the under-side of the arch, a huge depression opened up below the engine. The fireman, bringing up the rear, managed to keep just a few steps in front of the rapidly opening gap. Behind him, under the immense strain imposed on the track, sleepers and chairs began pinging off the rails. A few moments later the arch completely collapsed leaving No.661 supported on just the rails, but after a few minutes they buckled and the engine crashed 85 feet to the valley floor below. An attempt was made to recover the engine, but the recovery was not a success so it was cut up and removed in parts to Horwich Works. The picture opposite also appeared as a whole plate illustration in John Marshall's *History of the Lancashire & Yorkshire Railway*, showing No.661 smashed between piers number three and four. The devastation is obvious, but recovery was attempted in order that repairs could be effected. Despite the fact that number three pier looks to have completely collapsed, it was number four where the movement began. PHOTOGRAPH: AUTHOR'S COLLECTION.

---

engine assisted the 31 vehicle freight train, working smokebox-first behind the guards van. As it did so, the banking engine was showing a red light on the front and green one on the bunker, but it would seem that this dangerous practice was not uncommon on this branch. As bankers were not coupled to the trains they were assisting on the incline they could often return quickly from the main line to the branch, and having to change the lamps was a time consuming practice. With their duty completed No.2182's crew stood on the main lines (with their lamps showing wrong aspects) and popped their whistle for the signalman to set the road back to the branch. However, the signalman did not hear them, and furthermore he had not even considered that the freight train had used a banker. Having seen a cluster of red lights pass his box (two on the brake van and one on the banker's smokebox door) he believed that he had seen three red lights at the back of the train. Having witnessed that, he obviously missed the green which was showing on No.2182's bunker. So the 0-6-0T was left waiting on the main line and in due course the driver sent his young fireman (a passed cleaner) to carry out Rule 55. The lad could not remember the rule, so the driver explained it to him, but it was foggy and someone should have gone to the box immediately the train came to a stop. So whilst the essence of Rule 55 was being discussed, its application was ignored for a period of not less than 17 minutes. As he approached the box an up passenger train from South Shields came racing down towards his stationary engine. Hauled by 0-4-4T No.1867, the Newcastle train hit the light engine and derailed it on to the down line into the path of a 2-4-2T, No.671, which was working an empty coaching stock train from Heburn. This engine hit No.2181 and another multiple collision had been achieved. Eighteen people died in the wreckage, some of whom were badly injured and unable to escape before fire broke out and consumed the wreckage.

PHOTOGRAPH; AUTHOR'S COLLECTION

BURNT OAKS BRIDGE, CROWBOROUGH

London, Brighton & South Coast Railway
3rd April 1916

As we have observed, the use of tank engines on high speed passenger trains was associated with a number of derailments, but there was also a degree of controversy surrounding the use of some types of tank engines on even moderately timed workings. For years there had been a strong debate about the use of tank engines with their driving wheels leading, for there was a considerable body of evidence which suggested that this also led to derailments. Compared with tank engines which had a pony truck at either end, we can certainly see those classes which had a driving axle leading were more prone to accidents; particularly engines with four driving wheels and one pony truck such as 0-4-2s. Whilst the proof is by no means conclusive, the facts rather tend to speak for themselves. Compared with tender engines, tank locomotives are considerably less stable than other types and to this we must add other factors. For a start tank engines tended to have rather lighter springing, and this often combined with water surging through the tanks which caused a rolling or swaying motion. Most tanks were fitted with baffles to prevent the water sloshing about uncontrollably, but these did not completely prevent the water from moving. When we consider that a tank engine's water capacity could be anything up to nine tons, it is easy to see how this would dramatically alter the weights being imposed on each axle at any given time. For example, when going down hill, greater weight would be thrust on to the leading axle. If there was not a pony truck to help support the front end of the engine, this produced an effect know as 'nosing' where the leading axle would dig deeper into the track as the water forced it down. With these conditions coupling with rolling, swaying and 'hunting', it is little wonder that tank engines tended to discover weak spots in the permanent way. This seems to be what happened at Crowborough on the line between Lewes and Tunbridge Wells when the 8am passenger train to Brighton was dramatically derailed on 5th April 1916. As it made its way south-west, 0-4-2T No.273 was running smokebox-first drawing a train of mixed bogie coaches and 6-wheel brake vans at a speed of around 25mph. As it ran down an incline (varying from 1:66 to 1:80), the engine left the rails on a gentle right-hand curve with a 65 chain radius. It would seem that for some time prior to the actual derailment, only the leading wheels were off the track, but as the engine went round the curve it became 'derailed all wheels' and tipped down an embankment to the side. The line was lightly laid with 84lb bull-head rail in 30' lengths, but it was generally maintained in a good condition. On the day in question a ganger and two platelayers had been working on this section of line removing clay and packing the sleeper ends with ballast. The three men thoroughly asserted that the line was perfectly fit for trains to pass over it, but the crew felt the engine dip as though the permanent way had given slightly when the train passed over it. On this basis the Inspector, Lt.Colonel Von Donop concluded that it was a weakness in the line which led to the derailment. In view of the benefit of insight into what happened in so many other accidents, I would tend to think it was more likely a combination of where a particular type of engine exposed a weakness and then tragically exploited it. Yet, in the Crowborough accident, despite the heavy damage to the train only five passengers were hurt. The fireman was badly knocked about however, and the driver seriously injured.

PHOTOGRAPH, ABOVE: THE LATE ARTHUR TREVENA COLLECTION
BELOW: AUTHOR'S COLLECTION

RATHO

North British Railway
3rd January 1917

In the vast majority of accident reports we encounter that most understandable of causes, human error, where a momentary lapse led to disaster. Occasionally, we find accidents caused by individuals deliberately flouting the rules, but rarely do we see rules persistently being broken by a large number of railway personnel. Yet, such a situation had developed on the NBR at Ratho, where an incorrect operating procedure had developed in connection with the empty stock trains on the Queensferry Branch. Near the junction, the single-track branch split into two loops, and the train would run into the down loop where it detached the stock. The engine then ran 'light' on to the down main, crossed to the up main, before coming back through the up loop on to the single track, this accomplished it would reverse back onto the other end of the train standing in the down loop. This unusual procedure involved the 'light' engine running in a facing direction on both main lines which, of course was both completely against the rules and also asking for trouble. There had been a major collision at the junction just over five years earlier, but this was put down to a misunderstanding between the driver of a goods engine and the signalman. Yet, two or three other later incidents seem to show that it was the irregular working which was causing the near-misses. Such problems were soon to be compounded by the greater use of the Queensferry Branch, brought about by World War One.

On the afternoon of 3rd January a 4-4-0, No. 421 *Jingling Geordie*, came up the branch with an empty stock train, and the signalman noticed the crew begin to detach the coaches. However, he kept his branch signals 'on', because he had just accepted a down express from Edinburgh. But, to his horror, as the express (behind 4-4-2 No. 874 *Dunedin*) approached the junction, No. 421 burst through the points at the end of the down loop. As trap-points were only installed on the up loop, it ran unhindered to the main line. Running in a facing direction tender first, No. 421 struck *Dunedin* head-on. The goods engine's tender was completely wrecked by the impact, and the front end was badly damaged as it was driven forward by the force of the No.874. The express was fully loaded and 12 passengers were killed as the front coach completely broke up. A magnificent job of rescue work was undertaken by servicemen travelling on the express, but 44 people were badly hurt, including both drivers. Colonel Pringle's report observed that this accident had only occurred due to this irregular turning of trains on the wrong road, and it was at once stopped by the NBR's traffic superintendent. However, it must be said that it seems incredible that such a practice could have gone on for so long without it being brought to management's attention.

PHOTOGRAPHS: NBR OFFICIAL COURTESY: SCOTTISH RECORD OFFICE

THE YORKSHIRE DALES

North Eastern Railway
September/October 1917

At the end of 1916 the locomotive shortages of World War One were reaching critical proportions, with more engines being stopped for repairs than at any other time in railway history. With growing demands for the railways, particularly railway workshops, to get involved in war work, there was simply insufficient capacity to carry out scheduled running repairs. Every engine was worth its weight in gold, at a time when all the spare locomotives, coaches and wagons were being sent to work for the Railway Operating Department overseas. For example, the NER had loaned 50 engines, so it could ill-afford to lose any more, but that is exactly what happened in a five week period in the autumn of 1917. The first incident is pictured top showing what happened after a train of ten coaches ran away down an incline at Catterick Camp. Four of the coaches were brake-thirds and each one of these had been left overnight with their handbrake screwed down, no engine was attached to the rake and somehow the brakes were subsequently released. What is worse, these vehicles had been left standing on a falling gradient. As they ran away down the Camp Railway towards the NER station of Catterick Bridge, they picked up more and more speed. Just before they reached the station, however, the rake derailed and three soldiers were killed as a consequence.

Our next problem occurred at the opposite end of Wensleydale, in the tiny shed at Hawes Junction. This was situated not far from the 'box in which the Midland signalman had made such a terrible error just seven years earlier. In October 1917 fire broke out against the stark Pennine backdrop, but this time it was the engine shed and its occupant that were to go up in flames and not an actual train. The diminutive building was used primarily to house the tank engine which worked the service from the Midland main line down to Hawes, and at this time it was occupied by an NER 0-4-4T No.207. As the picture, taken outside Darlington engine shed shows, the fire must have been exceptionally fierce. All the paint has burnt away and the spectacle plates have cracked, as might be imagined, but in addition it will be observed that a considerable amount of plating has buckled due to the heat.

The final picture in this small montage is NER 2-4-0 No.265 which, like *Cardean* at Crawford, shed a wheel whilst it was in motion. Thankfully it was going much slower than the Caledonian locomotive had been in 1909, but it could still have been fatal. However a diligent crew managed to bring their engine safely under control and disaster was averted. Quite where this accident took place in upper-Wensleydale is not specified, and no Railway Inspectorate report was necessary, but the NER records on this accident, shown to me by Ken Hoole a few years prior to his death, stated 'mechanical failure to train working Hawes - Hawes Junction'. All three accidents are highly representative of the motive power difficulties which the Railway Executive Committee were experiencing in these bitter days of war.

PHOTOGRAPHS: ALL THE LATE KENNETH HOOLE COLLECTION

LITTLE SALKELD
Midland Railway
19th January 1918

We now progress to the final year of what was then known as the Great War, a period of both international conflict and significant trouble on the railways. To do this we must return to the Settle & Carlisle line where it runs through the fertile Eden Valley at the tiny (now closed) station of Little Salkeld which stands between the stations of Langwathby and Lazonby. Down this line came the Thames - Clyde express which had left Leeds at 1.45pm behind Class 4 4-4-0 No.1010, and passed over Ais Gill into the rain-covered valley at a speed of about 55mph. After passing through Little Salkeld under clear signals the driver looked up for the Long Meg distant, even though this block post had been closed as a wartime economy measure in 1915. But we must suppose that old habits die hard, and in this instance it was most fortunate that they did! Looking up for the signal which was no longer there, he suddenly saw something much worse, for a mass of deep mud, stones and earth had become spread across the tracks. They had long experienced problems with Long Meg Cutting, and in the days of construction it had been one of those locations where earth rapidly turned to free flowing mud when exposed to prolonged periods of wet weather. In the three days prior to 19th January, conditions had been ripe to cause another movement of earth; it had frozen quite heavily before a 3" fall of snow covered the valley, then came substantial rise in temperature followed by a rapid thaw. Ironically, just the same conditions would occur in the valley precisely seventy-eight years later, when a series of landslides at Culgaith, Kirkby Stephen and Ais Gill created their own problems; the latter being the aforementioned derailment of a Sprinter DMU and the subsequent fatal accident when another train ran into it. At Long Meg Cutting in 1918 the whole embankment, with its underlying bed of impervious clay, had become a sodden fermenting mass which was ready to slip at any time. It looked alright when a ganger walked through the cutting just 23 minutes before the crash, but in the intervening period it had then slipped down the 1:3 slope and covered the base of the cutting. Into this No.1010 sped with its 11-vehicle train, and the crew had just time to get the brakes on before the engine mounted the muddy mass. The engine ran for 180 yards, the crew getting showered with mud and stones, until the compound finally came to rest leaning over to the left. The 8-wheel van behind the tender turned over on to its side on the up line, and into this the first coach ran, mounting the wreckage and smashing down into it. Seven passengers died in the crash and a further 50 more were injured, some quite seriously, but in his report Colonel Pringle put this accident down as being due to 'An Act of God' which could not have been reasonably prevented; but would his successor adopt a similar approach with the landslide that claimed yet another life on the Settle and Carlisle under similar circumstances as the 20th century drew to its end? Even more strange than a repetition of the accident happening 78 years on, was what would happen to the same engine and the same location just 15 years later!

PHOTOGRAPHS: BOTH AUTHOR'S COLLECTION.

REDHILL TUNNEL
London, Brighton & South Coast Railway
18th April 1918

Of all the accidents and disasters which befell the railways during the war years, much could be said, but it is appropriate that we close this section with a few words about munitions and explosive trains which encountered problems. In 1916 there were two accidents involving munitions trains on the Caledonian Railway, but none of devices being carried detonated. A bigger problem was encountered on 22nd September 1917, when a van in a munition train running on the LBSCR caught fire; fortunately a goods inspector managed to uncouple the van whilst his colleagues succeeded in extinguishing the flames. As our lower picture shows, the same vigilance was not demonstrated by their fellow workers on 18th April 1918, when an LBSCR munitions train broke in two inside Redhill Tunnel. Ignoring the rules of train protection, the guard demonstrated negligent inactivity for a good ten minutes and as a consequence his train was struck by engine No. 541. These two trains were then struck by a third train that was carrying naval artillery shells, as a signalman had let it enter the bore being under the impression that nothing was amiss. Despite the fact that all three trains were compressed into the confines of the tunnel, it is incredible to report that no fire started in the wreckage of the 26 smashed wagons, nor were any of the explosives detonated.

PHOTOGRAPH; THE LATE ARTHUR TREVENA COLLECTION

PADDOCK WOOD

South Eastern & Chatham Railway

5th May 1919

With the end of World War One things began to get better on the railways, and the awful disasters of the preceding four years seemed to be a thing of the past. However, things were not automatically going to improve over night. For example the track and locomotives were all badly worn out, whilst the men who worked upon them were exhausted by the efforts which had been put in during the war years when 12 hour shifts were quite normal. It is no wonder mistakes happened. One such was recorded around 3.40am on the morning of Monday 5th May 1919, when a violent collision occurred between two goods trains underneath the bridge carrying the Brenchley - Maidstone road, immediately to the west of Paddock Wood Station. The trains involved were the 12.50am Margate train, drawn by 0-6-0 No.721 with a 50 vehicle load, and the 2am Folkestone train comprised of 40 vehicles and drawn by 0-6-0 No.61; both trains originated from the yard at Bricklayer's Arms. It was a warm dark night and it had been raining, which caused a veil of mist to rise from the ground and limit visibility. At 2.27am the first of the two trains left Tonbridge East on its way to Paddock Wood, on arrival it ran on to the Maidstone Branch down line, with the intention of carrying out various shunting operations. After about 40 minutes the shunting was complete and the train proceeded to shunt back along the down line in order to clear the facing points. The signalman had given permission for the movement, but the engine driver had some difficulty making the movement and the Keylands Siding Pilot Engine was sent to assist. The operation was completed by 3.39am.

When the train came to rest clear of the facing points, a few vehicles and the brake van were still actually sitting on the down main line. At about 3.26am the Folkestone train had been offered by Tonbridge East, and though the signalman at Paddock Wood accepted it, he did so under Rule 5 'Section clear but station or junction blocked'. He kept his advance signal at danger and waited until the Folkestone train had come to a stand there. When the driver whistled to show he was ready, the signalman pulled off the advance signal but kept his home signal at danger, but the driver ran past this at a speed of around 15 mph. The man had only held his post for about 15 months and had only ever been over this section once before, though he knew the road well enough as a fireman. Therefore fault lays squarely on this man for failing to observe the signals, but the signalman at Tonbridge East did not get off completely free as the Inspector was not satisfied that he had done all within his power to give the driver an adequate warning about the obstruction ahead. The fireman on No.61 who died of his injuries later that day was the accident's only fatality. The Folkestone train was conveying no less than three brake vans; of these two were 15-tons, both empty and the other No.2007 was 20-tons. The guard was riding in the latter van, which our picture shows to be badly damaged, it is therefore quite amazing that the guard got away from the accident with as little as three broken ribs. Our photographs give a general view of the scene showing the damage to the Folkestone train, and the vans piled up against the road bridge. Note the SECR horse-van used as a Parcels Delivery Van for Fast Train Traffic, which was being conveyed to Margate, smashed up against the side of the bridge.

PHOTOGRAPHS; M. WILCOX COLLECTION

ABERMULE

Cambrian Railway
26th January 1921

This disaster which claimed the lives of fifteen passengers and the footplate crew of a local train in a collision on a single line is a tale of incompetence and woefully inadequate working practices in the period just prior to the Grouping of 1923. The four incompetents who had a major role to play in the fulfilment of the accident were the relief station-master, the signalman, a 17-year old porter and a 15-year old 'odd job lad'; between them they were to work the Abermule end of the Tyer signalling system which protected the single line. Now the operation of this system required a signalman at either end of a single section of track, and the tablets which gave authority for trains to enter that section were kept in a locked cabinet. These could only be withdrawn when the signalman at the opposite end of the section pressed a plunger, and when this tablet was withdrawn an electric circuit was broken and further tablets could not be withdrawn until the first tablet was locked into the cabinet at the opposite end of the section or returned to its original instrument. The only people authorised to operate the system were the signalman or station-master, but because the tablet instrument cabinet was kept in the station buildings and not the signal box, it had become common practice for one of the two young lads to be sent to fetch the tablets and sign the train book. This was strictly against the rules! On the day of the accident two trains, an express and a local passenger, were due to pass each other at Abermule, and at 11.52am the local was allowed into the section from Montgomery by the signalman who then left the station for the signalbox. At 11.56am the express was belled from Newtown and, left on his own, there was only the 17-year old there to deal with this. He thus pressed the plunger and the token was released at the other end. Sadly he failed to tell anyone that he had done this. At 11.59am Newtown sent 'train entering section', but no-one was near the instrument to hear this, three minutes later the local train arrived in Abermule, and the 15-year old was the only one available to collect the tablet. The relief station-master then came hurrying up and was given the tablet by the boy, but due to the youth having a speech impediment the station-master thought he said 'take this tablet, the train is going on'. With that the lad went off to collect the tickets as the porter had turned up on the platform. The station-master, without looking at the tablet handed it back to the local train's fireman who accepted it without checking and then put it into his pouch. The porter was then sent to change the ground-frame levers and tell the signalman to pull off for the local; he began to do this with apprehension, and his concern increased when he could not pull the ground-frame levers, but when he saw the station-master give the local the right-away he assumed that the express had not been accepted from Newtown even though he had plunged for it. He did not notice the position of the down starting signal at all. The mix up which occurred in the working of that platform, sent the local train into the section to Newtown carrying the Montgomery-Abermule tablet, and a train carrying the correct tablet was already speeding its way down that single line of track. When the men at Abermule returned into the station buildings they saw, to their horror, what had happened and tried to recall the local, but it had passed the last signal. The express crew only saw the local coming towards them through a shallow cutting working hard as it came up the gradient: it was now too late!

PHOTOGRAPHS; AUTHOR'S COLLECTION

BUXTON

London & North Western Railway
11th November 1921

As a prelude to the Grouping of 1923, the London & North Western and Lancashire & Yorkshire railways, merged at midnight 31st December 1921. Just seven weeks prior to the event which created Britain's largest joint stock railway company, the LNWR had been literally shook to the core by an awful boiler explosion which occurred in Derbyshire. For years Buxton has been associated with heavy goods traffic, notably limestone (and its derivatives) which come from the many quarries which surround the picturesque spa town. There had been accidents in the area before, but most of these had been associated with derailments, collisions or runaways on the steeply graded lines through what is now the Peak District National Park. However, two of the most serious incidents in the Buxton area are associated with pressurised steam, the first of these being on 11th November 1921 when an engine exploded in the town's goods yard as it was preparing to depart with the 12.50am freight to Oldham. The tangled wreckage of tubes and bent plates in our picture shows what remained afterwards, when an LNWR 0-8-0, No.134, blew itself apart from within. As may be imagined the power of the explosion was enormous, and those who were in the vicinity when the blast occurred stood very little chance of escape; it will therefore go without saying that when the explosion occurred both footplatemen were killed instantly; but in view of the improvements we discussed on pages 8 and 9, how could such a terrible event happen at such a late date in locomotive development? Obviously this was a question which the subsequent inquiry would need to determine! When the Board of Trade ordered the enquiry it was to fall within the remit of the Railway Inspectorate, but as a boiler explosion was involved it also needed the specialist inspectors of the BoT's Mercantile Marine Department.

The boiler concerned was type B176 No.10, constructed at Crewe in 1905 but not actually fitted on to an engine (No.2567) until June 1907. It was designed to work at a pressure of 200 lbs. per square inch, and had a theoretical life-expectancy of 18 years. In December 1908, after various repairs, the boiler was put on engine No.2169, where it remained for six years before further repairs were undertaken. Next it went on to No.1017 where it stayed until the next set of repairs, before being transferred to No.134 in June 1918. In early 1921 the engine went for boiler repairs at Beardmore's in Glasgow, but the boiler was not actually removed from the frames on this occasion. After some light running-in during July, the engine was allocated to Manchester's Longsight shed on 4th August 1921, but in the 2,600 miles and three months that followed, strange things began to happen with the engine. Over 40 drivers had apparently noticed something wrong with No.134, and several had reported that they had difficulty in working the injectors and the engine was high in steam. In addition the steam gauge was reported as faulty on at least four occasions and it was duly exchanged, the last time being at Buxton on 10th November. Other drivers reported that the engine did not blow off freely, and several must have suspected that it was the safety valves which were at fault and not the injectors or the gauge. There was nothing to suggest that Beardmore's had made any error in their workmanship, but four or five of the other boilers that had been repaired by this firm showed a tendency to high pressure.

The remnants of the boiler were therefore meticulously examined by Mr. H. Cranwell who was a specialist in this field. His report was extensive and it revealed that, in reality, there were several causes for the explosion. In the final analysis the inspectors decided that no responsibility could be assigned to any individual and that the accident was not caused through negligence, they did however feel that all concerned should have realised something was indeed wrong with the safety valve during the numerous inspections that were carried out for so called 'boiler' problems. Fortunately problems with boilers were now the exception rather than the rule, and never again was such a fearful incident to take place, however the problems were not entirely eliminated, nor could they be where live steam is concerned. A particular difficulty with boilers was noted amongst the 778 members of the 2,100 strong American Transportation Corps S160 class 2-8-0s which were sent to work in Britain during World War Two. These engines, common with American practice only had a single water gauge, whereas British engines had two. As a consequence the chance of letting the water drop was significantly increased and this led to no less than three serious boiler explosions in the mid-1940s. These accidents were at Honeybourne (No.2403), Thurston (No.2363) and, worst of all, South Harrow Tunnel where No.1707 suffered a complete firebox collapse.
PHOTOGRAPH; ROD LEACH COLLECTION

DIGGLE

London Midland & Scottish Railway 5th July 1923

The Grouping of the railways into just four major stock companies at the end of 1922 was, as far as safety matters went, a positive step forward. Admittedly a few of the progressive private companies were held back by this merger, but generally it was the other way around and smaller, under-funded railways were assisted in bringing their signalling and safety procedures up to date. This was particularly noticeable with those absorbed into the GWR, a move which could only benefit companies like the Cambrian. Yet change did not occur over night, and old habits died hard. One such practice was noted at Diggle, which despite being to the west of the Pennines, was then in the old West Riding of Yorkshire. Diggle station was situated at the western portal of Standedge Tunnel, which was formed with one double bore and two single ones, the first of which was engineered by my great-great-great grandfather. The two outer station platforms were hard up against these tunnel portals, and an island platform was located between them; at the western end of these platforms a series of crossovers permitted an exchange of traffic between the fast and slow lines, and beyond these stood a number of sidings in which waiting traffic would be set back. It was near the entry to these sidings that a double-headed express from Leeds collided with a goods train from Crofton Junction on 5th July 1923. At 10.06am the goods train, drawn by 0-6-0 No.1062, had arrived at Diggle and come to a halt at the up home signal. As there were no fixed signals to cover the shunting operations, it was being moved by hand signals. The signalman first displayed a red flag from his window, but then lowered the home signal to allow the engine to pull forward to take on water if it was needed; all other movements would have been controlled by verbal instructions from the shunter or signalman. At 10.10am the goods train fireman came to the box to carry out Rule 55, though it did not occur to the signalman to tell either him or the driver that the red flag would shortly be removed in order not to impede the express or verbally instruct him to stay where he was until a green flag was shown. The driver of the goods train, must have then misunderstood an instruction from the shunter and, at about 10.20am the 0-6-0 began to pull slowly forward. This put it foul of the main line, and in the path of the express which was just emerging from the tunnel. Fortunately, the Manchester train had reduced its speed in order to cross over the junction onto the Micklehurst loop but even so the pilot engine, No.1027, struck the goods engine immediately to the rear of its tender. The pilot engine turned over on its side and No.1062's tender was derailed; the train engine, Experiment class 4-6-0, No.1406 *George Findlay*, forced its way past the stricken engines before it too was derailed - fortunately the debris of smashed wagons from the goods train prevented it tippling over. The first two coaches were telescoped and two passengers and the goods train driver were killed; but the real tragedy was the death of the pilot-engine's fireman who had exchanged duties as a favour to another Huddersfield Hillhouse man who had been rostered onto that fatal working.

PHOTOGRAPH, ABOVE; AUTHOR'S COLLECTION BELOW, PETER FOX COLLECTION.

LYTHAM

London, Midland & Scottish Railway 3rd November 1924

Our second accident in the Grouped era is again on the LMS, which was to suffer another of those fluke 'one-in-a-million' accidents on 3rd November 1924. We have already seen that few of the accidents in this book could be called (in insurance jargon) Acts of God, for most were entirely preventable. However, like Little Salkeld and Bullhouse Bridge, the one which occurred at Lytham was one which would have been difficult to prevent. It happened on the old L&YR-LNWR Joint line which ran round the southern Fylde Coast to Blackpool, and involved ex-L&YR 4-40 No.1105 which was still in its pre-Grouping livery that day. For years the L&YR had been one of the poorest railways in the realm as far as passenger comfort went, and it had been the subject of much adverse criticism in its operation due to the high proportion of accidents which it sustained. Yet by the time of the merger with the LNWR at the end of 1921, the L&YR had picked itself up by the boot strings and really worked hard to get itself up into the 20th century. At the time of its demise the company was considered one of the safest and most efficient railways in the land, its crack expresses and 'club trains' hauled by the huge 4-4-0 Atlantics being amongst the best forms of rail travel then available. Therefore it comes as a great surprise to note what happened to the 4.40pm express from Liverpool/Manchester - Blackpool which was full of businessmen returning to their homes after a busy day in Lancashire's principle cities. As the train approached Lytham station at a speed of 50mph it suddenly left the rails and demolished the signal box at Wharton where the signalman was seriously injured but lucky to escape alive. The engine then pitched round and ended up on its side, facing the direction it had been travelling in. Two coaches also overturned and these then spilled on to the up line, but the gas-lit vehicles did not catch fire. The driver of the express was killed in the derailment, as were 14 of the trains passengers, but rescue of the injured was speedily effected by men from the nearby Lytham Gas Works who brought precisely the right type of equipment needed to release people trapped in the wreckage.

Yet why did No.1105 end up in such a situation, particularly when it had only been released from Horwich works ten days earlier after undergoing a thorough overhaul. The accident investigators found the answer laying in a field 400 yards back down the railway, where the tyre of the engine's leading left-hand bogie wheel was discovered. It had broken wide open, and a large flaw was clearly visible at the centre of this break. The tyre was part of a batch of 34 which had been machined at Horwich in 1920, but since its manufacture it had run over 100,000 miles on various engines. Even when the engine had gone in for its overhaul this flaw had not been detected despite rigorous tests on every component, so its presence went unrecorded and it was left as a potential time bomb. This 'bomb' exploded on that November night when No.1105 took a violent knock on the points leading to the Gas Works' sidings, and in turn this caused the wheel tyre to spilt and thus derail the bogie. In this condition the train ran on until the displaced bogie wheel caught a low girder on a bridge which spanned a dyke near the signal box. With the bogie now fouling the obstruction, the engine was tipped over at speed and demolished in such a way as to achieve the results demonstrated in the accompanying pictures.

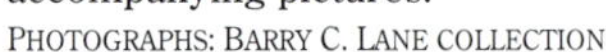

PHOTOGRAPHS: BARRY C. LANE COLLECTION

OWENCARROW

Londonderry & Lough Swilly Railway 30th January 1925

Many historians who have studied the account of the Tay Bridge disaster accept Bouch's argument that the lightly constructed coaches of the train were lifted bodily from the track and thrown against the weakened superstructure of the bridge. On 27th February 1907 a train travelling across the Leven Viaduct on the edge of Morecambe Bay was dramatically derailed as a result of high winds.

To prove just how Bouch's theory might have happened, we now turn to Northern Ireland and the Burtonport extension of the L&LSR which ran for almost 50 miles through some formidable countryside west of Letterkenney Junction. As it passed through the highlands of North Donegal, the line crossed the two great glens of Laheen and Veagh. There is no shelter or trees to break the force of the south-westerly gales that prevail, and across this wild, open valley runs the Owencarrow Viaduct.

It had long been noted that drivers should only cross the line with caution during gales, but on 30th January the Burtonport train was running over the viaduct in a strong gale. As it did so a particularly savage gust battered the train and three coaches were blown off the track and on to the side of the viaduct where they burst through the parapet. Fortunately the break occurred near to the point where the stone arches gave way to iron girders carried on piers, for at this point there was a large embankment of stones which prevented the train from being catapulted into the valley below, and our pictures illustrates just how the two coaches were prevented from being dragged over and thus to their doom. However the passengers in the coach next to the goods van did not fare so well, as their coach was turned upside down, and its roof was stove in, allowing the luckless inhabitants to be disgorged onto the valley floor. Two men and two women died as a result and nine others were injured, but they had to lay in their exposed position for two hours until a relief train could reach the scene. As a result of the accident, it was decided to fit wind-speed recorders to all viaducts where similar wind problems might exist. Fortunately accidents on viaducts are rare, but were Owencarrow and the Leven Viaduct incidents re-runs of the Tay Bridge Disaster, I personally believe they were, but we will never know for sure.

PHOTOGRAPH; ELTHAM - TIMES COLLECTION

CRAMLINGTON

London & North Eastern Railway
26th May 1926

It is a sad fact of recent railway history that vandalism has begun to play an increasing role in railway disasters, and in 1992 I was sitting in a train running towards Rice Lane on Merseyside, when a stone came flying through the window behind me; the culprit was a seven year-old boy. Other incidents have seen objects placed on the lines in a deliberate attempt to derail trains, notably the vandalism which wrecked a sleeper train at Prestonpans on 22nd May 1980. But this is not a new phenomena by any means, as an incident several miles further south on the ECML 54 years previously reveals. The event of 26th May 1926 took place during the General Strike when people were suffering terrible deprivation all over Britain, but notably so in mining communities like those in South Wales and the North East. Political protest was strong, but so too were acts staged by desperate men against the upper-classes who were viewed as the enemy. Even so this was no excuse for a deliberate act of vandalism which resulted in rail fastenings being loosened in front of the Gresley class A1 pacific *Merry Hampton*. The engine hit these rails and split the track and crunched through the ballast for about 80 yards before coming to rest against the wall of a disused signal cabin, its two leading coaches were also derailed but thankfully no-one was seriously hurt.

PHOTOGRAPH: NATIONAL RAILWAY MUSEUM.

MANORS STATION, NEWCASTLE

London & North Eastern Railway
7th August 1926

Nine weeks after the Cramlington incident the LNER suffered another accident in the North East of England, in the form of the Mystery of Manors Station. At 9.47pm on Saturday 7th August 1926 a six car electrical multiple unit left Newcastle Central Station on a circular journey to Whitley Bay and Tynemouth, where it turned west and headed back to Newcastle. As the train approached Manors (East) Station the guard suddenly noticed they were running too fast to stop, even though the signals were set against them. He at once applied his brake, but the train had already overrun the signals and the speed was too great to instantly overcome and it struck a special west-bound freight train, drawn by an 0-6-0 goods engine on a busy converging junction just beyond the station. The EMU collided side to side with the goods train striking it around the third wagon from the tender, damaging the motorman's end of the leading coach very badly. When the wreckage was examined, the driver was found to be missing, so rescuers went back along the track to see if he could be found. His body was discovered near Heaton, from which it was clear that the train had run a distance of 1 mile 96 yards at an approximate speed of 35mph without a driver. However, the technical operation of these trains meant that such an eventuality was almost impossible; yet two handkerchiefs had been fastened in such a way as to depress the dead man's hand. Quite why the motorman did this will always remain a mystery, but several theories were put forward at the time though the official investigation refused to be drawn into the speculation. Immediately behind the driving compartment was a luggage van with fixed and barred windows and behind that a small vestibuled gangway with doors on either side of the train. The luggage van was provided with sliding doors on each side and it was from the right hand side door in this compartment that the driver was swept by a bridge pillar. Behind this vestibule there was a first-class compartment, wherein a courting couple were travelling back to Newcastle. The presence of this couple may, some said, have led to 'dogging' which went tragically wrong. In railway terms the word 'dogging' was well known, for it referred to the practice of leaning out of carriage windows to watch courting couples in the compartments behind. This was invariably carried out by railwaymen, but this form of voyeurism was both disreputable and highly dangerous. Indeed, there are many instances recorded of this type of incident, and several deaths resulting thereform, perhaps one of most recent occurring near Liverpool in 1954. Of course there were many legitimate reasons why a driver might feel the need to look back down his train, but none of these would involve the dangerous practice of tying down the dead man's hand.

PHOTOGRAPH; THE LATE KENNETH HOOLE COLLECTION

LEEDS

London Midland & Scottish Railway 8th September 1926

Another accident associated with the Settle & Carlisle line is that which occurred at Leeds on 8th September when ex-MR 4-4-0 No. 304 found itself in quite a predicament after arriving with the night train from Glasgow and Stranraer - the same working which had come to grief at Ais Gill thirteen years before. On this occasion no-one was hurt but as the picture shows it could have been quite serious. As No.304 approached Leeds at 2.45am, it did so at a speed of about 35mph, the driver making his brake applications as he came up to the junction at the west end of the station. The weather now exposed the weakness of this long established practice! It had been a very dry August and September in the Leeds area, and everywhere was bone dry. However, like roads of today, when the rains finally came, the rails turned extremely greasy. When the driver from Leeds (Holbeck) shed applied his brakes, he found that a heavy thunderstorm at 1.30am had made the rails so slippery that the engine would not grip them. On the downward gradient the engine's wheels locked, and it skidded down into the buffer stops at the end of Number One platform road. The force, speed and weight of the engine was so great that No.304 overrode the buffers and it was lifted over the concourse and smashed into the station's generator house. The whole station was plunged into darkness and confusion reigned, but by a miracle the power-house attendant had left the building just moments prior to the 4-4-0s arrival.

PHOTOGRAPH: TIMES NEWSPAPERS

BRAMSHOT HALT, FLEET

Southern Railway 5th November 1926

We have mentioned, in the case of Ais Gill, it was absolutely essential for a guard to protect the rear of his train when it became detained on a running line, by the use of detonators at distances of ¼ mile, ½ mile and ¾ mile from the back of the stranded train. This simple act can prevent one of the most horrific of all accidents, rear end collisions, by giving a secondary warning device to fixed signals. As we will see over and over again, this rule was repeatedly flouted by some railwaymen, possibly because of the distance which had to be walked when the train might, at any time, be ready to move off again. A classic case was seen on the Southern Railway at Fleet when an empty milk train became divided due to a faulty coupling near Bramshot Halt, at around 6.30am on the morning of Bonfire Night 1926. When the division took place, the train's vacuum pipe was damaged and the driver had to go back to his cab to get a hammer to 'knock the thing into place'. This all took time, and just 10 minutes behind the milk train, an express was following on the down through line. For some reason, and in the absence of AWS/ATC to warn him of his errors, the driver of the express overran the distant signals on No.4 signal bridge just under a mile to the rear of the train, and then did the same at No.5 signal bridge 131 yards away from the last vehicle. This could have been due to a number of reasons, most probably connected with either the early morning mist or the fact that smoke was curling round his boiler casing. Whatever, having missed the signals, he had no means of knowing that the milk train sat in his path just a few yards ahead. Still steaming hard the driver smashed into the unprotected rear of the train, and lost his life in the process. Whilst he was mainly to blame for ignoring signals, the guard was also heavily censured for his failure to carry out the rules governing protection.

PHOTOGRAPH : TIMES NEWSPAPERS

PARKGATE & RAWMARSH

London Midland & Scottish Railway
19th November 1926

Just two weeks on from Fleet, disaster struck again when fate played an awful trick which subsequently claimed 11 lives. It was a grey, foggy day on 22nd November when an express passenger train encountered an obstruction near Parkgate & Rawmarsh station, which ripped out the sides of the coach compartments as one of our pictures shows. Three trains are involved in our story; the first of which was the 7.20am special mineral freight running northwards from Westhouses to Royston. The next was the 10.10am York-Bristol express passenger, and then there was the 8am special empty wagon train from Normanton to Toton, both of which were heading south. The mineral train was double headed with engines No.270 (2-4-0) and No.3980 (0-6-0), hauling no less than 90 loaded coal wagons and a 15-ton brake. Unfortunately one of the wagons in this train, Hickleton Main Colliery wagon No.1264 was in a seriously defective condition, its dominating problems being a fractured drawbar, a rotted timber sole-bar, perished rubber springing, and corroded through rods. As the train travelled north the bottom doors of the wagon began to open as the vehicle started collapsing. This scattered large quantities of coal on the line, and in turn this accelerated the demise of the wagon which began to break up whilst the train was in motion. This caused a sudden check to the train as it was travelling between 10 and 15 mph, which in turn made the crew apply the brake so that the derailed wagon would not be thrown over into the path of the oncoming empty wagon train.

Unfortunately, with the application of the brake, the front six wagons began to mount up and these derailed to the other side, bringing down the signal post for the up fast line. This occurred just as the express, drawn by 4-4-0 No.387, came upon the scene. Some part of the signal post was then deflected into the side of the train, tearing open the coach sides as it went past it at about 45mph. This action was extremely devastating, for it resulted in the carriage sides being almost completely ripped away. Colonel Pringle found the circumstances of this accident exceptional, and some of them very unfortunate in character. If there had been no signal post at this point, or had the expressed passed a few seconds earlier, there would have been no collision. However this one structure turned the simple collapse of the wagon into an accident which had very serious consequences. Therefore some considerable attention was given to what condition private owner wagons should be in before they were allowed onto the railway running lines. It was subsequently recommended that all wagons should be submitted for a detailed examination every ten years, which would also necessitate owners to re-register them for use on railways lines. Without examination and subsequent re-registration they could not be permitted access to run on the national rail system, it was what we might term as the railway fore-runner of an MoT test.

ABOVE *A view of the wrecked private-owner wagons and the signal post which they brought down. This was the second part of the chain reaction which followed the collapse of the wagon, and in turn led to the consequences shown in the next picture.*

LEFT *The sides of the wooden-bodied coaches which were ripped open by the obstruction which projected into their path, and sliced them open with savage ferocity. It is ironic that this train was another of the Bristol-bound expresses which became wrecked during the period between the two wars*

OPPOSITE PAGE TOP *A general view of the scene at Parkgate & Rawmarsh showing the damaged wagons, goods engine and the remains of the signal ladder. An interesting feature of this view shows that some of the wagons were still retaining their pre-Grouping markings at the end of 1926.*

PHOTOGRAPHS: ELTHAM-TIMES COLLECTION

HULL: PARAGON STATION

North Eastern Railway
14th February 1927

In Parkgate & Rawmarsh we saw a one in a million disaster, but in the accident at Hull's Paragon station on 14th February 1927 the chances of a problem occurring were so extreme as to make it virtually improbable. Yet in just 0.3 seconds a signalman at Park Street signal box made a fatal error which claimed twelve lives who were travelling in the 8.22am train from Withernsea. This was drawn by ex-NER class F 4-4-0, No.96, and was just approaching Hull when it collided head on with an ex-NER class M 4-4-0, No.1628, working the 9.05am to Scarborough. Both trains were running at slow speed, but the stock they were drawing suffered severe damage from telescoping. Both trains suffered badly in the crash, but it was the one from Withernsea which came off the worst by far. Most of the dead were in that train, including two children who were on their way to school in Hull. How both trains had come to be on the same road was a mystery which the Inspector had to solve, because the interlocking of points and signals meant that this was theoretically impossible. The Park Street signal box was a quite modern one, having been equipped with an electro-pneumatic system in 1905, and manned by three signalmen this busy 'box was provided with every modern signalling device possible. For example, all the turnout's were equipped with facing point locking-bars, which were fitted ahead of the points; when these bars were depressed by the wheels of a locomotive, it would lock the points and prevent any movement before or during the passage of the train. Yet it transpired that when the Scarborough train ran out of Hull, the signalman returned signal No.171 behind it, while his colleague set the road for the late-running Withernsea train so that it could enter the station without any undue delay. The first man should have waited until the whole of the Scarborough train had passed before he restored lever No.171, but it was common practice to work levers in this way, particularly at busy locations. Normally nothing would ever exploit the weakness of this practice, but his premature action of 0.3 seconds on this occasion led to tragedy. As the Scarborough train went through, the signalmen heard a curious clicking noise in the frame; this was later discovered to have been caused by lever No. 83 moving as the No.1628 ran through points which were set against it. It was now on the same road as the Withernsea train, and a 'once-in-infinity' mistake was to lead to disaster. In his report the Inspector wrote 'It is human nature for men, who take an honest pride in their work, to avoid if possible having to book the stoppage of a train, especially one already late.' But he concluded that both men had acted more hurriedly than they should have done, and that the brief delay of the Withernsea train would have been much more preferable to hasty actions.

PHOTOGRAPH; THE LATE KENNETH HOOLE COLLECTION

PENISTONE

London Midland & Scottish/London & North Eastern railway 27th February 1927

We now make our fourth, and final visit to Penistone where, on 28th February 1927, another serious accident occurred. That evening an ex-L&YR 2-4-2T, No.10760, left Bradford Exchange with a 4-coach local train for Penistone where it arrived at 5.32pm. When the passengers had alighted, the locomotive was then detached from the train and taken across the former GCR main line to the turntable on the opposite side. Around this time, the signalmen in the LNER box changed turns, and a new man came on at 5.56pm for his evening shift which would last until 2am the next day. One of his first tasks was to turn No.10760 and send it into the down loop, where it was held whilst a coal empty went through on the up main line. At 6.21pm the signalman began to send the light engine across through No.34 points, from where he intended to send it through the points from the up main on to the up branch line. However, when he forgot to set the points for this second movement things started to go very wrong, but as yet no-one noticed what was happening. As No.10760 put on steam the driver found himself running alongside the up main platform, instead of diverging away to the right and on to the Huddersfield branch line platforms. The signalman said that he had then ordered the engine to set-back by showing a white light to the driver, but no-one else saw anything of this and the 2-4-2T finally came to a halt near the station's west end. Preoccupied with a telephone call the signalman failed to see that the engine had not obeyed his commands to set-back (if such were given), and he then acknowledged a train which was offered to him by Dunford Bridge. He did not accept this immediately, but checked with Barnsley Junction before doing. From the man's own evidence we can see that he was not expecting it to be the 5.35pm Manchester - London, Marylebone express at all, but a slow goods train which had been preceding it over Woodhead.

The crew of the light engine were also breaking regulations, first of all Rule 134 (later Rule 132) which stated 'Except where authorised and in case of trains where the engine or driving cab is single manned, no engine must be allowed to be in motion on any running line unless both the Driver and Fireman are upon it.' But in direct contravention of this, after signalling his readiness to leave the turntable road the LMS driver had sent his mate to fetch a brew of tea from the station canteen. In moving off from the turntable road, he then broke Rule 185 as there was no-one with him to see that the points were in their proper position. Anyway, there he was on the up platform road, his fireman having just returned, when he saw the signals come off for the express. Realising that these could not apply to him he began to set back as fast as he could, running bunker first in the direction of Sheffield. The express was drawn by LNER class D10 4-4-0 No.5437 *Prince George,* which had dropped to a speed of 20mph in order to negotiate the sharp curve leading to the station. In the reflection of the platform lights the crew of the express saw the 2-4-2T scurrying backwards at a speed of 15mph, but despite braking heavily, the inevitable happened. The two engines collided front buffer beam to front buffer beam, and the pair carried on locked together for a distance of 465 yards. The first five coaches suffered damage, but casualties were relatively light and were mainly confined to slight injury or shock. However, the LMS driver was badly hurt and for a while it was thought that his injuries were life threatening. Despite having bravely stayed with his engine in order to lessen the severity of a collision which would have otherwise taken place within the confines of the platform area, the driver was duly censured for his errors; yet the bulk of the blame was attributed to irregular working in the signalbox for which the signalman was solely responsible.

PHOTOGRAPH: AUTHOR'S COLLECTION

BEARSTEAD

Southern Railway 20th August 1926

Another tank engine was in trouble the following month when Southern Railway 2-6-4T No.890 *River Frome* was derailed on a poor section of track at Wrotham. Although this incident was without any serious consequence, it was the prelude to a series of accidents that would affect the SR's 'River Class' tank engines. These engines had been developed by the South Eastern & Chatham in 1917, but they were not put into full production until 1925. They had been designed for express work, but because of their high centre of gravity they were inherently unstable at high speed. In the months which followed, many drivers complained about severe rolling at speeds over 50 mph, especially on poor sections of track and a number of near derailments were reported. On 2nd August No.800, *River Cray* was derailed on the sharp curve at Maidstone, then 18 days later an even more serious incident occurred at Bearstead, near Maidstone when imperfections in the track caused No.890 to come off the track again. The official report took the view that the 'River Class' was not in any way to blame for the derailment, but in view of what happened to No.800 after it re-entered service on 23rd August, we may be led to other conclusions.

PHOTOGRAPH: KENT COUNTY LIBRARY SERVICE

SEVENOAKS

Southern Railway
24th August 1927

Moving on from Bearstead we now look at the accident which occurred on 24th August when River Frome, was derailed whilst running at high speed with an express passenger train. This time it would be harder just to blame imperfections in the track, as the catastrophic events of that summer evening were to show that the 'River class' were particularly sensitive to bad sections of the permanent way. As we have mentioned before, the use of tank engines for express duties was one which was prone to difficulties, not least because of the tendency of water to surge around in the side tanks. This caused them to rock and sway alarmingly at high speeds, and in the 'River class' this was usually encountered between 50 and 60mph. Most drivers knew about this nasty characteristic so they took preventative measures, and using their own initiative they lessened the effects of this surging by putting on coal and reversing the dampers. It was an effective trick, but as will be imagined it was one which had to be timed just right. One of the men who actually fired on No.790, doyen of the class, wrote to tell me that on one occasion the rolling was so bad as they neared Smeeth, he was pitched hard against the cab-side fracturing three ribs as a result. Little wonder that some railwaymen called them the 'rolling rivers'. On 24th August this tendency to roll was going to be revealed in a major catastrophe, as we now recall.

On what had been a day of atrocious weather, the 5pm to Folkestone, Dover, Deal and Minster left London's Cannon Street station behind No. 800, which was drawing seven coaches and the Pullman car *Carmen.* It was booked to run non-stop as far as Ashford, and as it ran down from Knockholt to Sevenoaks, it was doing about 57 mph. However, on emerging from Polhill Tunnel the engine began its 'rock and roll' and the driver at once adopted the aforementioned tactic. It seemed to have cured the problem, but as they carried on between Dunton Green and Sevenoaks a knocking noise was heard at the front end of the engine and he shut off the regulator. The noise was the sound of the flanges on the leading-driving wheels hitting the rail chairs, the engine had been derailed. Even so it was not automatically a serious problem, as it was still possible for the driver to brake and bring the train safely to a halt. Unfortunately, there was a set of catch-points just ahead, close to an over-line bridge. Despite the driver making a hard application of the brakes, the derailed No.800 was now swaying quite alarmingly and the engine began cork-screwing along the track. The left-hand cylinder struck the abutment of the bridge, whilst the right-hand cab side of No.800 scrapped against the central pier. The engine ran on for a further 300 feet, but most of the train piled up around Shoreham Bridge smashing the pier. The first two coaches forced their way past the debris and came to a stand on the opposite side, but regretfully the third and fourth coaches were smashed up. The Pullman car *Carmen* was thrown across the track, though its superior carriage design ensured that damage to it was limited. Thirteen passengers were killed and 21 others were seriously injured, but the sturdy construction of the locomotive saved the lives of the driver and his 'mate'.

As a result of this accident the 'River class' were all withdrawn and converted into tender engines, but before this work was completed one of the class was tested on the former GNR section of the LNER. I am indebted to two readers who were involved in these tests with the late H.N. Gresley, for the detailed notes forwarded to me after volume five was published. Trials were run between St. Neots and Huntingdon and the results clearly showed that there was no significant roll even at very high speeds, and this further demonstrated that the River Class was capable of speeds in excess of 85mph on a good road. But the Southern did not have a good road, and when the trials were resumed near Woking, excessive rolling was noted at speeds of over 70 mph. This demonstrated that it was not the engines that were to blame, but this does not eliminate the questions which must hang over the design. In recent times we have seen differences between mechanical engineers and civil engineers which have led to whole classes of locomotives and multiple units being left to stand whilst improvements of one type or another were carried out. Back in 1925 Maunsell must have known about the state of the track on the former SECR lines, or at best he should have found out if his new class was suitable to be run upon it. As such it was a catalogues of mishaps, accidents and a disaster of considerable magnitude which brought the fact to everyone's attention.

PHOTOGRAPHS: KENT COUNTY LIBRARY SERVICE

DARLINGTON

London & North Eastern Railway
27th June 1928

In the days of steam many young boys wanted to grow up to be an engine driver, a desire that was often linked with speed and the romance of far away places that were associated with express train working. However, such an elevated position was not easily attained, and drivers had an apprenticeship which lasted many, many years. Beginning in some humble role within the locomotive department, they would gradually progress to become a cleaner, then a fireman and finally a driver, but the progress of this development was not by any means rapid. In fact most express drivers were old men when they attained their goal, usually being in their 50s or even 60s. Other positions of responsibility were more easily achieved, and as a man progressed, he would be given additional limited duties over and above his regular work. This began by letting the man try a higher grade of work, but limit this to more menial duties such as shunting, yard trips and so on. Thus we hear of 'passed cleaners' becoming firemen and 'passed firemen' doing driving work, but such work was strictly confined to the limits of their own experience and route knowledge; that rule, however, would often be changed at holiday times when men were sometimes given responsibilities beyond their experience. On the night of 27th June 1928 it was the inexperience of a 32-year old 'passed fireman' which led to the death of 25 people at Darlington Bank Top station. A shortage of regular drivers, due to holidays and other pressures of work, led to a young fireman being given the task of taking an ex-NER 4-6-0 No.2369 on the 9.30pm semi-fast train from Newcastle to York. He had done the journey many times as a fireman, and once as a driver, but his knowledge of the route did not include sidings along the way.

Bank Top, Darlington's principle station is covered by a huge over-all roof which spans a large island platform; back in 1928 this island had the two main faces of today, and bays at either end. On the up side, there were three roads; a platform road, a middle road, and a back road. It was a very cramped layout and the distance between the points of convergence for these three roads was just 144 feet; this meant that any train wanting to shunt either the middle or back road would have to run on to the main line thus fouling the progress of any through trains. At 10.45pm the semi-fast arrived from Newcastle 11 minutes late, and was signalled to the south end of the up platform to allow passengers to alight and also make room for another train. The middle road was occupied by a rake of seven vans which had to be included behind the third vehicle in the York train. A shunter uncoupled the semi-fast and the 'passed fireman' was told to pull his train forward as far as the South Junction, however as the length of this shortened train was 135 feet, he had to pull out onto the main line. This required the observance of two calling-on signals, the first of which (No. 8) was duly cleared to let him proceed as far as the second signal, No.18, the middle-road starter. As an excursion from Scarborough to Newcastle was due the signalman kept No.18 at danger, unfortunately the driver failed to observe this and he ran past it. The signalman was unaware of the driver's error, but a 'curious clicking sound' in the frame (just like that evidenced at Hull), alerted him to the fact that something was wrong. He therefore promptly threw all the signals to danger, but it was too late. Atlantic class Z, No.2164 was racing towards South Junction with eleven coaches at a speed of 45mph under clear signals, when he saw the semi-fast's engine running into his road from the left. Although he applied his brakes, the two trains collided head on and the semi-fast's engine was driven back 1800 feet along the down main resulting in the four vans behind it being completely destroyed. The second and third coaches were smashed into each other and, in addition to the dead, 45 passengers were seriously injured, as were both drivers and the fireman of the express. Fourteen of those killed were members of the Hetton-le-Hole Mother's Union, and their deaths left four widowers in one street alone. Two outstanding recommendations came out from this incident, one was colour light signalling which was installed in Darlington a decade after the event, the other was the LNER's adoption of buck-eye couplings which would drastically reduce the terrible effects of telescoping as we will discover later in this book.

PHOTOGRAPH; THE LATE KENNETH HOOLE COLLECTION

PINWHERRY

London Midland & Scottish Railway
2nd July 1928

It is a matter of coincidence that our next accident, which occurred just 4½ days after Darlington, bears such a striking similarity to the disaster on the LNER. Whilst the accident which befell the LMS on 2nd July 1928 is completely different in its circumstances, it has exactly the same root - inexperience. As the 'passed fireman' should have never been sent out alone on the York road without a knowledge of the sidings into which he might have been shunted, a similar situation existed with a new driver on the route to Stranraer. In May 1928 the man was promoted from shunting duties in the Greenock and Glasgow area, and duly put on to the freight link to work the Stranraer service. It was a normal enough progression, and there were procedures to help men gain extra experience of a particular route but, at the same time, leave them in charge of the running of their engine. This was achieved by providing a conductor who would help the driver gain his route knowledge by showing the signals, speed restrictions, special regulations, and local knowledge that would be needed. Once he was fully satisfied that he knew the road, the driver would sign a 'Route Card' or 'Road Book' to show that he was familiar with the route and happy to drive it unaccompanied in future. The driver involved in the accident at Pinwherry had a conductor for his first five trips, after which he signed for the route and then did his first solo trip along the route on 2nd June. With that route learned, tuition was given on other routes, and this conductor training continued up to the end of the month. On 2nd July he was on his own again, once more working the Stranraer road with the 1am freight from Glasgow. At 6.30pm, after a suitable rest period, they took Class 3F 0-6-0 No.17759 on the return trip. Their load consisted of 29 4-wheeled goods vehicles (many of which were loaded with Scottish Seed Potatoes) and a 20-ton brake van. They managed to get away ten minutes early, but due to the crossing of a passenger train at Glenwhilly they had dropped to 7 minutes late; yet by smart working this had been reduced to 3 minutes at Barrhill. As the train began the long descent from Barrhill to Phinwherry, the guard noticed the speed increasing but failed to see any application of the engine brake and could do nothing himself to slow the speed as his brake was already fully applied. The train whipped down the incline and passed through the station at about 50 mph, and began to negotiate the two reverse curves at the far side of the Pinwherry. The enginemen did not appear to have been concerned by this, as one of them had taken the tablet from the tablet catcher and put it into the cab. This had probably been the fireman who, incidentally, did not know the road. As the train passed under the bridge at the north end of the station it gave a sudden lurch then derailed down the embankment. As rescuers arrived at the scene the engine and tender were found to be half buried in mud, and it was obvious that both footplatemen had perished. Why the driver had taken his train at such speed can only be a matter of conjecture, but the Inspector concluded that he was anxious to make up time and forgot the severe curvature at Pinwherry.

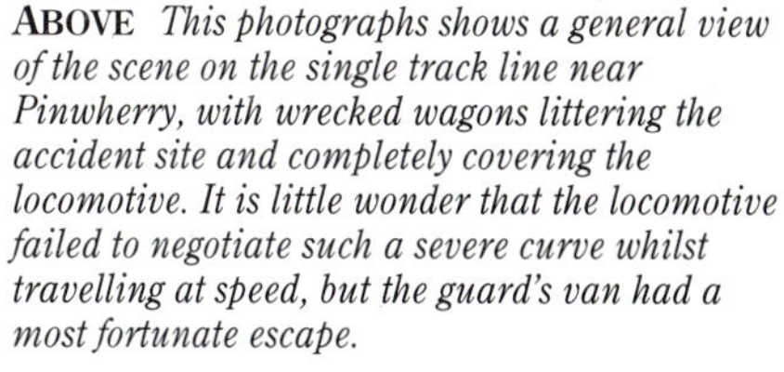

ABOVE *This photographs shows a general view of the scene on the single track line near Pinwherry, with wrecked wagons littering the accident site and completely covering the locomotive. It is little wonder that the locomotive failed to negotiate such a severe curve whilst travelling at speed, but the guard's van had a most fortunate escape.*

LEFT *This gives a detailed view of the wrecked wagons, with their loads of seed potatoes scattered all around. The upturned van by the policeman presents a superb view of the underframe detail, and will undoubtedly be of interest to model makers. Yet such a tragic view only became possible due to the driver's carelessness or over-confidence, or possibly a mixture of both.*

PHOTOGRAPHS; THE LATE J. BARR COLLECTION, COURTESY THE GLASGOW TRANSPORT MUSEUM

CHARFIELD

London, Midland & Scottish Railway 13th October 1928

From the Northern Division of the LMS, we shift our scene to the opposite end of the system and move to Charfield on the route between Gloucester and Bristol. The date was Saturday 13th October and the train, the Night Mail from Derby to Bristol. It was a typically Midland Railway scene, as the engine was a re-built Johnson Class 3, No.714, with a train of eleven vehicles, of which only four were used for passengers. It was also typical of many secondary LMS express services of the day, in that it employed far from modern stock. More significantly, and despite the tragedies of the high Pennines, three out of the four coaches were still gas-lit, as were five of the vans. Even eighteen years on from the Hawes Junction tragedy, the company's policy of coach modernisation was still found wanting; this was clearly an apathetic response to an already identified problem, and it was also to have a major part in what followed a driver's error at Charfield.

Preceding the Night Mail were three other trains, the progress of which have a direct bearing on the events in question. These trains were the 10.35pm from Washwood Heath to Bristol, the 9.15pm GWR freight from Oxley Sidings to Bristol, which would leave the LMS line at Yate Junction, and the 12.45am Leicester to Bristol parcels. As the latter was rapidly overhauling the former trains, it was decided that both these freights should be shunted in order to give precedence to the Leicester train; this shunting was duly achieved by setting the GWR back at Berkeley Road and the LMS train at Charfield. After this the controller at Fishponds, Bristol made the decision to pass the LMS freight on first, and send the GWR train to be set back at Charfield. To me this seems to have been quite illogical, as the much faster, lighter GWR train could easily have been clear of the LMS line at Yate by the time the Night Mail reached there. The signalman at Charfield ordered the LMS freight out of the sidings, and gave it a clear road to Wickwar, but unbeknown to him the driver decided to take on water at the station which took five minutes. As the GWR train was waiting to enter the section, the signalman realised that this could not now be passed before the Night Mail. He was in the process of setting back into the sidings when he saw his track-circuit indicator change from 'Clear' to 'Occupied', and realised that the mail was overrunning his signals. A minute later and the 50-vehicle goods would have been in the siding, or had the express been running at the speed limit of 45mph instead of the estimated 60mph, the results would have been completely different. As it was 2-6-0 No.6381 was still fouling the main line and the express struck its tender, turned to the right and smashed into the side of an up freight which was just passing. As at Ditton and Sevenoaks, the wrecked trains piled up around a bridge and this served to make the circumstances much worse than would have otherwise been expected. The roof of one coach was flung over the bridge, and some of its occupants catapulted out. The wreckage was then consumed by fire and the first six vehicles in the express were completely burnt-out. Officially the death roll was sixteen, but we may never know the exact figures at all. An often related story of Charfield tells of the two unknown children who were killed in the crash, and in the nearby village church yard there is a tombstone erected in their memory. The full story of this incident is recounted in *BackTrack* Volume 3 p155, whilst our next accident, that at Dinwoodie is extensively covered in Volume 7, p293.

PHOTOGRAPHS: ATLANTIC COLLECTION

DINWOODIE

London, Midland & Scottish Railway 25th October 1928

With the spate of disasters which rocked the LMS in the mid-1920s, we now have to return to the Northern division. Once again we look at an accident which was investigated for the LMS by the late Mr. J. Barr, who's family have been so helpful in providing information into the accidents he dealt with. Sixteen weeks after he had arranged the clear up of the Pinwherry disaster, Mr. Barr was again involved with sorting out a much more serious disaster. Although this one occurred on the West Coast Main line in Scotland, it was an almost direct repetition of the events at Thirsk on the ECML 36-years earlier. The night of 25th October 1928 was typical of late-autumn in the Scottish Borders, with dark storm clouds scudding over the uninhabited countryside between Lockerbie and Moffat. In the storms and rain, a worried 31-year old signalman made his way to the lonely signal box at Wamphray. His wife was not well, having recently undergone a complicated child-birth and their baby was very sickly and fretful. At this time the man was working the night shift, but instead of resting during the day he was having to care for his wife and small baby, as well as look after two older children and do all the household chores. Women living in the nearby railway cottages helped all they could, but it was a tired man who walked into the box at Wamphray that night. The rain and the stuffiness of the snug signal box did not help, nor did the fact that he had already got into the habit of 'cat-napping' in between the passage of trains. As his 'alarm clock' he relied on the signal bell codes transmitted by his colleagues in the neighbouring boxes, but such was the recipe for disaster. It had its fulfilment when the down 'Royal Highlander' express from Euston to Aberdeen and Inverness ran into the rear of a 35-vehicle freight train which had come to a stand due to a mechanical defect.

About 3am the signalman was roused by the bell-code signals for the express and, with his mind still fogged by sleep, he cleared the 'boards' without having ensured that the preceding train had left his section. Accordingly, the double-headed express was allowed to proceed under clear signals and whilst travelling at about 60 mph, it struck the back of a freight train from Carlisle to Dundee. Having come to a halt between Wamphray and Dinwoodie the guard of this train had failed to lay down detonators, nor had the driver sent his fireman to apply Rule 55. Without any secondary protection to prevent a back-up in case of a signalling error, the express train's pilot engine went through the freight's 20 ton brake van at floor level, completely demolishing it. In turn, the brake van's heavy ballast blocks ripped away the bogie of the pilot engine (an ex-Caledonian 4-4-0, No. 14435) and a good deal of the under-gear. It rolled over and ploughed down the side of the embankment, followed by the train engine, a standard compound 4-4-0 No. 1176. All four enginemen on the express were killed instantly, but due to the sturdiness of the coaching stock only five passengers suffered from slight injuries or shock as the all-steel construction prevented wide-spread injury. In fact, as a result of Dinwoodie, the Ministry of Transport recommended that where all-steel vehicles were included in a train, they should be marshalled next to the engine to prevent telescoping. However, in practice this rarely happened unless such a vehicle just happened to be at the right end of the train. Whilst Dinwoodie showed that the improved design of coaching stock could lessen the effects of an accident when it happened, it also seems that the same accident proves that simple expedient measures for protecting a stranded train were still not being properly carried out. Even though the signalman was clearly at fault for his lapse, the freight train crew were equally responsible, but sadly a belt and braces attitude was not was manifested that night at Dinwoodie for it was almost a quarter of an hour before they began laying detonators to protect their rear end. Again it was too little too late, but what of the signalman? Although he openly admitted that the accident was his fault, we surely cannot judge him too harshly for such a human error.

PHOTOGRAPHS: THE LATE J. BARR COURTESY GLASGOW TRANSPORT MUSEUM.

ASHCHURCH
London, Midland & Scottish Railway
8th January 1929

When writing about the accidents at Charfield and Dinwoodie, I should have mentioned that the principle recommendation which came out at the subsequent enquiry was once again the necessity for ATC/AWS apparatus and track-circuits. It will be recalled that the GWR had set the lead in this field, but elsewhere a major debate had raged over the merits of Automatic Train Control. In 1920 Colonel Sir Arthur Pringle had become so concerned over the lack of an adequate, standard system for train control he formed a Committee to look into the matter and when his report was published in 1923 it concluded that there was a case for warning devices at distant signals, but it was more essential that trip-stop control be provided at stop signals. Sadly, this was a plan that was killed by its own ambitiousness, for the cost of converting a minimum of 38,000 stop signals and 24,000 locomotives was placed at a figure approaching £5 million. A second committee was therefore convened, but less than a fortnight after its first meeting, the terrible disaster occurred at Charfield; no doubt this crystalised the Committee's thinking, but they were soon to be given further irrefutable proof of the consequences which could come from the lack of ATC/AWS. The accident which proved this happened on the same Derby - Bristol main line as Charfield, but this time it was much further north at Ashchurch between Cheltenham and Worcester.

The circumstances of the disaster at Ashchurch were uncannily similar to Charfield, for once again a driver overran a series of consecutive signals which were placed at danger. The signals were in this position to allow a slow-moving goods to be set back over a trailing cross-over from the up main to the down main. However, in thick patchy fog a Leeds - Bristol express which was travelling at a speed of around 50 mph, began overrunning the signals protecting this movement. As at Charfield, the die was now cast and the collision which followed was an inevitable consequence of operating a railway without any physical connection between the signals and the cab of the locomotive. Under full steam the LMS Compound 4-4-0 No.1060 barrelled through the patchy fog with a lightly loaded fourteen-coach express. As it overran the signals the driver seemingly had no sight of either them, or the freight engine which was passing through the cross-over at a speed of about 2 mph. Though the express made a last minute brake application, it was completely ineffective and the Compound struck the freight engine at a speed of about 40 mph. It was driven back for a considerable distance, whilst the wooden bodied coaches crumpled up around the tender of No.1060. The leading coaches telescoped and our picture shows the extent of the devastation, with wreckage spread over a wide area. However, despite the exceptional severity of the collision, the death toll was very light as only four people were killed. An interesting inclusion in the picture is 2-4-0 No.175 with the 8-wheeled engineer's saloon which is stopped just beyond the wreckage. Note the coach's open verandah and the almost pristine condition of the train specially assigned to the duty. Another interesting facet is noted in the wreckage which pictures splintered wood and severed gas-lighting systems, yet no fire attended this disaster as it had done at Charfield; for once, the self-sealing valves introduced after earlier disasters had proved their worth. But surely what was needed, was a means to prevent such accidents taking place, and not just methods designed to minimise the consequences therefrom. In short, Ashchurch demonstrated that the LMS badly needed an automatic train control system.

A year after this accident, the second Pringle Committee published their report with two defined ways of increasing railway security. When the committee's recommendations were presented to the Minister of Transport in 1930, the report came out in favour of two approaches to the improvement of railway safety. The first of these was the 'Direct' method, which involved the employment of a form of ATC equipment similar to that used by the GWR, the second was the 'Indirect' method' which placed greater reliance on the improvement of signal sighting, block controls, track circuiting and the introduction of colour light signals. Only the GWR went ahead and carried on improving its train control system, but had the other companies swallowed their pride at this time the future would have been very much different. Hindsight shows that this system was simply the best, most cost effective scheme that could have been introduced at the time. There was an added bonus in its application, in that huge fog-signalling and other associated costs could have been used to offset its introduction. (By the way I should state that, except on matters of safety, I'm not a GWR enthusiast)! As it was the GWR went its own sweet way, whilst other railways carried out experiments with track circuiting, colour light signalling and so on, and these 'indirect' approaches were subsequently introduced on the other three railways. In particular, the LMS placed its faith in the improvement of signalling installations by the replacement of semaphore arms with colour light signals - this was to be a woefully inadequate stance as we will see.

PHOTOGRAPH; BBC HULTON PICTURE LIBRARY

DOE HILL

London, Midland & Scottish Railway 12th February 1929

Five weeks on from Ashchurch, yet another disastrous collision befell an LMS express after errors occurred in the course of another shunting operation; however, on this occasion the Inspector clearly noted that 'No form of automatic train control, would have reasonably prevented this accident.' Events began in the early hours of the morning on 12th February 1929, at Morton Sidings where an express freight train was shunted from the up-goods line to the up-passenger in order to allow a fast train to pass. However, when the signalman gave the 'right away', he erroneously re-started the 10.50pm from Sheffield to Birmingham Soho on the wrong line. Now to explain how this could have happened, we need to mention that this section of the former Midland Railway near Clay Cross had four running lines, which ran (east to west) in the following order; up goods, down goods, up passenger, down passenger. On either side of these running lines were several sidings, those to the west serving Morton Colliery, whilst those to the east served Pilsley Colliery. The sidings were connected by a single through crossing road, with a trailing slip connection in the up goods and both passenger lines; the down goods had the benefit of a double slip with a facing connection. About 100 yards to the north there was another trailing connection leading from the down passenger line to Morton sidings. Now the prescribed movement for the type of shunt required involved, in this order, lever 13 (trailing crossover points in up goods), then lever 14 (crossover points in down goods leading to up passenger), followed by lever 16 (trailing crossover slip points in down passenger to up passenger). This would be followed by the lowering of shunting signal No.12 which would direct the train on to the down passenger. After it came to a stand the signalman would put back levers 12, 14 and 13, the signals protecting the shunt and the main line (Nos.25 and 39) would now be locked and the train protected. However, when reversing the process after the passage of the fast goods, the signalman omitted to pull lever 16 and the engine was therefore restarted on the wrong line. Although the crew knew they had to go through the cross-over after the shunt, because of the darkness neither the driver nor his fireman realised they had not done so. The class 4F 0-6-0, No. 4491, was thus allowed to proceed southwards on the down passenger line with its train of 34 goods wagons and a 20-ton brake van. In fact the error went unnoticed until they reached Doe Hill Station where, upon observing that the platforms were on his wrong side, the driver brought the train to a stand. On doing this he sent his fireman to change the head-lamps to show a red aspect and then set off to lay detonators, but as he walked down the track he saw the head-lamps of the 9.30pm from St. Pancras to Glasgow approaching him at speed.

Running at about 40mph at the head of a thirteen-coach train, was No. 5977 a standard four-cylinder Claughton 4-6-0. The express driver had no chance of avoiding the collision, and both he and his mate were killed by in the impact. The first two vehicles in the train were wooden bodied, both telescoped into each other and were totally wrecked, part of the body on the first one was thrown thirty feet to the west of the frame. The third vehicle was of all-steel construction built in 1927, and though almost completely destroyed it absorbed a lot of the lateral-force. As a result the three all-steel bogie brake vans which followed, Nos. 7067, 7352, and 7969, were all derailed, but with lessening degrees of damage. The remainder of the train was undamaged, and afterwards even able to go forward behind another engine. A few passengers were thrown from their seats in the sixth vehicle, corridor composite No. 9328, but the 12-wheel sleeping car which came next was hardly shaken - in fact one passenger slept throughout the whole incident and, when woken the following morning, was astonished to hear of the proceedings. Though a signalman's error and a lack of attention by the footplate crew of No. 4491 led to this disaster, it is a remarkably interesting accident because it emphasised exactly what Colonel A.H.L. Mount had tried to bring home about the correct marshalling of all-steel vehicles after the tragedy at Dinwoodie!

PHOTOGRAPHS NATIONAL RAILWAY MUSEUM

LEIGHTON BUZZARD

London, Midland & Scottish Railway
22nd March 1931

Although 1928 had been a very bad time for accidents on the LMS, the years 1929 and 1930 were remarkably trouble free. With the exception of a fatal accident at Culgaith on the Settle & Carlisle Railway on 6th March 1930, not a single life was lost on any railway during those two years. However when 1931 started the problems came back with a vengeance and, ironically, most of these were associated with high speed derailments. On 3rd January there was a serious accident at Carlisle when an engine approaching the city's Canal Junction was derailed and claimed three lives as a result. The driver was subsequently tried for manslaughter at the Cumberland Assizes on a Coroner's Warrant, but this reliable and truthful and obliging man (as he was described by his superiors) never once gave any entertainment to Colonel Mount's suggestion that he might have acted incorrectly. He remained resolutely firm that as he approached the point of derailment, he felt a sinking feeling and the engine just rolled over. The courts found him 'not guilty' but the Inspector's report heavily censured him, and the man could bring forward no evidence to rebut the suggestions that he had been travelling at speed over the points concerned. Yet barely had the dust settled at Carlisle than on 4th January the Royal Scot was derailed at Weaver Junction, and nine days later the Golden Arrow came off the rails at Kent House. On June 30th the Flying Scotsman was derailed at Beal, but the most serious accident of the period had already taken place at Leighton Buzzard as we now discuss.

It is a most unusual occurrence for accident reports to be issued within so short a period as five days of each other, but the similarities between Carlisle and Leighton Buzzard were so great that Colonel Mount delayed publication of the former to ensure that his message was clearly understood. The reason for this derailment is far less complex than it was at Carlisle, but the actual cause of the lapse on the footplate can not be satisfactorily explained because both of the crew were killed. At the time there was a necessary diversion from the down fast to the down slow at Leighton Buzzard, and a speed limit of 20 mph was subsequently imposed. To ensure that this limit was obeyed, the signalman was instructed to keep his signals at danger until an approaching train had slowed right down, before he could clear them and let it take the crossover between the lines. However, on 22nd March Royal Scot Class No.6114 *Coldstream Guardsman* was approaching the crossing at a speed of 55 to 60 mph with an up express, but it failed to slow down at all. The driver and fireman both had exceptionally good records, and it seems unlikely that such an error could have occurred unless something had distracted them. No mechanical defect was discovered, nor was there anything else which might have served to distract them, other than something like grit in the eye. However, it soon began to emerge that many drivers had their own theories about the cause of the accident, as the Royal Scot class were gaining a reputation for having smoke clinging to the boiler casing and thus obscuring the view. If smoke was indeed beating down on the boiler and cab windows, then the driver might well have missed the home signals completely. We must remember that the distant was showing clear, and he would only have the home signals in view 612 yards. At a speed of 70mph, this would only mean a sighting period of 17 seconds, little enough time to take avoiding action. Again, ATC/AWS could have played a part, even though this would have meant first checking the express at the distant. However, it would be a further fifteen years before the need for such a system was really demonstrated on the LMS as we will see in the accidents at Ecclefechan and Bourne End.

PHOTOGRAPHS; TIMES NEWSPAPERS LTD.

CRICH
London, Midland & Scottish Railway
17th June 1931

Sadly the LMS's problems of 1931 did not end with Leighton Buzzard, and just three months later another fatal accident occurred because of the absence of ATC/AWS. This time it was on the former Midland main line from Derby to Leeds, and the 17th June 1931 was just nine minutes old, when a violent rear-end collision took place near Ambergate. As the 10,00pm Leeds - Bristol postal express neared Crich Junction, Ambergate, it ploughed into the back of the 6.27pm up mineral express as it was slowly travelling towards Derby. Drawn by two engines, both 4-4-0s, the 11-coach express was running at a speed of between 30 and 40 mph. On being struck by the express, the 64-vehicle goods train divided at the 47th wagon and the front portion continued on for some distance behind 0-6-0 No. 4416 as the footplate crew were totally unaware that the collision had even taken place. The drivers of the two express trains, however were fatally injured, and their firemen were both badly hurt. The guard at the back of the goods train was also seriously injured, but passengers on the express were affected less as only five fare-paying travellers and 10 postal workers reported injuries, and of these none were particularly serious. Yet this was such a violent collision that a 5-ton tar boiler being transported on the freight train was thrown over 35 yards to land in a field without so much as disturbing the grass around where it landed. The accident was undoubtedly the fault of the express drivers as they had run past at least two signals when they were at danger. However, there is some doubt as to whether the crew had been given a false impression about the state of the road when a signalman at Wingfield pulled off his home signal as he could not be sure that the train had come to a halt. Even if we give them the benefit of the doubt for the distant signal, just how the express drivers could have run past two more red lights is totally beyond comprehension. The signalman did not escape criticism however, as the Inspector concluded that he too had committed a grave error of judgement in pulling off his home signal when he had no way of being sure that the express had been brought almost to a standstill as the rules required.

PHOTOGRAPH: NATIONAL RAILWAY MUSEUM.

DAGGENHAM
London, Midland & Scottish Railway
18th December 1931

The LMS accident record continued to take another battering as the year drew to a close, this time at Daggenham Dock on the London, Tilbury & Southend section. On 18th December 1931 Class 4F 0-6-0 No.4030 was making its way through a dense fog from Brent to West Thurrock, with a train of 38 wagons/empty oil tankers and a 20-ton brake van. As it neared Daggenham Dock the train parted between the 28th and 29th wagons due to a defective drawbar. As they were due to stop at the home signal the guard appears to have failed to notice the fact that the train had divided, but we will never know as the man was to lose his life a few moments later. In any case he remained in his guards van and did not get out and put down any detonators to protect the stranded rear portion. As visibility was down to 10 to 12 yards, it seems likely that he had not realised the precarious position that he was in. Unfortunately the signalman failed to see that the train had split, and as it passed he did not notice that the tail lights were missing. When the front portion of the goods passed out of his section, he cleared back for the following train, a passenger train from London (Fenchurch Street) to Southend which was being drawn by 4-4-2T No.2139. As it ran into the section under clear signals the crew had no chance of seeing the brake van until it was far too late, and in the ensuing collision a passenger was also killed. Of the 250 passengers on the train, 33 were detained in hospital due to their injuries, ten of these being of a very serious nature.

PHOTOGRAPH: ATLANTIC COLLECTION

GREAT BRIDGEFORD

London, Midland & Scottish Railway
6th June 1932

The troubles for the London, Midland & Scottish Railway continued in 1932, and as will be quickly appreciated from a review of the last 22 accidents, the one now under discussion means that the LMS suffered 14 major accidents in the first decade after the Grouping, This is a poor record by any standard, and we have not even discussed the near major disaster at Cowie Viaduct on 3rd October 1927 when an Aberdeen - Euston express had the narrowest of escapes. In that instance a brake reservoir came adrift as the train approached the high viaduct, the four front coaches were derailed and they smashed through the parapet but only escaped falling into the precipice below by the narrowest of margins. The LMS were lucky that day, but on 6th June 1933 they were once again abandoned to disaster. But this was a disaster which should have been readily avoided, particularly after what had been learnt following Leighton Buzzard. Indeed few commentators could believe that an almost identical derailment would take place only a year after that event but, at Great Bridgeford an up express passenger train once again ran through a cross-over from the up slow to the up fast at high speed. This time it was a train running from Crewe to Stafford and Birmingham which derailed near the south end of Great Bridgeford station. The engine 4-4-0 No.5278 *Precursor* overturned, the first coach was completely wrecked and the next was very badly damaged and those following also suffered. Some 80 passengers were travelling on the train when it derailed, and of these three were killed instantly with a fourth dying in hospital afterwards. The driver was buried in his cab under coal which slipped from the tender, but he was extricated and taken to hospital along with his fireman and nine passengers who had been seriously hurt, 42 more people sustained injuries to a lesser degree. That is the bare bones of the accident, but this is another of the great mysteries which have never been fully understood. Whereas the driver at Leighton Buzzard was killed, the one at Great Bridgeford survived and his story varied greatly with that of the signalman and it posed a question which the Inspector would have to resolve.

It was a very difficult case, for it was the word of one man against the other; the driver claiming that he had been running under clear signals, the signalman claiming that the express had passed the warning signal at danger. The driver's evidence seems to be the more reliable of the two statements, and much of the circumstantial evidence favours him although his fireman was unable to provide corroboration as he did not see what happened. The driver's version of events was that he was running at high speed under clear signals, but after he passed the distant the signalman reset the junction to divert the train on to the fast line in order for it to follow an express from Perth which had just gone through. Though the stop signals were showing danger, he could not possibly stop in time and he went into the crossover at too great a speed. Whilst the Inspector expressed grave doubts about parts of the signalman's evidence, he wrote; 'Whatever the criticisms may be in detail, however, with regard to the evidence of these two men, the fact remains that there is no proof that [the signalman] acted as [the driver] suggested; there is equally no proof that [the driver] passed the distant signal in its warning position. In the absence of such confirmation, one way or the other, as for instance existed in the Leighton Buzzard case, the evidence appears to me to be so balanced that I feel there is sufficient reason to refrain from even offering an opinion as to which man is the more likely to have been responsible. ....I regret such a finding, and in my inability to reach a definite conclusion, the more because there must necessarily remain attached to the unoffending party the suspicion of blame, in the one case for a serious momentary failure, and in the other for a still more serious lapse.'

PHOTOGRAPH: BBC HULTON PICTURE LIBRARY.

FRIOG (Vriog)

Great Western Railway
4th March 1933

The line from Aberystwyth to Pwllheli was opened by the Cambrian Railway in 1865, and the cash strapped little company had to do all that it could to keep costs to a bare minimum; this had an indirect bearing on a couple of incidents which mark the tiny hamlet of Friog as one of those unfortunate locations to suffer two railway disasters. The community, just south of Fairbourne, was never large enough to merit even the tiniest of halts but it did give its name to a substantial cutting where the single track line was carved into a ledge 90 feet above the sea. Above this the hillside climbed upwards as the Cader Idris range rose up towards Pen-y-Garn. On New Year's Day 1883 a landslide occurred in Friog Cutting, showering over 100 tons of earth down on to the railway line below, and into this Cambrian 2-4-0, No.96 *Pegasus* had the misfortune to run with a local passenger train. The passengers fortunately escaped injury, but the engine was precipitated over the cliff on to the rocky shore-line below and its crew were killed outright. Stabilising work followed this incident and a careful watch was kept on the peaty soil above the railway for quite sometime, however, by 1933 this practice had been discontinued and a chilling sequel to the 1883 accident was to be repeated 50 years on. Heavy snow on the hillside, just eight days earlier (itself a far from usual event) had been followed by a rapid thaw, and shades of Little Salkeld were being echoed in the ground. When the 6.10am mail train from Machynlleth to Pwllheli ran through the cutting the reverberation of its passage caused the loosened earth to slide and around 2,000 tons of soil and rubble swept down on to the track. Once again the passengers were spared, but the engine (ex-Cambrian 0-6-0 No.874) and its crew were carried over the cliff and dashed on to the rocks below. The crew were killed, but the line was later given the protection of an avalanche shelter, but like Little Salkeld (where its second accident also occurred in 1932) the circumstance between the two accidents at Friog bore an uncanny ring of familiarity.

PHOTOGRAPH: THE LATE ARTHUR TREVENA COLLECTION

RAYNES PARK

Southern Railway
25th May 1932

Before we can consider Little Salkeld, there is another accident which we must place in chronological order; and this is that which occurred at Raynes Park on 25th May 1932. To do this we return to the Doublebois accident of 1895 and the badly designed tank engines which the GWR were employing in the south-west of England. Ironically, the GWR were not alone in this because their near neighbours and close rivals, the London & South Western Railway, were also having troubles with tank engines around the same time. On 3rd June 1898 one of Dugald Drummond's 0-4-4 tank engines was involved in a spectacular, though relatively non-serious accident. Once again suspect track and high speed led to the derailment, at Tavistock, and as a consequence the company took note of the Inspector's criticisms and relegated the engines to suburban work around London. They performed sterling service on such workings for many years, but was their inherent instability a major factor in the derailment which took place at Raynes Park on 25th May 1932? Admittedly, there was a serious defect in the permanent way as a consequence of an inspector and the ganger lifting the track without authority or proper speed restrictions being put in place. Even so, a more stable engine might have stayed up right, but as it was No.107 and the 3.10pm from Waterloo to Alton was derailed on to the up through line. Approaching the scene was 2-6-0 No.1261, with the 12.11pm Southampton - Waterloo, and this engine ripped open the sides of the first three coaches in the Alton train. Five passengers were killed and 34 more were injured, as was the driver of No.1621.

PHOTOGRAPH: BBC HULTON PICTURE LIBRARY.

LITTLE SALKELD

London, Midland & Scottish Railway

10th July 1933

Our next accident, Little Salkeld, is unusual because (whilst some locations have suffered two or more serious accidents) as far as I have been able to discover none have ever twice involved the same engine. Several engines also had the misfortune to suffer two or more bad accidents, but always at different locations, therefore, 4-4-0 No.1010 is truly a unique locomotive as both accidents happened within a few hundred yards of each other. Whilst the first incident, detailed on page 79, was a pure freak of nature the second occasion on 10th July 1933 was due entirely to human-error. Little Salkeld was one of the small-type stations on the Settle-Carlisle line, and the signal box was equipped with one of the smaller Midland frames. The box was not continuously manned and therefore only 'switched in' when a train had to be set back to allow an express to pass, or when wagons were being dropped off in the yard. Therefore, it was operated by a passed-porter/signalman and, according to the report, the man doing the job in 1933 was not a very good one. That day he had knocked off an hour early to take his lunch at 12.30pm, because a down freight train which usually passed at 1.30pm sometimes had a wagon to drop off. He was just having his lunch when the freight train arrived 25 minutes early, and in something of a temper he left his lodgings to attend to it.

Sure enough, the freight had a single wagon of coal to drop, and he had to open up the box. However, he did not first check the traffic position with the adjacent boxes at Langwathby and Lazonby, before moving the inter-locked points which also threw the home signals to danger. The crew of the freight uncoupled the train behind the third wagon and the class 4F 0-6-0, No. 4091 ran forward, before being signalled to push the wagons over the cross-over onto the up line. At that moment

the up Thames-Forth express, came rushing out of Long Meg cutting under clear distant signals at around 60mph. The compound hit the leading wagon which was just fouling the up line, and then smashed into the tender of the 4F. Number 1010 was derailed to the left and ran on along a paved cartway in the goods yard, coming to rest 90 yards further on. Its coaches scraped though the wreckage and many had their sides ripped open, causing injuries to about half of the 60 passengers on board. The fireman of No.1010 was seriously hurt, but the 4F's driver was fatally injured. The 'signalman' later claimed he thought that the express had passed during his lunch but, as it was not due to leave Carlisle until 12.44pm, he had most likely forgotten all about it. The accompanying pictures clearly show the damage to No.1010 and the coaches as they stand in the station yard, whilst the bottom view taken at Carlisle Durran Hill engine shed shows No.1010 after being recovered.

PHOTOGRAPHS ABOVE AND CENTRE: NATIONAL RAILWAY MUSEUM. LEFT: THE LATE KENNETH LONGBOTTOM

HITHER GREEN

Southern Railway
4th September 1934

Our next accident, featured in Volume One of the original series, with the very brief caption 'The down local line was blocked outside Hither Green Station, Southern Railway, on 4th September 1934, when two goods trains collided.' Sadly I have not been able to find any more information to elaborate on this incident, but I have left it in as it allows me space to say a few more words about the incident at Hither Green which we feature on our cover of this book. On 20th February 1960, Battle of Britain Class 4-6-2 No.34084 *253 Squadron* moved out of the up goods loop against the signals. Like many of the other derailments we have already discussed, the engine ran into the dead end siding and smashed through the buffer blocks. It rolled down a high embankment and caused great damage to itself and seriously disrupted all other traffic when it sliced through the signalling cables. Fortunately there were no serious consequences, and R. C. Riley was able to take the photograph illustrated on the cover. As Mr. Riley has been of great assistance in compiling the *Trains In Trouble* series over the years, we would like to pay tribute to his efforts by recording his words on this accident which featured in *BackTrack* Vol. 1 Issue 1 in the spring of 1987. 'By the following day, a Sunday [21st February], temporary cables had been put in and the signalling was back to normal. The Bricklayers Arms' breakdown crane restored the leading van to the tracks by midday and the Stewarts Lane gang was busy stripping side plating from the engine and banking up sleepers beneath it. There had been the inevitable oil bath fire, attended to by two fire appliances. The sleeper bed beside the engine leading to the main line was completed and it was hoped to rerail 34048 on 24th February, but a 350 hp diesel became derailed a short distance behind the Pacific and by the time this was rerailed it was only possible that day to recover the tender. On Sunday 28th the Bricklayers Arms crane was on the up main and the Stewarts Lane breakdown train on the loop with the Kelbus lifting gear slowly jacking up the engine, which was attached to a hawser through a gear, kept taught by two 350 hp diesels. About 3.30 pm the engine was righted with a clatter.' Sadly, these two derailments were not isolated instances and, as we will discuss on page 173, on 5th November 1967 Hither Green suffered a terrible accident when 49 people were killed after a broken rail derailed a heavily loaded train from Hastings to Cannon Street.

PHOTOGRAPH: THE LATE ARTHUR TREVENA COLLECTION

BOWLING BASIN, Near HELENSBURGH

London & North Eastern Railway
8th September 1934

An unusual lapse of memory occurred on the second Friday in September 1934, when the crew of a Class J36 0-6-0, No. 9280, left four trucks on the running line at Bowling Basin. The shunting operations taking place at a little after 9am that day saw the 0-6-0 taking ten trucks from the up line sidings to the nearby High Basin Sidings, but in the process four of these were somehow forgotten.

How the two GWR and two SR vehicles were left behind was a matter of some disagreement, and conflicting evidence between the driver and the guard centred around a hand signal. But even if the driver had moved prematurely as the guard claimed, the guard could have given a hand-signal to set back. As it was the guard did not do so, nor did he carry out Rules 110(b) or 69 and ensure that the line was clear and no trucks had been left behind. When questioned he could not explain why he had not done this, but it was a potentially fatal error. In the absence of a continuous track-circuit to advise the signalman of the obstruction which was sitting on the main line, the 9am train from Helensburgh to Glasgow was allowed into the section.

At 9.23am precisely, Class V1 2-6-2T No. 2902 and its six-vehicle load came racing down and collided with the wagons, two of these were smashed to atoms, but the other pair were hit with such force as to send them racing up the track for a distance of 500 yards. Thankfully injuries to the passengers and crew were only very slight, mainly due to the improved construction of the rolling stock.

PHOTOGRAPH: THE LATE KENNETH HOOLE COLLECTION

PORT EGLINGTON, Nr. GLASGOW

London, Midland & Scottish Railway 6th September 1934

When I covered the accident at Port Eglington Junction on 6th September 1934 in *Trains In Trouble* Volume 7, it was highly remarkable in that it revealed photographs of an LMS class 2P 4-4-0, No. 639, which was previously thought to be one of the few members of the class to elude the camera's lens. It is also of interest, because the collision occurred after a period of almost a year's immunity from passenger fatality in train accidents, which had thus far been one of the longest periods so recorded in British Railway history. Sadly, that evening was to claim the lives of three footplatemen and six passengers, whilst one driver and 10 passengers were seriously injured. Eighteen more passengers and both guards were detained in hospital, and a further 27 others reported injuries of various kinds. Number 639, was working a 6-coach Glasgow (St. Enoch) - Kilmarnock train, when it was hit head-on by sister loco. No. 591 on a Paisley - St. Enoch train with a similar number of coaches. The Kilmarnock train thus weighed 233 tons, whilst the Paisley train was probably about 257 tons. Only the driver of the Paisley train survived and, though seriously injured, it was his evidence that provided the central point of reference for the accident investigators.

The driver said that as he had pulled away from Shields Road station he noted the junction signals were off. He was running tender first, and had to turn round to 'notch-up' the regulator, however he claimed the home signals were reversed and when he next looked up they were showing danger. He had no chance of touching the reversing gear, and judged that he had got to a speed of 20 mph when he realised the situation. The engine was then little more than 165 yards from the point of collision, and No. 591 was heading towards them at a speed of between 25 and 30 mph. Colonel Mount thoroughly examined the situation at Port Eglington, both in the signal box and by twice riding on the footplate of a 4-4-0 running tender-first. For the trains to have met when they did, and at the speeds at which they were running, the home signal could not have been clear 40 seconds after No. 591 left Shields Road. Even though it would have been possible for the signalmen to have reversed the signals in 29 seconds, Colonel Mount concluded that the driver had actually seen another set of signals and was thus misled. He commented, 'I noted myself how deceptive these signals might be, and, as stated, there was unnecessary obscuration of [signals] No. 73/75 which I understand has since been dealt with. ......The circumstances of this collision illustrate the necessity for safeguarding the fallibility of drivers in respect of junction operation.' With semaphore installation at the junction it was difficult to improve the position, but had the St. Enoch colour-light signalling system been extended as far as this extremely busy junction, the accident would probably have been preventable. There was also a question of irregular operation of a signalling system which could allow three trains in the same section at the same time, no matter how long this method of operation had been worked on the basis of Regulation No. 4. The company therefore came in for a degree of criticism, and were advised to apply standard instructions for junction block working. The luckless driver was tried on a charge of culpable homicide before a Sheriff and Jury in Glasgow on 28th January 1935. The trial lasted three days, but in the end the jury returned a unanimous 'Not Guilty' verdict and he was acquitted.

ABOVE *The accident scene at Port Eglington shortly after the collision, with the tender of No. 591 pressed hard into the side of No 639, behind which can be seen the wreckage of the two leading coaches in the Kilmarnock train; these being third-brake No. 24350 and third-class No. 17483, both of which had wooden bodies and underframes and were thus unable to stand the impact.*

BELOW *A view of Class 2P 4-4-0 No. 591 taken shortly after the collision, when the engine had been removed from the scene. By now it has been separated from its tender which understandably suffered the worst of the damage in the Paisley train. It was a particularly sad accident, not only in human terms, but also in as much as there was a heavy loss of capital equipment. For example, although locomotive No. 639 was also recovered its bogie truck had to be cut up on site then, on examination at the works, it was found that the engine had been so seriously damaged in the collision that both the boiler and frames were completely beyond repair.*

PHOTOGRAPHS ALL COURTESY: THE LATE J. BARR COLLECTION, GLASGOW MUSEUMS

WINWICK

London, Midland & Scottish Railway

28th September 1934

A contrast in the accidents at Ais Gill, Darlington and Charfield with those at Dinwoodie and Doe Hill will clearly demonstrate the efficiency of the newer types of rolling stock; as all-steel construction, buck-eye couplers, shock-absorbing buffers and the elimination of gas-lighting all served to improve passenger safety. Indeed, as the control by the big four companies led to progressive improvements, we note that recommendations in many railway accident reports concentrate more on minimising the effects of an accident rather than their prevention. That is not to say that the cause of accidents had been completely eliminated (indeed the continuing demand for train control clearly showed it had not), but the emphasis was now put very much on the minimisation of the effects of an accident. We can probably demonstrate the increased superiority of the new railways in the accident at Winwick Junction which, had it not been for these advances, could have had similar consequences to Quintinshill. On 28th September 1934 a local passenger train came to a halt at Winwick Junction, just north of Warrington, where it would diverge to the left and take the ex-LNWR branch to Earlestown. This was a busy junction on the WCML, and having received the local from Winwick Quay he had intended to offer it Vulcan Bank, but he forgot to do so. The driver had sent his fireman to the 'box to carry out Rule 55, but the section was such a short one that he had not reached this when the accident occurred. Running under clear signals a 4-6-0 Prince of Wales Class locomotive, No. 25648 *Queen of the Belgians*, was heading a Euston to Blackpool express. Little did its crew know that the block instruments had been cleared erroneously and as a result 12 people died on that dark night as the coaches telescoped into each other. If such a serious amount of damage and injury could occur in steel stock, one can but imagine how badly wooden-bodied coaches would have fared.

PHOTOGRAPH; THE LATE ARTHUR TREVENA COLLECTION

WHARF ROAD OCCUPATION CROSSING

London & North Eastern Railway

27th November 1934

In between the two periods of World War, a significant increase in the number of accidents at level crossings was noted. Like Bagworth on the Leicester & Swannington and Hixon, which we will cover later, it was a problem which increased as technology moved forward. In the 1920s there had begun a significant increase in the ownership of private cars and commercial motor vehicles, and in those days there was no requirement for a driver to take any form of test before going out on to the main road. When it came to an understanding of railway operations as well, some drivers were even more sadly lacking. Such was the case of a man who decided to take a 2-ton Chevrolet truck across an occupation crossing between Broxbourne and Cheshunt, for in foggy weather he drove his vehicle across the sleeper paved crossing without informing the nearby signal box that he was doing so. In exceptionally poor visibility he pulled out in front of the 8.31am Cambridge - London express, which was travelling at 50 mph behind 4-4-0 No.8986. The train driver failed to see the truck, and it struck the obstruction causing the engine to derail down an embankment, where it was mounted by it tender. No serious injuries were recorded among the passengers, but both footplatemen on the Class D16/2 were killed outright.

PHOTOGRAPH; BBC HULTON PICTURE LIBRARY

ASHTON-U-HILL

London, Midland & Scottish Railway 25th February 1935

I have already endeavoured to make the connection between the design of tank engine types, imperfections in the track, high-speed and accidents. More than any other case thus far, we come across the Midland's 2000 Class 0-6-4Ts which had been introduced in 1907 and colloquially become known as 'Flatirons'. Forty of the engines had been built, and they were notorious for their rough riding and frequent derailments. In June 1928 No.2015 bounced itself off the rails at Swinderby whilst heading the Tamworth mail train at 60 mph, then No.2029 split the track at Ashton-under-Hill between Ashchurch and Redditch/Evesham in August 1929. The track had been partially re-sleepered, but six years later No.2023 came to grief nearby, on 25th February. At the time it was running at 55 mph on a Class 3 branch (where speeds were not expected to exceed 45 mph), although no specific rules had been laid down about the maximum speed which engines could travel. However, there is always the exception to the rule and on that grey February day, No.2023 was not required to stop, so it was travelling at high-speed when it came off the rails and killed the driver. To determine the effects of this type of engine on poor track, Colonel Mount took No.2011 along the branch. He concluded that track variations were likely to cause the engine to oscillate rapidly and violently, thereby inducing heavy lateral forces which might tend to bodily displace the track. He noted that the track variations on the branch had come about because of the practice of merely replacing occasional sleepers and not completely renewing the road after the 1929 crash, consequently criticising the Permanent Way Inspector for under-estimating the seriousness of the work at hand. He also criticised the 'Flatirons' because of their 5' 7" driving wheels but recommended no improvements as the class were about to be withdrawn, however before this could be achieved, No.2011 was derailed at Moira on the Burton - Leicester line.

PHOTOGRAPH COURTESY: NATIONAL RAILWAY MUSEUM.

KINGS LANGLEY

London, Midland & Scottish Railway 14th March 1935

Just three weeks later, a signalman's negligence at King's Langley led to a another fatal accident. A multiple collision was caused after No.5496 (on the 4.55pm up express meat train from Alexandra Dock to London Broad Street) came to a stand on the main line due to a fractured brake pipe. The train was delayed for about six minutes while repairs were effected, however it had just got under way when they were run into by the 5.50pm milk train from Stafford to London (Euston) which was being drawn by No.1165 at a speed of about 25 mph. The debris spilled over on to the down line, and this was run into by No.5511. The accident caused the death of the driver of the milk train and the Inspector concluded that this was because the signalmen were more preoccupied with other matters, namely a telephone conversation on an unauthorised subject. He further stated 'there is no redeeming feature in this case, and I find nothing to relieve [the signalman] of responsibility for this accident, which fortunately had no worse consequences.

PHOTOGRAPH; THE LATE ARTHUR TREVENA COLLECTION

WELWYN GARDEN CITY

London & North Eastern Railway
15th June 1935

As we have discussed, the LNER sat back on its haunches and did very little about the recommendations in the Pringle Report. In a way this was quite understandable as the LNER were particularly affected by the fall in traffic during the Depression, and it took a fatal accident at Welwyn Garden City on 15th June 1935 to prompt them into action. That evening three express trains left King's Cross in a fairly short period of time, commencing with 10.45pm departure. Eight minutes later No.4441 left with an 11-coach train for Newcastle, with the express passenger/mail train for Leeds leaving at 10.58pm. This third train was drawn by class K3 2-6-0 No.4009 which was considerably more powerful than the Atlantic on the Newcastle train which had the additional burden of a heavier load. As the Newcastle train reached Welwyn the driver noted that the distant signal was at caution so he slowed down to 20 mph and gently coasted forward until he saw the home signal come off. He rolled on towards the starting signal and when he saw it was clear he began to put on steam, but barely had he done so than his train was struck in the rear by the K3 travelling at almost 70 mph. The signalman at Welwyn had committed the unforgivable sin of accepting a train into his section when one was already in it, and in the subsequent enquiry it emerged that he had become utterly confused; this had led him into sending and receiving signals to adjoining boxes and pegging up his trains on the wrong set of instruments and he had probably cleared a down block instrument for an up train. Not even the most modern rolling stock could have withstood such a terrific onslaught; the rearmost coach was so completely destroyed that not a soul therein survived. The bogies and the coach frame were wrapped around the buffer beam of No.4009 and were pushed forward a distance of 419 feet. Thirteen passengers and one member of staff died in the accident, and 29 more people were seriously injured; but such an incident should never have arisen. Fortunately, the injury toll in the offending train was not high and though damage to the Leeds engine was substantial (as will be seen in the lower picture taken at Doncaster Works early in July 1935), it remained upright and thus protected the train behind it.

The evidence is complicated and difficult to describe briefly, but the Inspector was clearly of the opinion that the man with responsibility for such a busy section of track was completely unsuited to the job. He also felt that the confusion had been caused by the block instruments all being the same colour and all having a similar tone, so he suggested modifications which might be undertaken to help busy signalmen to differentiate between them. More importantly this accident identified another weakness, the area of track circuiting, and the LNER subsequently adopted a system which only allowed for 'Line Clear' to be sent once an occupied track circuit had been cleared. Not unnaturally, this system became known as Welwyn Control. If this type of arrangement had been accompanied by colour-light signals and ATC/AWS, then the LNER would have had a very safe railway indeed. However, as events at Castlecary in 1937 were going to show it was only a partial measure.

PHOTOGRAPHS: JOHN ADAMS

SHRIVENHAM

Great Western Railway
15th January 1936

Having talked at length about the GWR's enviable safety record, it is rather a pity to have to write about a most tragic accident which even the superb ATC system could not prevent. Indeed, it is sad to say that on this occasion the crew of the overnight Penzance - London, Paddington express, were even misled by its existence into believing they had a clear road for GWR 4-6-0 No. 6007 *King William III*. They had taken charge of the train at Newton Abbot in Devon and raced through the night, with their passengers either dozing in their compartment seats or having the luxury of a berth in one of the sleeping cars. They left Swindon at 5.15am and made their way through the Wiltshire countryside at speeds of around 50 mph. As they approached Shrivenham the clear signal bell sounded on their ATC apparatus, but when the crew next looked out of the spectacle plates they witnessed three red lights straight ahead of them. The lights were on a brake van (these being its rear and two side lights), which was standing at the rear of five loaded coal wagons which had become detached from the preceding train due to a drawhook failure. This train was hauled by 28XX class No.2802 and had originated in South Wales, but it was running three hours late after suffering an interminable delay at Swindon. As the crew passed Marston Crossing they had looked back and checked that their train was intact, as the rules obliged them to do every so often.

Unfortunately just after this the drawhook of the 48th wagon failed, leaving the brake and the five wagons behind it. The goods train then continued on as far as Ashbury Crossing where it was put into a loop in order for the night express to pass, however no-one looked to make sure that the train was complete (Rule 148). As it was the stranded portion was slowly rolling to a stop and the guard thought he had come to a halt at the Shrivenham home signal, but he didn't check because was busy trying to work out by which train he could get a lift home from Didcot to Severn Tunnel Junction. Once he came to a halt he should have looked at the signals immediately! However, there was considerable doubt attached to his statements, and the Inspector concluded that the guard could have begun to protect the train considerably sooner. Mind you the signalmen at Shrivenham and Ashbury Crossing 'boxes were also at fault, as they were obliged to keep a good look out as each train went past and ensure that it was showing a tail light. If not their obligation was to set all their signals to danger and send the message 'stop and examine', as Rule 183 clearly shows they should never give the message 'train out of section' until they are completely sure it has passed. But both these signalmen were convinced they had seen a red light, so we can only imagine it was what they should have seen, what they expected to see, and what they 'saw' even though it was not there. So, under favourable signals *King William III* raced on at speed, and the driver got his ATC signal to confirm the road was clear ahead, even though it was not! The brake-van and the last three wagons were splintered into matchsticks, but the other two wagons were propelled up the tracks for 1½ miles. The express engine rode up over the wagon wheels and ballast blocks of the brake van, then turned over onto its right hand side. This accident had a very sad outcome in the death of the driver and one passenger, but it was ironic that the stranded portion had come to rest between the distant signal and the track circuits for the up home signals. Had continuous track-circuiting been in place, then the accident would never have taken place!

PHOTOGRAPHS; BBC HULTON PICTURE LIBRARY

SLEAFORD: NORTH JUNCTION

London & North Eastern Railway
15th February 1937 and 19th July 1939

On 15th February 1937 a group of five platelayers had just 'knocked-off' for their lunch and retired to a cabin alongside Sleaford North Junction on the Lincoln - Spalding line, when a York - Lowestoft express passing through the junction became derailed. Three of the leading coaches broke away from the train and, being diverted to the left, two of these ran over the permanent way cabin, killing three of the gang instantly. A fourth man died in hospital later that evening and the fifth was seriously injured. It would appear that the experienced driver of LNER class B17, No. 2829 *Narworth Castle* had seriously over-estimated his speed at Sleaford North distant signals and, instead of negotiating the junction at the prescribed maximum of 20mph, the Inspector concluded that it must have been in the neighbourhood of 40mph. In view of the fact that the 10 coach train was well loaded, it is perhaps fortunate that only 15 minor cases of injuries and shock resulted among the passengers. However, what is quite remarkable is the fact that, later that day, there was another derailment at Sleaford - this time at Upton. During the latter part of the day, a diverted freight train worked across the junction, but once again took it at speed.

Yet Sleaford was not to escape with just this double trouble, as reader A. R. Horton pointed out showing that another accident took place at Sleaford South Junction on 19th July 1939 as a 31-vehicle express goods became derailed whilst travelling from Lincoln to Spalding. The engine (no number recorded) had taken the 'avoiding line' at 3.30am and was just approaching the south junction when it left the track near the ballast bins. The engine 'sliced through the sleepers as if they were made of cheese' and rolled down a small embankment, pulling many of the empty vans down behind it. These were smashed to firewood as the picture shows. Breakdown crews were summoned from Colwick, Peterborough and Grantham, and the line was reopened for single-track operation by 2pm in the afternoon. The only injury in this spectacular derailment was sustained by the guard who suffered a dislocated hip. Unlike the earlier Sleaford derailment this was a considerably less serious event, but it turned the area into one of those locations which suffered multiple incidents. Ironically we will return to nearby Langrick on the following page.

PHOTOGRAPHS; ELTHAM-CHRONICLE COLLECTION

LANGLEY
Great Western Railway
1st March 1937

In the accident at Shrivenham the issue of continuous track-circuiting was clearly demonstrated, as it had been at Welwyn a year earlier. However, of all the major accidents reported in the first half of the 1930s, only four could have been prevented by continuous track-circuiting, whilst 14 might have been averted had simple track-circuits been installed at the home signals. It was clearly evident that as a first stage, the simple systems were ultimately more preferable as a short-term measure, with continuous systems being installed as a secondary programme. Yet it was the GWR who were again going to suffer due to this policy, this time it happened at Langley in Buckinghamshire on 1st March 1937, just six weeks on from Shrivenham! That evening a 25-wagon empty spoil train, the 7.45pm from Reading West to Old Oak Common derailed on trap points at Dolphin Junction, after 2-6-0 No. 6320 ran past the signals when they were set at danger. Two of the steel ballast wagons were thrown across the up relief road, and these were then struck by 2-6-2T No.6167 which was running on that line with the 6.35pm ex-Oxford. The driver of the spoil train was unable to explain this lapse, which was entirely out of character for a man who had previously been commended for vigilance in protecting an accident, and who had also saved a child from drowning in 1924. Unfortunately, one of the guards involved in the accident sustained fatal head injuries, and for once the GWR's safety system was found to be inadequate. As a consequence the Inspector concluded that a sand trap and drag should be installed at the end of this loop rather than just simple catch-points.

PHOTOGRAPH: BBC HULTON PICTURE LIBRARY

LANGRICK
London & North Eastern Railway
22nd May 1937

Many accidents were due to the defective condition of the permanent way as we have already learned, but equally many of these problems were compounded by the running of certain types of locomotives at high speeds. Usually we have talked about tank locomotives, but it equally applied to some classes of tender engine as became evident to the LNER in Lincolnshire during the 1930s. For example, just three weeks after the Sleaford accident, and only a few miles to the north, there was another lunch-time derailment. Whilst working the 12.44pm Boston - Lincoln express, class K3 2-6-0, No. 126 split the rails at 40 mph and left the track. The train forced its way past the tender, causing the damage shown in the picture opposite. The investigation into the accident laid the blame on the condition of the permanent-way, in particular the condition of the sleepers, of which 68% dated from when the GNR had first laid the track in 1895. In 1931 it was proposed that this complete section should be re-laid the following year, but head-office deferred the request, and apparently the matter was thereafterforgotten.

PHOTOGRAPH: ATLANTIC COLLECTION

LONDON; BATTERSEA PARK STATION

Southern Railway
2nd April 1937

The need to prevent more than one train being in a section at a time was a paramount matter as we have already discussed. To this end the 'Sykes Lock & Block' mechanical signalling system was a great improvement, particularly on very busy lines, as it accomplished its purpose by preventing a signalman from being able to lower the signal controlling the entrance to the Block Section ahead, until that signal has been electrically released by the signal box in advance. In turn, he could not release the signal until the preceding train had passed the signals controlling the entry to the section ahead of him and that signal then placed to danger. As such a system of working was attained through the interior portions of the Block Instruments being connected to the signal levers, it goes without saying that signalmen had to work such levers and equipment with great care. It was a relatively fool-proof system, but as events at Battersea Park showed on 2nd April it was not infallible.

In 1932 Battersea Park 'box was handling 712 train movements each day, but by the end of 1936 this had increased to 838. In peak periods the signalman had to make 972 bell, block and lever movements every hour; that is one operation every 3.7 seconds. It was not outside the capability of an experienced man, but even so a booking lad would have helped considerably. There had been one up until 1936, but the company withdrew this valuable assistance and decided to dispense with the train register instead. Now, if an experienced man could barely manage to keep up to the work load, what chance would a relief signalman have after just seven hours of training in a particular 'box? Ironically that training was given on the day proceeding the accident, and some readers will quickly realise that this is celebrated as April Fool's Day in Britain. It was certainly foolish of the railway to send this man into a busy signal box the next day with just this basic training, for trouble appears to have begun very early on his shift. Around 7.59am he held a London Bridge - Victoria train at the approach to the station with the intention of letting a South London line - Victoria on to the main line ahead of it; unfortunately he set the slides for the electro mechanical system in the wrong order, thus causing a fault which manifested itself as though the train cancelling indicator had malfunctioned. In an effort to redress the situation and restore the apparatus, the signalman cut the seals of the instrument panel and moved the slides to the normal position.

Whilst this was an authorised procedure (in an emergency) it was a highly unorthodox and totally unnecessary act. Neither did it entirely resolve the situation and it only served to confuse the signalmen on either side of him, particularly the relief man at Pouparts Junction. He was evidently under the impression that the section was now clear and he thus offered Battersea Park the 7.31am EMU from Coulsdon North to Victoria. What happened next is a matter of debate; the Pouparts signalman said Battersea Park accepted the train, but the signalman there emphatically denied that he had. In all events the 8-car set was cleared and because of the mist and poor visibility it ran into the rear of the stationary train which was still standing in the Battersea Park section. The ensuing collision claimed the lives of 10 people and injured a further 72. In the Report into the accident both train crews were cleared of negligence and the Inspector accepted the version of events put forward by the Pouparts Junction signalman. Evidently his colleague nearby should have never been given the responsibility for such a large, important box, but whether his act of breaking open the apparatus was a gross error or sheer act of over-confidence will never be known. To prevent a repetition of such an event the Sykes Lock & Block apparatus cabinets were sealed with padlocks and the rule allowing signalmen to manually re-set them withdrawn.

PHOTOGRAPH: KEYSTONE PICTURE LIBRARY

DURHAM

London & North Eastern Railway

13th June 1937

The matter of automatic train control was an issue which raged on throughout the 1930s, for a great many accidents continued to needlessly occur, when they could have been prevented by ATC/AWS. Not all, however, were attended with serious consequences, as the gradual improvements in coaching stock design and construction began to reduce the number of older vehicles in service. One incident which would have been exceptionally serious had it not been for these improvements was seen at Newton Hall near Durham, where the absence of ATC/AWS led to a spectacular derailment during the early hours of 13th June 1937. After being delayed in departing from Scarborough's Londesborough Road station, 300 passengers on a return excursion to Newcastle were running homewards behind Class C7 4-4-2 No.2197. It had turned midnight as they passed through Darlington, but because it had lost its path the excursion train was frequently being put on to slow lines to let faster moving scheduled trains pass it. As it approached Newton Hall, a few miles south of Durham City, it was running on the down slow line in order to let the Bournemouth - Aberdeen express overtake it. Beyond Newton Hall the line reverted to two tracks, and because of this successive signals were placed at danger. Unfortunately, as the signals were still protecting the down fast, the crossover at the end of the loop was still set pointing to a short sand drag and a set of buffers. Though the driver had seen the signals for the down slow he disregarded them, thinking that he was on the up line. His engine ran across the facing points of the crossover, into the sand drag and through the buffers. These were unable to withstand the impact and they were pushed on for about 150 feet in front of the excursion train. Running through the ballast considerably slowed down the train, and it might have escaped serious injury all together, but it ran out of room and struck the abutments of an over-line road bridge. It was deflected across the up line and managed to block the ECML completely. Only nine people were injured, most only very slightly and the *Northern Echo* reported that all the glasses and mustard pots in the dining car escaped unscathed.

PHOTOGRAPH; NORTHERN ECHO COURTESY DURHAM COUNTY LIBRARY SERVICE

LONDON; EALING BROADWAY

Great Western Railway

16th November 1937

The problem of short roads and buffer blocks was not limited to just the LNER in 1937, as we discover with this picture taken near Ealing Broadway station on a foggy 16th November 1937. The GWR steam railcar pictured here operated on the service from Ealing Broadway to Denham which was the first station on the GCR/GWR Joint line to Princess Risborough. Dense fog made signal observation very difficult, and in addition an absence of fog-signalmen meant that extra coverage was only being given at the distant signals. Mistaking another signal for his starter, the railcar driver set off forward but, as the points were locked it was directed into a short dead-end siding which ended in a set of buffer stops just outside the signal box. In view of how close the driver found himself to the signalman, we might even ask whether or not he was going to enquire in person about the position of the signals!!!

PHOTOGRAPH; BBC HULTON PICTURE LIBRARY

SWANLEY JUNCTION

Southern Railway
28th June 1937

The accident at Swanley Junction pictured here happened late one Sunday evening, after control had decided to stop the 8.17pm Margate - Ashford - London to pick up passengers who had missed their connections with an earlier train. As 4-4-0 No.1768 approached the station, the signalman set his levers so that the train would draw up into the platform, and this involved protecting the junction on which the direct line from Margate came in from the right. To do this the signalman pulled lever 31 and set the road for a short branch which ended by some EHT Switch-gear equipment. On this line stood two empty coaches and a loaded wagon, but minutes later these would be reduced to firewood as the 4-4-0 burst through them before running into the electric station, where it smashed the concrete support pillars and hit the large transformer. As the train approached the station the signalman had endeavoured to slow it down by keeping his distant signal on, but instead of waiting until the train had properly slowed down at this signal he released it too quickly. Even though the driver had the stop signals against him, the psychological impression he received must have greatly convinced him that he was clear to run over the junction - after all he was not booked to stop at Swanley, and there had never been any reason for him to do so with this train in the past. Accordingly he put on steam and ran straight into the short, dead-end siding. Of the 100 passengers on board the train, four were killed outright and 8 were seriously injured. The Inspector commented, 'Whilst this was a case of admitted failure to observe and obey signals on the part of the driver, the fundamental cause of this accident was failure in operation, that is to say, the omissions of precautions usually taken against a driver's fallibility.'

PHOTOGRAPHS; BBC HULTON PICTURE LIBRARY

CASTLECARY

London & North Eastern Railway
10th December 1937

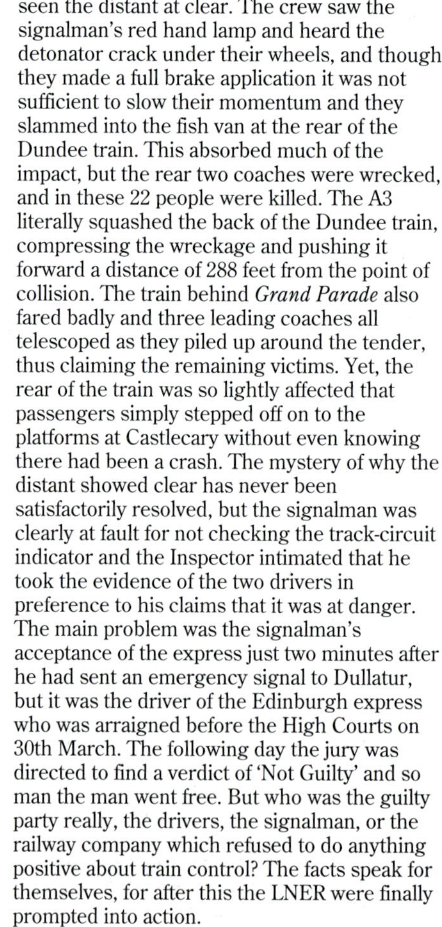

Whilst the LNER had escaped serious consequences from the lack of ATC/AWS at Newton Hall, six months on from that event they were not going to be so lucky. It was once again on the troubled metals of the old North British Railway that Scotland was to suffer a major accident, and with 35 dead it became the country's third-worst disaster to that date. It had been snowing all day in the central part of Scotland and the clouds were building up against the Campsie Fells causing a particularly heavy belt of snow to fall between Kirkintilloch and Denny. Along the course of this heavy fall of snow lay the LNER main line from Edinburgh to Glasgow, and the railway faced growing problems as a consequence. At Gartshore a pair of facing points had already been put of action by the snow, and as a consequence the down line had to be closed for over half an hour and two trains were held up; a passenger train at Croy, and a goods train at Dullatur. The next station back towards Edinburgh was Castlecary, where two express trains were due around 4.30pm; the first of these was the 2pm from Dundee to Glasgow behind D29 4-4-0 No.9896 *Dandie Dinmont* which was hauling seven coaches and a fish van; the second was A3 pacific No.2744 *Grand Parade* which was drawing the 4.03pm Edinburgh - Glasgow express. As the Dundee train approached the Castlecary signal distant, it was (the driver later asserted) showing clear, but the signalman said he had set all his signals to danger in view of the obstruction at Dullatur East. Thus, as the train went past, he hurriedly waved a red lamp from his window and sent the signal 4-4-5 'Vehicles Running Away On The Right Line' to his colleague at Dullatur. Had he but checked, he would have seen that the train had come to a halt. Admittedly the view of its tail light was obscured by the corner of the goods shed, but the track-circuit indicator in his box would undoubtedly have confirmed its presence. Oddly, having handed over the problem to Dullatur, he went on to accept the 4.03pm as he did not want to delay such an important train. He could think of no rule which would prevent him from doing so, and to this end he even telephoned a colleague to ask him if he knew of any regulation that would forbid him from doing so. The fact that an accident at Dullatur would have delayed the express seems to have been an irrelevance in this man's mind. During the next three minutes he did nothing to find out what had happened to the Dundee train, or if there had been a collision at Dullatur at all. Then, at 4.35pm the fireman of *Dandie Dinmont* came up to the 'box in accordance with Rule 55, a minute before the 'train entering section' signal was received for the Edinburgh express.

Realising the possible danger the signalman said 'I'll have to see about getting the four o'clock stopped', and he took out detonators and a hand lamp and went down to the track. He had got down just a single detonator when Grand Parade came rushing out of the veil of snow at speed of 70 mph, the driver also having seen the distant at clear. The crew saw the signalman's red hand lamp and heard the detonator crack under their wheels, and though they made a full brake application it was not sufficient to slow their momentum and they slammed into the fish van at the rear of the Dundee train. This absorbed much of the impact, but the rear two coaches were wrecked, and in these 22 people were killed. The A3 literally squashed the back of the Dundee train, compressing the wreckage and pushing it forward a distance of 288 feet from the point of collision. The train behind *Grand Parade* also fared badly and three leading coaches all telescoped as they piled up around the tender, thus claiming the remaining victims. Yet, the rear of the train was so lightly affected that passengers simply stepped off on to the platforms at Castlecary without even knowing there had been a crash. The mystery of why the distant showed clear has never been satisfactorily resolved, but the signalman was clearly at fault for not checking the track-circuit indicator and the Inspector intimated that he took the evidence of the two drivers in preference to his claims that it was at danger. The main problem was the signalman's acceptance of the express just two minutes after he had sent an emergency signal to Dullatur, but it was the driver of the Edinburgh express who was arraigned before the High Courts on 30th March. The following day the jury was directed to find a verdict of 'Not Guilty' and so man the man went free. But who was the guilty party really, the drivers, the signalman, or the railway company which refused to do anything positive about train control? The facts speak for themselves, for after this the LNER were finally prompted into action.

PHOTOGRAPHS; AUTHOR'S COLLECTION

OAKLEY JUNCTION

London Midland & Scottish Railway 21st January 1938

Another accident which should have been averted by track-circuits was that which took place at Oakley Junction just six weeks after Castlecary, but on this occasion improvements to signalling actually led to a signalman being unable to quickly rectify an error he had made. This time it involved the mid-afternoon express from St. Pancras to Bradford Forster Square which had left London at 2.10pm, behind Jubilee class 4-6-0 No.5568 *Western Australia* and seven coaches. Running in the opposite direction was an empty stock train of 20 bogie corridor coaches, which was destined from Bradford to Olney. It had been due at Oakley Junction at 11.15am, but it was running over 3 hours late so the control advised the signalman to shunt the train there; putting as many coaches as possible into the 'Way & Works siding' that ran off the up line of the Northampton Branch which diverged from the Midland main line at this point. It arrived at Oakley Junction at 2.30pm and the signalman shunted it on to the down branch in order to clear the up fast and leave the up branch free. An up express ran through at 2.46pm and the signalman set the road to the up fast, but the crew of the ECS train did not respond to his hand-signal so he reset the points as he was expecting the down Bradford express about 3pm. He then decided that he might be able to get the 2-6-0 and nine coaches into the 'Way & Works siding' so he set the road for this and showed a hand-signal, it was now around 2.55pm. The guard of the ECS train took some time over this operation, first screwing down the brakes in the 20th coach and then scotching the wheels of the tenth to prevent it running away when the nine coaches in front were withdrawn. He then observed the green flag from the 'box, and the driver drew his engine forward and came to rest on track-circuit 866 which had only been installed 6 weeks before.

The newness of the signal box may have had much to do with this accident, it was only the signalman's 27th turn of duty since the junction had been re-signalled. Unfortunately he failed to block back on the main line for the shunting operation, and during the second movement of the train he accepted the express at 2.57pm. Unfortunately he had failed to reset the points for the junction and this meant that the express would be diverted down the Northampton branch at speed. Realising his error, the signalman quickly attempted to reset the crossover (levers 20 and 26), unfortunately because the 2-6-0's front wheels were just 2 feet beyond the insulated track joint, the track-circuiting bolt-locked the points so that they could not be moved. As the express crossed Bromham Viaduct it was running about 70 mph, but the driver failed to observe the down distant signals. He said that this was due to the steelwork of the girders which only gave him a view of 260 yards, but the actual sighting distance was another 60 yards on top of that. He freely admitted that he had never expected to see the signals at danger, and this might be a more likely explanation. Even though the driver applied the brakes the Jubilee turned off the main line and ran head-on into the 2-6-0 at a speed of 25 mph; two passengers were killed and a dining car attendant was fatally injured, whilst 46 other people were injured to varying degrees of severity.

PHOTOGRAPHS; KEYSTONE PICTURE LIBRARY

NEWPORT

Great Western Railway
19th August 1938

In a number of accident reports which I have studied, the potential for disaster on an enormous scale was averted by only the narrowest of margins, but very few of the photographs of these incidents portray just how narrow the escape actually was. Yet, a picture taken at Newport, Monmouthshire, on 19th August 1938 clearly shows an accident which had the potential to be one of the most disastrous ever experienced by the GWR. The train involved was an express from Crewe which divided at Newport into portions for Bristol and Cardiff. It was the rear section of this train, the 11.54pm to Bristol, which was involved in the accident. It was some 16 minutes late when the 4-6-0 49xx class engine, No 4925 *Eynsham Hall* backed down onto the train. The driver was on the right hand side of the engine, and he incorrectly allowed his fireman to read the disc signals on the left hand side of the train as he could not see them. If he had not been too anxious to get his train away (in order to meet a guaranteed London connection at Bristol), he could have crossed to that side of the engine to check the signals for himself. Unfortunately, this error compounded a mistake which had already been made by the signalman, who had pulled off the wrong levers. Though the signals showed a green light, the road was actually set for a release siding at the east end of the station. This short spur led to a stop-block which was adjacent to the parapet of the bridge over the flooded River Usk, and if the fireman had not been observant, the engine would have ploughed through the buffers and dived into the river below. Fortunately, the man redeemed his earlier mistake by seeing the the red light on the stop-block and shouted for his driver to brake. As it was, the force of the impact tore apart the fishing of the last rail joint and forced the buffer stop forward, with the train only coming to a halt when its buffers struck the bridge parapet; only three passengers suffered minor injury.

PHOTOGRAPH: ATLANTIC COLLECTION

HATFIELD

London & North Eastern Railway
26th January 1939

The year 1939 got off to a bad start on 26th January, when a multiple collision took place at Hatfield in Hertfordshire. An accident had happened earlier in the day when a fish train collided with the rear end of an empty passenger train, but little damage was done. At the time trains were running on the 'time interval' system, because a heavy fall of snow during the previous day and overnight had brought down the telephone and telegraph wires. As a consequence of this trains were beginning to queue up at Hatfield station. Approaching this bottle-neck from the north was Train No.269 from Peterborough to Kings Cross, with 2-6-2 Class V2, No. 4813. Running at an estimated speed of around 30 -35 mph, it ploughed into the back of the 7.34am Cambridge - King's Cross train behind 4-4-2T No.4437. The force of the impact was such as to drive this train forward so that it smashed into the back of train No.238 which was stationary behind 4-6-0T No.2840 as it also awaited its turn to move south. The driver of the V2 was adamant that he was only running at 20 - 25 mph. when the accident occurred, but the Inspector did not accept this and stated that the blame squarely rested on the shoulders of the driver 'for his lack of care in adverse conditions'. One passenger was killed in the Cambridge train, and 27 more were to suffer injury or shock. The footplate crew on No.4813 were also injured, the driver quite badly. The lines were blocked for over 14 hours, and extensive diversions were required. In conclusion the Inspector recommended modification of the block working, but worse was yet to come.

PHOTOGRAPH; THE LATE ARTHUR TREVENA COLLECTION

HILGAY FEN

London & North Eastern Railway
1st June 1939

As the clouds of war gathered over Europe, one of the LNER's three Royal Train drivers faced an unenviable situation as he took the 11.02am express from Hunstanton to Ely behind ex-GER 4-4-0 No.8783. Like the driver of No. 8986 five years earlier, he was travelling at speed under clear signals when he suddenly saw a 2-ton truck negotiating an occupation crossing ahead. There was no legal agreement about the use of this occupation crossing between the LNER and Norfolk County Council, as it was only designed to allow access to a number of council-owned smallholdings on the opposite side of the track. The road approach to the crossing did not afford good visibility of the railway line, but once a vehicle pulled up to the gates a driver could see a mile down the line in either direction. On 1st June 1939 the driver of a Ford truck decided to take a short-cut over the crossing, but when they pulled up at the railway, neither the driver or his mate were keeping a good look out. The signals were standing clear for the express, and the gates to Long Drove Level Crossing (400 yards away), were clearly visible as being shut against road traffic. However, at the subsequent inquest the lorry crew said that they did not understand railway signals so they started across. As the 4-4-0 approached the crossing, the train driver saw the truck at a distance of 300 yards and watched in horror as it began to move across when he was just over 200 yards away. Blowing his whistle he tried to make a full brake application, but No. 8783 hit the lorry just as its driver jumped clear. The engine derailed and the train behind followed suit, but the buck-eye couplings prevented any telescoping from taking place and they might have escaped unscathed. However, the coaches were now foul of their gauge, and just ahead a rake of wagons and vans stood in a siding adjacent to the cattle dock at Hilgay Station. These were struck by the bogie of the engine, then as the coaches passed them, they ripped out the sides causing injury to twelve people and killing four more.

Reader Alan Garraway writes that his father was given the job of clearing up the site, and on the second day he was greatly surprised to see the driver involved in the crash driving past the scene with another train on the same duty. Normally it was practice to suspend a driver from work after such an incident, but evidently someone had forgotten on this occasion. Mr. Garraway also recalled the earlier level crossing accident at Shepreth on 17th August 1928, when No.3253 hit a motor lorry as it was travelling south with a Cambridge - King's Cross express. This accident (shown in our lower picture) drew attention to the urgent need to bring commercial motor vehicles within the scope of existing regulations which governed the passage of traction engines across railway lines, but his memory was of a much more different nature; 'Next to the engine was a horsebox containing a valuable racehorse from Newmarket, the van was completely reduced to firewood, yet the horse escaped and walked on the line to Shepreth station with only a scratch on its shoulder.' Interestingly the farmer who's field was invaded by the wreckage from this crash tried to sue the railway for trespass!

PHOTOGRAPHS: TOP, KEYSTONE PICTURE LIBRARY
RIGHT, BBC HULTON PICTURE LIBRARY

SALTCOATS

London, Midland & Scottish Railway 5th August 1939

Our look at the next accident takes a somewhat different approach, in that it comes from the memories of one of the survivors. However, the lady in question was no ordinary traveller, a her father was Mr. J. G. Barr whom we hav already discussed in this series. He had lon been involved with railway accidents, indee hi was a real baptism of fire as he had been gi en charge of the recovery operations at Quintinshill in 1915. In the succeeding years he dealt with one accident after another, cleaning up the scene but constantly striving to make substantial improvements in first the Caledonian's, and then the LMS's, breakdown and recovery procedure. However, in 1939 he retired as Motive Power Superintendent for the Northern Division of the LMS, and had just begun to enjoy more leisure time with his family. Few thoughts of railway accidents could have occupied his mind that summer as his daughter, Mrs. Edith Fox remembers that her parents had just returned from a three and a half week long holiday overseas. They had arrived home at the end of July and still enjoying their new found leisure, they decided to take an evening cruise with the Caledonian Steam Packet Co. the following Saturday, 5th August. Intending to go to Arran in the afternoon. Mr. and Mrs. Barr and two of their daughters, Marion and Edith, caught the circular 12.30pm Glasgow Central - Ardrossan train service from Cathcart at 12.40pm. Sitting in the third coach they approached Saltcoats North at 1.20pm, but then they got what Mrs. Fox described as 'a bad shake up'.

In an interview in 1992 she told me 'we each had a window seat, mother was knitting and father was reading his paper. All of a sudden there seemed to be a funny noise, and father put down [illegible] which suddenly turned into an alarming bumping sound.' The train had obviously become derailed, for as Mrs. Fox recalled, 'even we girls knew it meant that the wheels were off the track. Then the carriage started to tilt down the embankment, and though this seemed a long way it wasn't really. The first and second carriages telescoped, and also came into the third. Marion got the impression that the coach was being telescoped, and urged me to come across the carriage in case anything came into my back.' When the train finally came to rest Mr. Barr jumped out, made a brief examination then came back to his family and told them that stones had been placed on the line. Although he was officially retired, there was no-one more capable to take over the rescue operations so Mr. Barr took charge and remained to direct the work until arrival of other senior officers. The Miners Welfare establishment was immediately adjacent to the site of the accident, and Mrs. Barr went down to the welfare place to help. Mrs. Fox get people out of the wreckage, bringing cups of tea and so on. The driver, fireman and two passengers died through what was either an act of vandalism or a childish prank, but of course the real reasons were never uncovered. It is really ironic that things went they way they did, for this was the first fatal accident on the Northern Division since Mr. Barr had retired and he was bang in the middle of it.

The police report into the accident indicated that vandalism was the most likely cause, but whether this was by a child or an adult could not be ascertained. If a child was the culprit, this was bad enough, but if it was an adult we can only guess at the type of warped mind which would achieve pleasure from doing this. It is a problem which continues down to this day, and one which is evidenced with increasing regularity I am sad to say. On 16th February 1971 a fully loaded Inter-City HST set was travelling through Reading at a speed of around 65 mph when it hit two pieces of rail which had been cleverly arranged across the tracks so as not to interfere with the track circuiting. The HST hit the obstruction, derailed and suffered a split fuel tank which subsequently caught fire. Fortunately the incident did not turn out to be serious, but police believed that the accident was caused by someone with a grudge against the railways. Another act of vandalism (with a piece of rail being dragged on to the track) occurred near Prestonpans in May 1980, but here the offender was caught and sentenced to a term in borstal. Perhaps the terms of the Offences Against The Person Act 1861 (often used to prosecute errant railwaymen after an accident), should still be applied to those who commit wilful vandalism: 'Whosoever shall unlawfully put or throw upon or across any Railway, any Wood or Stone or other Matter of Thing, with Malice or Intent to endanger the safety of any Person travelling upon such Railway, shall be liable to be kept in Penal Servitude for Life, or for any Term not less than three years, or to be imprisoned for any Term not exceeding Two Years, with or without Hard Labour, and if a Male under the age of sixteen years, with or without whipping'.

PHOTOGRAPHS: THE LATE J.G. BARR

WORLD WAR TWO AND THE PRE-NATIONALISATION ERA

BLETCHLEY

London, Midland & Scottish Railway 14th October 1939

As the accident at Saltcoats violently interrupted the Barr family's summer, a series of even greater tragedies were to interrupt the lives of millions after Britain declared war on Germany a month later. The circumstances surrounding the blackout and air raid precautions which were introduced to protect the railways are detailed in my book *Britain's Railways At War* but, briefly described, the principle measure involved the elimination of any lights which might be seen by enemy aircraft. Locomotive cabs were fitted with anti-glare screens, coach windows were obscured and station lights extinguished. The accident which occurred at Bletchley at 8.35pm on 14th October is considered to be the first major victim of this ARP regime, in that the blackout had a serious part in the events which led up to the disaster. That night as the Euston - Inverness express was standing at the up platform of Bletchley station, a shunting engine 0-8-0 No.9169 began to attach a parcels van at the rear. The 0-8-0 was just backing the van on to the rear of the train when it was struck by pilot engine 5MT 4-6-0, No.5025, as it was leading train engine Royal Scot Class 4-6-0 No.6130 *The West Yorkshire Regiment* which were pulling the Euston - Stranraer express. The Black 5 struck the front buffer beam of the 0-8-0 at a speed of about 40 mph and it was pushed back into the Inverness train, destroying the van it had just attached and the two vehicles beyond this. As the picture shows, the 0-8-0 was then forced up on to the platform where it demolished the refreshment bar and waiting rooms. The official report shows that four people were killed as a consequence, including an RAF serviceman travelling as a passenger, a postman, a porter and the driver of the 0-8-0; 6 people were seriously injured, and 35 others suffered minor cuts, bruises and shock.

The weather was extremely bad at the time, and the rain was being driven by an easterly wind. However, this was no excuse for the crew to fail to keep a good lookout, but this is evidently what had happened, because they had run past no less than six signals showing danger, and done this at 75 mph. This was 10 mph faster than the limit imposed by the Railway Executive Committee in September 1939, but as the engines were not fitted with a speedometer, this may have been an error any crew might have made. Another factor which may have had a bearing on this accident is the fact that the more experienced driver was on the train engine, when he should have been on the pilot engine as so many of the usual landmarks were obscured by the blackout. Indeed, the virtual blackness of the scene, coupled with that awful rain was claimed to be the main reason for the lapse and it is evident that the Inspector agreed with this view in many ways, even though he did not exactly say as much. What he did do, was to recommend more training for footplate crews and suggested that this might be achieved by doing route training through showing films in cinemas or specially adapted railway vehicles near to principle engine sheds. His other recommendation was once again train control, but in the constrained finances of the war years, he might have been asking for the moon. Interestingly, despite the heavy damaged sustained by No.5025, it was quickly repaired and returned to service. On final withdrawal from BR the engine escaped once again, for it had the great fortune to be preserved.

PHOTOGRAPH; BBC HULTON PICTURE LIBRARY

WINWICK
London, Midland & Scottish Railway 16th October 1939

Just two days after the terrible smash at Bletchley, the LMS suffered another multiple collision on the West Coast Main Line. This time it was at the scene of the 1934 accident at Winwick Junction, and just barely 5 yards from where No. 25648 *Queen of the Belgians* came to grief. The full circumstances of the accident at Winwick have eluded my research, and only a very sanitised report of the event appeared in the railway press at the time. Coming hot on the heals of Bletchley (and just five weeks into World War II), it was a problem of some considerable significance, and it appears as though the censors got to work on the job very quickly. It would seem as though there was a general feeling that reporting such a second major accident would seriously undermine public confidence in the railways at a time when they were carrying extremely high levels of traffic. However, readers of *Trains In Trouble* pointed me in the right direction and after Volume 6 was published, a much clearer picture emerged. The (now) late-C. D. Moat wrote 'I was a fitter at Preston Loco Department at the time and also a member of the breakdown gang, and we were called out to the smash late on the 16th. I remember getting quite a shock when we arrived there, because my dad was the driver of the first express engine, No. 5544.' Another reader recalled the circumstances, saying 'the goods train had come to a stop in the loop, but somehow a light engine then ran in the rear portion of the goods train and killed the guard who was sitting in his van. The wreckage fell over on to the fast line, and this was hit by the double-headed express which was going about 60 mph. The locomotives were derailed over on to their side but the coaches stayed upright and none of the passengers in the train were badly hurt. There was a suggestion that the blackout had a part to play in this accident, as the train crews were not exactly sure of their location.' Ironically, fate had struck twice at the same location in almost identical circumstances.

As the autumn progressed, the dark nights of winter continued to present more difficulties with the black-out, but as the weather worsened, so too did the problems for the railways. After several snow falls in December and January the railways began to get ready for what bad weather would mean in times of a blackout, but nothing could prepare them for the snow which started to fall on 19th February 1941. Snow blanketed the north of England and blizzard conditions prevailed for 56 hours, severely disrupting train services across Lancashire, Yorkshire, Durham, Northumberland, Cumberland and the Scottish Borders. The LNER's Divisional Manager, Mr. Jenkin Jones said 'it was the greatest dislocation which has ever occurred in this country'. Up to that time it certainly was, although the winter of 1946-7 proved much worse, the following examples will reveal just how bad 1940 turned out to be. For instance, the 11.30am train from King's Cross which left on the Saturday, failed to arrive at Darlington until 3am on the Monday. Shap, Beattock and Grayrigg were all blocked on the WCML and in Derbyshire many lines were closed for over a week. The lower picture on this page conveys the general impression of how bad it really was, as it shows an LMS train which was stuck between Adlington and Blackrod for four days.

PHOTOGRAPHS: ABOVE KEYSTONE PICTURE LIBRARY
BELOW, NATIONAL RAILWAY MUSEUM

WEMBLEY

London Midland & Scottish Railway
13th October 1940

It happened at Wellingborough in 1898, and it happened again at Wembley on 13th October 1940, proving that history has a very nasty habit of repeating itself. Those readers who will recall events detailed on page 34 will undoubtedly have a feeling of déjà vu as they look at this page. It was just a year on from Winwick and the LMS had been coping well in spite of all the pressures of the blackout, increased traffic, lack of materials for maintenance and the loss of railway personnel to the armed forces. However, the accident which befell them at Wembley Central occurred in broad daylight, on a good, fast section of track, and with experienced railway personnel around. The fact that it was wartime had nothing at all to do with the events we now relate, because, like Wellingborough, it was a sheer whim of fate which led to the derailment of the 11.50am from Liverpool to Euston that afternoon. Just prior to this train being passed into the section at Wembley Central, two men had decided to take a loaded barrow from one side of the station to the other. Unfortunately they had completely misjudged the weight of the truck, and on taking it down the slope at the end of the platform, it ran away from them and ended up on the barrow crossing just as the express was approaching. Drawn by Patriot Class 4-6-0 No.5529 (named *Sir Herbert Walker,* but not actually bearing the nameplates at the time), the train raced into Wembley at speed. As it hit the the trolley, the front bogie was derailed in a similar manner to Midland Railway 4-4-0 No.1743 at Wellingborough. The trolley was smashed to pieces, but the engine overturned immediately and it was pitched on to its right-hand side. The engine slewed round at a 45 degree angle to the track, but the tender turned a full 90 degrees, crushing the cab of the engine and the footplate crew. The engine and tender now completely blocked all four roads, and the coaches ran up against them causing severe damage; the first was wrecked completely and the second and third telescoped, but those behind this stayed upright, even though they had derailed and zig-zagged across the tracks. A number of people were killed and over 50 seriously injured. The parachute water column at the end of the platform was smashed at its base and hurled bodily through the air before coming to land some distance away. Over 250 yards of permanent way were torn up and severe disruption followed. By good fortune and presence of mind, the signalman at Wembley Central was able to prevent other trains which were approaching the station from running in to the wreckage. Needless to say this minimised the effects of the tragedy, which could have had even more serious consequences than those which were experienced. Indeed, had there been a multiple collision, one can imagine that in the days of highly packed trains (which had people standing cramped in the aisles and vestibule ends), such a disaster would have even worse results than the awful accident which followed at nearby Harrow & Wealdstone just twelve years later on.

PHOTOGRAPHS: KEYSTONE LIBRARY

NORTON FITZWARREN

Great Western Railway
4th November 1940

We have been to Norton Fitzwarren before, and just a week shy of the 50th anniversary of the boat train disaster on 11th November 1890, tragedy once again struck this tiny Somerset village. At 3.47am on 4th November the GWR were to face their first major disaster since that accident, and it was to cost them dearly as it took the lives of 26 passengers and the fireman of an express passenger train from London to Penzance. The train had left the capital's Paddington station at 9.50pm, but it had done so during an air raid, and its progress very slow as a result, so that it did not reach Taunton at 3.30am. Being 68 minutes down, the signalman took a decision to let a following train overtake the express, and so he set the road for the 12.50am newspaper train to take the fast line out of Taunton. The express, behind King Class 4-6-0 No. 6028 *King George VI* and its thirteen coach train was put on to the slow line. The line west of Taunton had been quadrupled in 1931, and despite the fact that the layout was a little cramped, it had considerably improved the traffic flows. The four line section ended just beyond Norton Fitzwarren (where the lines to Minehead and Barnstaple diverged). There was nothing wrong with the signalman's decision to put the King on to the slow line, but it was an event which had rarely (if ever) happened before. The driver of the express was unaware of the fact that he was on this line, and in all probability it seems as though he had automatically assumed they were on the fast line. Intent on making up some of the time back, the crew rapidly set to work to build up speed, and as they approached Norton Fitzwarren the express was up to about 40 mph. Had the lights not been blacked out for the duration, the crew would have undoubtedly seen the station ahead and realised that something was amiss, but as it was they were unaware of their true position until the 5-van newspaper train began to draw ahead of them within the confines of Norton Fitzwarren station.

The driver realised his error and told his mate that they were on the wrong line, but as the cross-over was only a few yards past the end of the station it was far too late to do anything. The engine went through the trap points at the end of the loop and ran on to the soft ground beyond, before it tumbled down the embankment and came to rest in the boggy ground below. The driver pulled himself clear and began wading through the water, waste deep in places, to warn the signalman at Silk Mill Crossing of what had happened. Badly shaken he approached the 'box and told the signalman that he was afraid he was responsible for the accident. But how could such an event happen, particularly on a line where ATC was fitted? The Inspector concluded that in a mistaken belief that they were on the main line, the driver had been reading the signals for the newspaper train as applying to himself. The cramped nature of the site and the position of the signals, along with the blackout all undoubtedly played their part in deluding a man with over 40 years railway service. Even so, it is clear that he must have over run at least two signals showing danger, and cancelled the ATC warnings these gave. In this he would be like his counterpart who wrecked a Britannia Class locomotive at Milton, Didcot in 1958, and both these cases showed that even the best system could be subject to human fallibility. It is, however, entirely fortunate that the disaster was not attended by even greater consequences, as the newspaper train could literally have been but seconds away from colliding with the derailed coaches of the express. When this train was stopped for examination at Wellington, it was discovered that the fourth and fifth vans had been showered by debris and ballast thrown up from the accident, but it had just pulled clear in time.

PHOTOGRAPH: BRISTOL UNITED PRESS

HAROLD WOOD

London & North Eastern Railway
11 February 1941

As the dark days of World War Two continued, the German offensive against Britain heightened during the winter of 1940-41, but fortunately the railways were not the focal points of Luftwaffe attack that the British Government had feared them to be. Even so tragedy continued to strike the railways as the winter progressed, and the next major incident took place on 11th February when a Southend train collided with the rear of a Norwich train which had come to halt in mid-section. It was a warm, sunny day as the 10am Norwich Express left Liverpool Street Station on 10th February 1941, a rare day when the gloom of wartime winter seemed a long way away. The locomotive assigned to the job was one of the LNER's newest 4-6-0s, a class B17 No.2828 *Harewood House,* though it would have its work cut out that day as the engine struggled with its heavy train. However, things on the footplate were not so good, with the poor war-time coal supplies burning sullenly in the firebox it reduced the head of available steam pressure. In turn the engine began running slower and slower, and it was unable to ascend the 1:100 bank bctween Harold Wood and Brentwood. In view of good visibility, and the protection of colour-light signals, the guard he did not position all his detonators. The rules required him to place one at least two hundred yards to the rear, but another rule had obliged him to walk to the front of the train to find out why they had stopped. On returning from the engine he decided that it wasn't really necessary to put down all the detonators as prescribed, as this would mean that he had to make two long walks so he laid down just one charge 30 yards from the rear of the train. Unfortunately, he had not reckoned with the driver of a Southend train making a much larger blunder.

The Norwich train was still standing there when the Class B12 4-6-0, No. 8556, under full steam ran into the back of it at 30mph. As a consequence it was pushed forwards about 20 yards, with the last vehicle being completely destroyed. The B12 literally tore through it, with the roof coming down on the engine's boiler casing as the accompanying pictures clearly show. Seven lives were claimed as a result, and 17 more were seriously injured, though the rest of the train escaped with only minimal damage. The front two coaches on the Southend train telescoped, but there were no injuries as the first vehicle, a brake third, and the first three compartments at the leading end of the next coach were empty. At the time of this accident, much of the line from Liverpool Street to Shenfield and Southend had been equipped with colour-light signalling. When the driver of the B17 brought his train to a stand, he did so by colour-light signal DT17 and used its telephone to advise the signalman. Furthermore, because the Norwich train had not cleared the track-circuit, the automatic controls kept signal DT16B behind it at danger, and had signal DT16 showing a yellow aspect. Why the driver of the B12 over-ran these two signals in good visibility is unknown, but the Inspector concluded that he must have fallen asleep and missed seeing them. If the guard of the Norwich train had managed to lay detonators 200 yards back down the line instead of just 30 yards, the explosions may have warned the crew of the B12 and roused the driver in order for him to take preventative action. Once again, this showed the need for ATC/AWS, which would have provided an audible warning when a signal was over-run.

PHOTOGRAPHS; KEYSTONE PICTURE LIBRARY

SLOUGH
Great Western Railway
2nd July 1941

It has to be said that even though ATC had played a significant part in reducing disaster, incidents like Norton Fitzwarren had proved that it did not completely eliminate them. This problem was made even more acute when engines were run on lines equipped with ATC, yet did not have the warning equipment fitted in their cabs. Such a situation was to increase dramatically during the war years, as the GWR saw more and more locomotives running on their lines when they were not so fitted. Ironically, it was at Slough (where the need for ATC was first realised by the GWR) that disaster struck. On the night of 2nd July 1941 a signalman diverted an up express from the main to relief line, because he had mistakenly put another (late running) train on to the up main thinking it was the express. This should have put things right, and the signalman certainly thought that he had resolved the situation. However, the GWR report indicates that this incident seems to have flustered him, for thereafter he did not properly adhere to Block regulations. Without checking that a freight train had come to a stop on the down relief line, he may have reversed the distant signal on the down relief in order to reset the crossover. Alternatively the driver of the down goods may have over-run the signals. Normally it would have been fitted with ATC equipment, but this was a Stanier designed WD 8F 2-8-0 which was allocated to the LMS, but on loan to the GWR and as such it had not been deemed necessary to fit it. However, the Inspector gave the driver the benefit of the doubt and the fault was placed on the signalman for irregular working, and a badly sighted home signal which was later removed to a new location. The engines met head on at a diamond crossing at a relative speed of 35 mph. The resulting collision wrecked the two leading coaches of the express and killed 5 people. The driver of the 8F, his fireman and six passengers were all seriously injured, with 19 others also hurt to a lesser extent.

PHOTOGRAPHS: KEYSTONE PICTURE LIBRARY

TODMORDEN
London, Midland & Scottish Railway
4th September 1942

Another accident involving a loop line and the black out occurred at Todmorden on the former L&YR trans-Pennine line, when LMS 0-6-0 Class 4F No.4541 derailed down an embankment. As the slow moving, 28-wagon coal train from Crofton Sidings (Wakefield) neared Todmorden, it was diverted into the sidings to allow a passenger train for Manchester Victoria go past. In the darkness (which was complicated by the black out) the driver lost his bearings and, looking out for a landmark, he missed the ground signal at the end of the loop. He carried on along the short road which ended in a set of buffer stops, but he forced his way past these and the engine plunged down a fifty feet high embankment. The crew were completely buried under an avalanche of coal and it took two hours to extricate the driver, but he was fortunately none too badly hurt. However, this was the third accident to happen here during the black out, so it was decided to improve the signal lighting regardless of what other risks this might entail.

PHOTOGRAPH: G. GREENWOOD COLLECTION

ENEMY ATTACK
All Railways
1939-1945

The view on this page shows Schools Class No.934 *St.Lawrence* at London's Cannon Street station after suffering a direct bomb hit on 11th May 1941 which devastated the cab and literally blew the tender apart. In the debris on the ground, between the two main driving wheels, readers will observe the engine's nameplate laying like so much scrap. This engine was just one of many casualties of the Luftwaffe's attacks on mainland Britain; another, A4 Class No.4469 *Sir Ralph Wedgwood* was shown on page 26 of Volume 6 in the original series, whilst LMS Black 5 No.5425 was illustrated on page 29 of Volume 2. These views clearly show that despite all the precautions, the inevitable still happened, and the railway network suffered quite major damage. All over the British Isles, railway installations were affected; yet the country's major asset was its plethora of routes (a legacy of pre-grouping competition), which gave the Railway Executive a variety of alternatives for re-routing trains away from damage affected areas. As I mentioned in *Britain's Railways At War,* 'lines which had almost been a virtual liability in the pre-war years were now proving to be of vital strategic importance.' However it was not all plain sailing, and the picture above shows a train which had run into a crater on the line between London and Harwich. This was the 8.45pm departure from Liverpool Street, and it serves as a classic example of problems which affected the railways in the war years. As reader E.G.W. Summerfield recalls 'It was a somewhat contentious subject at the Emergency Operating H.Q. (located at Shenfield) as to whether the train should have been used to search the line for bomb damage. The situation was that the train had come to a stand at Shenfield with the colour light signals at red, and the telephone and track circuits dead. Communications had also been lost with Ingatestone, indicating that the telephone wires were down and the signalling cables cut. Notwithstanding that something must have happened close to the track, Stratford Control sent the train into the section. One possible reason for the controllers' attitude was that a room at the Emergency HQ had been wired for occupation by Stratford Control, but they remained in exposed offices on the top floor of the loco erecting shops throughout the war.' In my earlier books I stated that no-one was hurt, but I have been subsequently informed that the driver and fireman were killed and a passenger slightly hurt when the train fell into a bomb crater near Ingatestone station.

PHOTOGRAPHS: ABOVE: KEYSTONE PICTURE LIBRARY
BELOW: SOUTHERN RAILWAY OFFICIAL, COURTESY KENT LIBRARIES

SOHAM

London & North Eastern Railway
2nd June 1944

In the early hours of 2nd June 1944, the sleeping market town of Soham in Cambridgeshire was devastated by the explosion of forty 500 lb. bombs. However, unlike the incidents pictured on the previous page, these were 'friendly' bombs which were being carried by rail to bomber bases for use in the 'softening up operations' which would preface the D-Day landings. They were being carried in the leading wagon of a 52 vehicle train which was packed with high explosives behind WD Class 8F 2-8-0 No.7337 which had left the Whitemoor Marshalling Yard at March, around 11.40pm the previous night. Forty-four of the wagons were carrying a mixture of 500lb and 250lb bombs, the other seven carried detonators. The load had been landed at Immingham and was destined for the United States airbase receiving station at White Colne in Essex, which would be reached via Ely, Bury St. Edmunds, Ipswich, and Colchester. Because of the heroism of the crew, I will reveal their names as driver Ben Gimbert and fireman Jim Nightall. They travelled along the single track line as far as Soham, but as they approached the station Gimbert saw flames coming from the first wagon in the train. We will never know what started that fire, but it was assumed that it was probably sulphur dust left over from a previous load that had been ignited by a spark from the engine. As Gimbert slowed down, he began sounding his whistle to warn the guard, as they came to a halt 90 yards from the station. The fireman jumped down from the footplate and ran to uncouple the wagon, before rejoining Gimbert who quickly put on steam to draw forward. It is obvious that it was there intention to get the blazing wagon clear of the station before it exploded, but he was worried about going on to the double track section ahead because the mail train from Newmarket was due any time. He slowed down in the station to ask the signalman whether the next section was clear, but as he did so the wagon exploded at 1.43am.

An explosion of 20,000 pounds of high explosives must be an awesome sight, and this massive force of destructive energy blasted apart the tiny station. Only the train guard and Gimbert escaped, although the driver was very badly injured. The explosion blasted out a crater 15 feet deep and 66 feet wide, and destroyed the track for a distance of 120 feet. Five villagers were seriously injured by the blast, including the Soham station-master. His house alongside the peaceful little station was reduced to a pile of rubble, but the rest of his family were more fortunate, escaping with only minor injuries. Elsewhere not a single house in Soham escaped from the damage caused by the shock of the explosion, and fourteen homes were completely destroyed; three dozen more were so badly damaged as to cause their families to be relocated whilst repair work was undertaken. Inside a mile radius 700 buildings were affected, but we must temper this devastation with what might have happened had Gimbert and Nigthall not acted so bravely and just left their train for all 51 wagons to explode. As it was their courage was recognised by the award of the George Cross to both of them.

PHOTOGRAPHS: ALL AUTHOR'S COLLECTION

ECCLEFECHAN

London, Midland & Scottish Railway 21st July 1945

On Saturday 21st July 1945, the war in Europe had been over for six weeks though fighting in the Far East was still going on as the 1pm express passenger train from Glasgow Central to Euston was running southwards in the rain. The drizzle beat about the cab of No. 6231 *Duchess of Atholl* as it hurried down to Carlisle from Beattock with a comparatively light load of eleven coaches and two bogie vans. Running just ahead of it was a train of 45 4-wheeled wagons and a brake van being drawn by Class 4F 0-6-0 No.4234. Its driver had expected to be set back at Dinwoodie or Lockerbie, but because the express was running late the goods train had been allowed to go on to Ecclefechan, where it was to be set back into a lay-back siding. It was just manoeuvring back into this when No.6231 came charging down on it and struck the 4th van in the freight train at the fouling point of the trailing connection. This was about 50 yards from the north end of the up platform, and thus in the worst place possible; the leading bogie van was thrown across the tracks, blocking both lines. Fortunately the sturdy construction of the all-steel stock stood up to the impact and the remaining twelve vehicles remained upright in a straight line. The first five were derailed because 140 yards of the permanent way was badly disturbed by the engine, but the others stayed on the track. The Duchess was badly damaged however (as our picture at Crewe Works shows), whilst the freight engine sustained heavy injury after being pushed forward for 110 yards. The station did not escape either, and the face of the platform were torn away and the footbridge wrecked. It is by very good fortune that no-one was waiting on the station at the time of the accident, as debris and ballast was showered against the up platform and signal box with a malevolent force which caused the station clock to stop at 3.07pm precisely. Station staff were dazed and stunned by the disaster, but they immediately set emergency procedures into operation. Clouds of steam enveloped the scene as No.6231's safety valves were torn away, but rescue workers quickly ran to the cab of the Duchess to help the crew. Unfortunately the driver was dead, and the fireman fatally injured.

Yet despite the tragedy which had occurred on the footplate, the passengers were to fare considerably better. Fifty were injured, but only 31 of these needed hospitalisation - and of these just twelve were still in Dumfries Royal Infirmary at the end of the week. The casualties were therefore thankfully very light, but it could have been much more serious. This accident is quite inexplicable, for the two men on the footplate were both very experienced, conscientious and extremely capable. It was a hard case to investigate, and Ecclefechan is therefore another of those great railway mysteries which have never been really explained. There may have been some condition caused by the drizzling rain which obscured the signals momentarily, but the driver of the freight train who had passed through eight minutes earlier saw nothing which suggested this as being the case. Another theory was that black smoke was beating along the boiler casing of the Duchess, and if so this could have obscured the driver's view. In fact this was a problem which had been experienced elsewhere, and was only resolved when smoke deflector plates were fitted to the non-streamlined members of the class as our lower picture shows. However, once again none of these circumstances mitigated against the fact that it was a driver's responsibility to closely watch out for and strictly observe the signals on his route. Yet within a few weeks the same problem would hit the LMS as a crack express behind a very conscientious driver derailed at high speed near Bourne End.

PHOTOGRAPHS; BOTH AUTHOR'S COLLECTION

BOURNE END

London, Midland & Scottish Railway 30th September 1945

This story begins early on a Sunday morning in Crew station, where a driver was awaiting the late-running 8.20pm express sleeper from Perth which was due in to Crewe at 4.20am. As he waited he sat reading the Rugby - London section of the 'Fortnightly Notice' which, in part, said Sunday Sept. 30. Between Boxmoor and Watford, 23 and 18′ m.p. Up and Down Fast. 7.0am to 5.0pm..... All trains to travel over the Slow lines between Bourne End and Watford No.1 At that time the bulk of passenger traffic was still connected with men being repatriated from overseas, leave traffic and servicemen travelling on civilian trains to and from demob centres. However, now that the war was over there was something of a reluctance on the part of several 'special link' drivers to work Sunday services, and this threw a burden on the men who were. One of the drivers who would do these duties was asked if he would do the train at 4.23am to Euston, 'Yes, I will gladly' came the reply, 'London and back home for dinner'; with that he went away to prepare his engine. London and back by dinner may have been the plan, but the driver and fireman were dead by breakfast.

Yet this was one of Crewe's most careful drivers who was well known, both as a temperate man and one who knew his job. His study of the notices of special engineering works was so well known, that other drivers would often ask his advice on where restrictions would be encountered before they set out on their trips. Having accepted his London trip, the driver got his engine No. 6157 *Royal Artilleryman,* over to No. 4 engine siding to await the arrival of the Scotch Express. As usual up trains were running late and during the 1 hour 22 minutes he had to wait, the driver was seen studying the notices. Those who knew him well told the Inspector that he would not have missed any point concerning a route he would have to take. The official report recorded 'It has been a matter of comment at Crewe Motive Power Shed that [the driver] has always been very methodical in the way he looks after his Fortnightly Notices.... he was the very best man at Crewe for reading the Notices.' In view of this, what happened a few minutes after 9am as his train raced down to Bourne End from Tring Summit is therefore quite inexplicable. At the point where he would crossover from the up fast to the up slow, the colour light signals were showing a double yellow. A Royal Scot could have safely negotiated the crossing at up to 40 mph, but No.6157 must have been doing at least 60 mph. As it hit the crossover, it burst through the points, and then turned over the embankment on the left. It crashed down some nine feet below the line, and was followed by the first coach which was impaled on the tender, the second broke free and spread itself across the running lines, but the next four coaches all crashed down the embankment. Of the 398 passengers on the 15 coach train, no less than 38 were killed in the crash, in addition to the driver, fireman and five others who succumbed from their injuries later. Some 124 passengers were injured, over half of whom were very serious. Rescue work was prompt and the first casualties were in hospital in less than half an hour. Like the mysterious case at Ecclefechan, there was much conjecture as to why this most efficient driver had failed to react to the colour light signals correctly, and it was suggested that, like Ecclefechan his view may have been obstructed. This time the theory was not smoke or rain, but sunlight and haze which may have caused him to miss the signals as he came down on Bourne End in that first autumn of peace. Why the driver continued across the crossover at speed will ever remain a mystery, but in common with the accident at Ecclefechan, it was the type of situation which could have been readily prevented by an ATC/AWS system.

PHOTOGRAPHS; THE LATE H.C. CASSERLEY

LICHFIELD

London, Midland & Scottish Railway
1st January 1946

The New Year of 1945/46 got off to a very bad start, when a serious accident occurred on Monday 31st December 1945. For many, this was the first day back at work after the first peace-time Christmas holiday since 1938. But as the public began their daily travel once again, a series of disasters were waiting to pounce on the railways. It struck first at 9.12am on the Metropolitan & Great Central Joint Railway between Northwood and Northwood Hills, when a London Passenger Transport Board electric locomotive ran into the rear of a 6-car electrical multiple unit in dense fog. Had we been able to find an adequate illustration of this incident, we would have detailed it in this book, but only views of the very poorest quality have so far emerged. So we will make very brief reference to it before moving on to Lichfield. At 9.12am London Transport electric locomotive L19, from Baker Street to Aylesbury ploughed into the back of a stationary Watford train near Northwood Hills, telescoping its rear two coaches. Damaged electrical circuits in the coaches caused arcing, and due to a failure to switch off the current, the arcing continued and fire ensued. Three passengers lost their lives and seven more were injured.

Disaster struck the following day at Lichfield Trent Valley station when another local train was struck from the rear by a moving train. This time it was the 6.08pm Stafford to Nuneaton, drawn by unnamed Prince of Wales class No.25802 and comprised of four wooden-bodied bogie coaches on steel or composite underframes. As per normal practice the train was put into the up slow (platform) line at around 6.54pm, and the guard slipped across to the station buffet for a cup of tea. This undoubtedly saved his life because at 6.58pm his guard's compartment was completely shattered by 5MT 4-6-0 No.5495 which was heading an express fish train from Fleetwood to London Broad Street. This had been following the local all the way from Stafford, but at Lichfield the formation of the line changed to four tracks, and the fast lines passed between the two slow loops which served the platforms. Having put the local into the front half of the loop, the signalman cleared the up fast for the express freight which was running at a speed of about 35mph. However, as it ran into the station it also ran on to the up slow on which the local was standing. Despite braking hard, the class 5MT hit the stationary train with such force as to drive it forwards for a distance of over 100 yards. The Prince of Wales class loco was driven right into the sand drag situated beyond the outlet of the up slow to up fast line. The four coaches were completely demolished and two of them were thrown upon the platform. Of the 100 people on board the local, 13 were killed outright and seven more died later. Twenty were seriously injured and many more complained of minor injuries - however both sets of train crews escaped unscathed, although the driver of the express fish train was badly shocked by the events. A tragic feature of the accident was the death of five people from North Lancashire and one from Cumberland, who would not have been travelling on this local train had it not been for a timetable change which had been implemented that day. These passengers had travelled south on the Blackpool - London train which had always stopped at Nuneaton. Unfortunately, with this stop being omitted, they now had to catch the local train to Stafford to make a connection. In the official enquiry which followed the disaster the blame was attributed to a twisted point rod and the driver misreading signals, however, this is a case where a great degree of doubt was attached to the findings by the railway unions and I must agree with those who take the view that it was easier to find a human scapegoat than blame the railway company for this most tragic accident.

PHOTOGRAPHS: ALL AUTHOR'S COLLECTION

BROWNEY SIGNAL BOX

London & North Eastern Railway
5th January 1946

Investigations into the accidents at Northwood Hills and Litchfield had barely got under way when the third accident of the week occurred on the East Coast Main Line in Co. Durham just north of Ferryhill. As it heads north to Durham City, the line descends to cross the River Browney, creating a sharp dip with falling gradients on either side. At the bottom of this dip once stood Browney Signal Box which, over the years, had witnessed many runaways, particularly breakaway portions of unfitted freight trains. This was a direct consequence of the geography of the line which provided the ideal conditions for couplings to snatch and break, but all of the incidents prior to the first week of January 1946 had been very superficial. Yet as the viciousness of British railway's Black Week continued, all of this was about to change. It began innocently enough as a Class B16 4-6-0, No. 842, left Low Fell Yard at Gateshead for Doncaster at 4.30am on 5th January. The train of two fitted vans, 42 4-wheeled unfitted vehicles and a 20-ton brake van was some fifty minutes behind its scheduled departure time, and it was out of path as it progressed slowly southwards. At Bridge House near Durham it was stopped at the up home signal, where a signalman was waiting in the six foot. As the goods train slowed down to a crawl he climbed on to the footplate and told the driver that he was authorised by control to obtain a lift to his duty at Ferryhill No.3 'Box. Seeing his colleague climb onto the footplate, the signalman at Bridge House cleared the signal, so the engine driver released his brake but did not put on steam. The train had not actually stopped, and as they moved away the signalman told the driver he had felt a slight jerk and ' hoped he hadn't divided the train'.

Though there was no indication that this had happened, a dangerously weak draw-bar on the seventh wagon from the engine had fractured. The Bridge House signalman saw the division and sent the 'train divided' bell signal to the next box at Browney, where the relief signalman wondered whether or not to let the front half of the train run on to the Hett Mill section, and allow the rear portion to come to a halt somewhere in the dip at Browney. However, as there was a serious threat of this rear portion overtaking the front half, he reasoned that the possible consequences of a derailment on Croxdale Viaduct meant he should bring the B16 to a halt within the protection of his 'box. He also placed his down home signal to safeguard the 11.15pm King's Cross - Newcastle express which was almost due. Unfortunately, when the collision occurred, wreckage from one of the wagons slipped down the embankment and caught the signal wires leading out of the box, pulling both the down home and down distant signals off. Tragically, the crew of the express engine, Class V2, 2-6-2 No. 4895, were therefore misled as to the state of the line, so they ran on at about 50 mph and smashed straight into the wreckage. Ten passengers were killed and eight were badly hurt in the concluding episode of the first week of 1946, bringing the casualty figures to 33 killed and a similar number injured. On the face of it, this accident seemed completely beyond prevention, for the signalman had acted in good faith by bringing the front half of the goods train to halt within the protection of his signals, even if the correct procedure would have been to let it run on to Hett Mill; it was a tragic culmination to British Railway's Black Week.

PHOTOGRAPH; ABOVE: KEYSTONE PICTURE LIBRARY
LEFT: THE LATE KENNETH HOOLE COLLECTION

POTTERS BAR

London & North Eastern Railway
11th February 1946

It was cold and dark on the night of 11th February 1946, and many of the trains in and out of King's Cross were running behind schedule. The delays were not excessive, but they were leading to path displacement of long distance trains and so Control gave precedence to local trains. Consequently, the signalman at Potters Bar accepted the 9.32pm Hatfield - King's Cross local passenger service, which was also running late. Drawn by 0-6-2T, No. 2679, it was comprised of two quadruple sets of inner suburban stock. In his evidence given at the subsequent enquiry, the driver of the local train said he was approaching Potters Bar at a speed of 35-40 mph when he ran past the distant, where he shut off steam for the outer-home. Through the dark ahead he could see the aspects of the two inner-home signals, one of which was showing red, the other green. The driver was convinced that the green applied to him, and he continued his run into the station at a speed of about 15mph. In doing this he began to brake in order to crossover from the slow line to the platform line but to his great surprise the 0-6-2T collided with the buffers at the end of the slow road. His train carried on past him to the right and derailed itself across the adjacent running lines, but the female guard quickly got herself together and dropped down to track level in order to protect the train. As she did so she could hear the approach of another up train, so she ran towards it shouting and waving her red hand lamp. However, she had not realised that a down express was also approaching the scene from the opposite side.

A multiple collision was now inevitable, and in total 1,075 people were travelling in the three trains that were going to be involved. About 50 to 60 seconds after the 0-6-2T collided with the buffers at the short dead end to the up slow, the wreckage of its train was struck forcefully by the north-bound 9.45pm Edinburgh express hauled by V2 2-6-2, No. 4876. Travelling at 45 mph under clear signals, the V2 could not avoid hitting the second coach and pushed its underframe in front of it for 115 yards. As it came to a rest the tender lifted up behind it, and the first six coaches of the train became derailed. Then as No. 4876 came to a halt, it was ploughed into by sister engine No. 4833 on the 5pm express from Bradford Exchange. It was every railwayman's nightmare, a collision between two trains with a third running into the wreckage. Miraculously, only two people died but seventeen other people were injured. The official report eventually determined that the driver of the local was primarily to blame and contended that he had passed the signals at red. Obviously we will never know the true sequence of events that night, and we can only take the view incorporated in the official report which attributed the blame to the local train driver for passing a signal at red, but the signalman's action was highly questionable and his evidence seems quite open to question.

PHOTOGRAPHS: ALL THE LATE ARTHUR TREVENA COLLECTION

GIDEA PARK

London & North Eastern Railway

Our next accident comes at the beginning of 1947, the last full year before nationalisation, and we begin our story at London's Liverpool Street station. On an extremely foggy night two trains were preparing to start a journey along the ex-GER main line just three minutes apart. The first was the 10.25pm express to Peterborough, but as it had been delayed on its journey into Liverpool Street by the fog, Control decided to let the 10.28 pm semi-fast to Southend precede it. Although this was a slower train, it would be given the fast line as far as Gidea Park, where it would transfer to the down local in order to let the express go past. Class B12 4-6-0 No.1565 left Liverpool Street right on time, but by the time it reached Gidea Park Station it was 16 minutes late due to the thick fog. The Peterborough express, behind class B17 4-6-0, No. 1602 *Walsingham,* left Liverpool Street at 10.50 pm but it made surprisingly good speed through the fog and began clawing back the 25 minute deficit. Now all should have gone according to plan, but control had not reckoned with the lax fog signalling arrangements employed in the Romford area. The men here were called out to operate Clayton fogging equipment and show hand lamps as an additional means of protecting signals which were set at danger/caution. The critical signal in this incident was the Romford down distant, to which the fogsignalman was called out at 8.50pm. This was some 2½ hours before the accident, but the lengthsman assigned to this duty decided to go to a whist drive and he did not arrive at Romford 'box until 10.20pm. When he did so he picked up a batch of ordinary detonators, even though these were totally inadequate for the Clayton apparatus. According to his own statement it took him a further thirty minutes to reach the signals, situated just 1,328 yards away, and when he got there he supposedly fitted a partly filled detonator magazine to the down through line, just before two trains went past in quick succession. When the first of these went through he took off the detonator by means of the apparatus, but replaced it before the second train arrived. He further claimed this was then exploded by the B17, but no one on that train ever heard it. Evidence from other witnesses suggests that the magazine was actually stored at the nearby Crowlands signal box, and the lengthsman was still walking to collect this when the trains raced past him in the fog. From the Southend train the guard actually saw someone walking down the track carrying a hand lamp and he took this to be the fogsignalman, so it is fairly safe to say that there was no secondary warning provided at the down distant!

About this time the signalman at Gidea Park tried to cross the Southend train over to the down local line, but could not do so as a train for Shenfield was still occupying the next track circuit. According to the rules he protected the Southend train with the down through outer home signal. As the track-circuit cleared, he began to start No.1565 when the telephone rang from Romford 'box, warning him that the express had 'overrun the boards at a fair old rate'. No sooner had this happened than the train describer apparatus buzzed and the signalman knew it was racing into his section and the back of the Southend train. As he was over 400 yards from the station he could take no effective steps to warn them of the impending danger, other than to try ringing up on the telephone. At that moment the express passed the last signal protecting the back of the Southend train and, at a speed of about 33mph, it subsequently buried itself in the rear coach just as the train had begun to move away. Sadly, the wooden bodies of the three rear coaches of the stationary train were completely wrecked and the trailing end of the fifth coach was also badly damaged. Seven people died and a further 45 were detained in hospital, and once again the need for an adequate form of ATC/AWS was clearly demonstrated.

PHOTOGRAPHS: ALL AUTHOR'S COLLECTION

GRENDON, NEAR POLESWORTH

London, Midland & Scottish Railway
21st July 1947

A feature of the postwar period was the high number of railway accidents which were either directly due to the effects of deferred maintenance, or ones which could have been prevented if the war had not interrupted planned modernisation programmes. On this page we look at just two examples, beginning at 10.38am on 21st July 1947 on the WCML at Grendon, not far from Polesworth station. The train was the 8.30am express passenger from London to Liverpool, that was made up of 16 vehicles behind streamlined Duchess class 4-6-2 No.6244 *King George VI* which ironically had the same name as the GWR engine that came to grief in the high speed derailment at Norton Fitzwarren in 1940. This time, however, the LMS engine was running on the fast line when it overturned at a speed of 65-70 mph. As it came into the left-handed curve at Grendon the gauge began to shift because of the seriously worn condition of the track, which had last been relaid with 95lbs. rail in 1929. It would have been relaid again in 1944, but due to shortages of materials and manpower the work was deferred and it was put into the 1948 programme. However, whilst it was technically within the limits for high speed running the track was nearing the end of its life, and as *King George VI* came into the curve the gauge widened and the engine became derailed. It fell on to its right-hand side and came to rest 400 yards from the point of derailment, but thanks to its streamlined casing it was not badly damaged, and after being righted by cranes from Wellingborough, Rugby, Crewe and Derby it was towed to Crewe without having its motion disconnected. The coaches did not fare so well and the ends of six of these were crushed in, which had serious consequences due to the fact that the train was heavily loaded and crowded with over 800 passengers, of which 130 were standing. Four were killed outright and one later succumbed in hospital, whilst 19 people were seriously injured, most of the fatalities and injuries being sustained by those standing in the vestibule ends.

PHOTOGRAPH; TOPHAM PICTURE LIBRARY

DONCASTER

London & North Eastern Railway
9th August 1947

Just 19 days later it was the turn of the ECML to suffer disaster, this time in the form of a rear-end collision just south of Doncaster station; it involved the 1.25pm train from King's Cross to Leeds which ran into another Leeds express that had left London 15 minutes before it. Once again the trains were heavily loaded, with around 700 passengers in each, and many standing in the corridors. This time 18 passengers lost their lives and 118 more were injured to some extent, of which 51 were detained in hospital. The events began when A3 Class 4-6-2 No.50 *Persimmon* came to a stand at Bridge Junction home signal, and V2 2-6-2 No.936 was improperly allowed to enter the same section under clear signals. The last three coaches of the 1.10pm train were completely destroyed as a result, and the V2 was heavily damaged around its front end. Examination of the debris, one could not call it wreckage, revealed that the last three coaches of the leading train had been completely destroyed; the majority of casualties occurring therein. The signalling of this section had long been due for modernisation but the work was suspended with the outbreak of war in 1939 and restarted in 1946, but until it was completed at the end of 1947 there was a transitional section between Balby Junction and Bridge Junction. Sadly the man working Balby Junction does not emerge in the accident report as a very good signalman, for he had every opportunity of seeing the 1.10pm standing just 177 yards from his box. However, he accepted the following express and lowered his signals for it before obtaining 'Line Clear' from Bridge House or receiving the 'out of section' message for the preceding train. Stating that very serious responsibility lay upon the signalman, the Inspector wrote: It might be said that [the signalman's] lapse could be attributed in part to clearing the block prematurely for the first train, and this was his first blunder; but he could not account satisfactorily for his actions during more than 5 minutes, namely, from the time [the first train] passed his box soon after 4.35pm till the collision occurred at about 4.41pm.'

PHOTOGRAPH; THE LATE KENNETH HOOLE COLLECTION

SOUTH CROYDON
Southern Railway
24th October 1947

Usually the 8.04am 6-car commuter train from Tattenham Corner to London Bridge was very well-patronised, and by the time it reached Purley people were often standing in the aisles. At Purley the 3-car EMU service from Caterham was attached to this train, and the combined set of nine vehicles which resulted offered a seating capacity of 750. However, on Friday 24th October fog was causing severe disruption and many trains were running late and out of sequence and commuters were adopting their usual custom and practice of squeezing into the first suitable train which came along, regardless of how full it already was. Living in a town which does not even boast a set of traffic lights, I find my visits to London a fraught experience, but what I dread most is travelling on suburban or tube trains when people jam themselves in rush hour commuter trains without a care in the world. It must have been the same that October morning in 1947, for the seating capacity on the 8.40am was exceeded by a third and around 250 passengers had to stand. Not only was this train crowded beyond capacity, but the preceding train, the 7.33am Haywards Heath - London Bridge train had around 800 passengers in an EMU set which could seat 536. A number of minor accidents had previously been sustained in the operation of over-crowded services such as these, but fortunately this had not been attended by any major disaster. Yet the Southern Railway could never have expected the consequences of this, and just two months prior to nationalisation disaster struck. In the thick fog hundreds of unsuspecting passengers were being trundled and jolted up to London, though a series of events were already in progress which would leave 31 of them dead or dying and another 183 suffering injury or shock. For as the Haywards Heath train cautiously made its way across Croydon South Junction, it was struck violently from behind by the Tattenham Corner service which was running under incorrectly cleared signals after the signalman used a release key to free the Sykes 'Lock & Block' equipment. Debris falling from the trains at once short-circuited the electrified lines causing the breakers at Purley Sub-station and South Croydon Track-panelling Hut to open simultaneously. The impact of the second train smashing into the first was exceptionally severe as the leading buffers of the Tattenham Corner train underrode the rear buffers on the rear coach of the Haywards Heath train. This coach was torn off its bogies and thrown over on to its side, and this caused the body to separate from the frame. The van and rear motorman's cab were completely demolished. The next coach in the Haywards Heath train, that is to say the second last, was also badly damaged by the force of the collision but it remained on the rails. The Tattenham Corner train was, as might be imagined, very badly damaged at the front end. The motorman's cab was literally swept clean away and the control gear therein thrown some 50 yards along the track from the point of collision. The rest of the coach, as far back as the last two compartments, just disintegrated. It was in this coach that the bulk of the fatalities

occurred! The second, third and fourth coaches were also damaged and derailed due to track being ripped up by the leading coach. Fire service, police, railwaymen and the inhabitants of nearby Sussex Road all rendered invaluable service and comfort to the dazed or injured passengers, 41 of who were detained in hospital.

The subsequent enquiry was an exhausting one, and it could not fail to determine that the fault lay with a signalman who lacked the experience to work on such a busy main line' He had joined the Southern Railway in 1936, but when war broke out he enlisted in the army and spent three years as a prisoner of war after the fall of Torbruk. He rejoined the railway service in May 1946, commencing his training for the post of signalman in March 1947. Five weeks before the disaster the regular signalman at Purley Oaks box was taken ill, and the novice was ordered to take over the 'box in his absence; even though he only had nine weeks experience of manning a 'box for a whole shift, and five weeks of manning one for just two hours per day. The Inspector subsequently questioned the logic of placing so much responsibility in the hands of one who was so inexperienced. In his summary he said; 'it seems to me that [the signalman] was allowed too rapidly to assume duties with too much responsibility'. However, whilst this accident may have been caused by inexperience, the misuse of the release key was an ongoing problem, we encountered it at Battersea Park and in the 1955 accident at Barnes we will come across it again!

PHOTOGRAPHS; ELTHAM TIMES COLLECTION

GOSWICK

London & North Eastern Railway 26th October 1947

Our next accident took place at the tiny station of Goswick, three stops south of Berwick-on-Tweed, and it is one of distinct similarities. First of all, this was the scene of a serious accident on 28th August 1907 which is shown in the smaller of the two pictures on this page. That incident is very similar to the one now under discussion, for it involved an engine derailing on the entry to the up independent line having overrun the distant signal and negotiated the crossover too fast. The driver and fireman of 4-6-0 No.2005 were killed, but it was not determined why an experienced crew should ignore signals and take a restricted crossing at four times the permitted speed of 5 mph. The next similarity will be identified with the accident at Bourne End, for when disaster struck at the entry to the crossover just 100 yards south of Goswick in 1947, the circumstances were almost identical to the high speed derailment on the WCML two years earlier. The next interesting fact is the name of the locomotive A3 class 4-6-0 No.66, *Merry Hampton,* which is associated with the disaster at Cramlington shown on page 86. It was also a day of contrasts, for unlike the accident at foggy Croydon two days earlier, beautiful autumn sunshine bathed the Northumberland coast.

We begin our story at Edinburgh's Haymarket Engine Shed where a driver was slipping in through the back entrance, accompanied by a shadowy figure in a borrowed fireman's uniform. The intruder, a railway mad naval rating, was quietly directed across to the A3 before the driver went to 'book on'. Now, but with all this subterfuge, the driver missed seeing a special engineering notice pinned up on the driver's bulletin board. Meanwhile, the regular fireman who should also have seen the notice arrived late for duty, booked on and went straight to the engine. So, as *Merrie Hampton* rolled into Edinburgh Waverley and on to the 11.15am 'Day Scotsman', neither of the crew members had seen a notice which warned them that re-scheduled bridge work meant that trains were being diverted from the fast road on to the independent lines at Goswick. Like Bourne End, the train was made up of fifteen coaches and with 420 aboard, its passenger list almost the same as the night sleeper from Perth. At 12.45pm the signalman in the little 'box on Goswick station platform received 'train entering section' from Scremerston, so whilst keeping the distant at caution he set his home signal at danger intending the train to come to a near standstill before pulling it off. Seeing a wisp of steam he thought this was coming from the safety valve after the driver had shut off steam; after all the driver should have had this signal in view for a good time and been bringing his train to stand. When the train was about 360 yards from it the signalman pulled the lever to clear, assuming it would have slowed down sufficiently to negotiate the crossover in safety. However, as the train got closer to the 'box, the signalman realised that it wasn't slowing down at all; the driver had failed to act on the distant and was still running at a great speed under what were now clear signals. The signalman acted quickly and threw his signals back to danger and used one of his levers to place a detonator in front of the train, but whether or not even this was observed is not know; true the driver now seemed to have shut off steam, but the brakes had not yet been applied. How much the presence of the unauthorised passenger on the footplate played a part in this we will never know, but the A3 barrelled into the crossover at a speed of at least 60 mph. It then burst through the trackwork, rolled over and ended up in precisely the same ditch as No.2005 40 years 1 month and 29 days earlier. Twenty-eight passengers died and many were seriously hurt including the three men on the footplate. It was a tragic finale to the LNER's accident record!

PHOTOGRAPHS; THE LATE KENNETH HOOLE COLLECTION

FARNBOROUGH

Southern Railway
26th November 1947

Whilst the Southern must have had high hopes that South Croydon was going to be the last serious accident of their regime, tragedy was going to strike one final time when nationalisation was just 35 days away. It was, like Croydon, another rear end collision and also an incident in which a signalman is recorded as having been flustered by exceptional circumstances. This time the problems began with a power failure on the line between Fleet and Farnborough which caused all the colour light signals to fail safe at red. Such a fail safe, was initially an ideal arrangement, but as traffic had to be quickly restarted it could, and did prove to be a quite dangerous situation. To pass trains along, the signalman was empowered to authorise a movement under the 'proceed at caution' rule by issuing a form to the driver allowing him to pass the signal at danger. Obviously this arrangement had to be worked under the very greatest care, and was dependent on all the signalmen working in harmony. Unfortunately, harmony was not much in evidence on the day that disaster struck in Farnborough. A little before 6pm the 3.05pm Bournemouth West - Waterloo train came to a halt at an auto-signal just west of Farnborough, but the signalman on duty in the Farnborough 'box was getting flustered with the general situation and he delayed 4-6-0 No.860 *Lord Hawke* much longer than was necessary. As the train 9 of coaches and a GWR milk van stood at the lights, it was struck violently by the 11 coach Ilfracombe - Waterloo train behind No. 453 *King Arthur* which was running at a speed of 20 mph. The rear coaches split wide open and two people died with 11 more being badly injured. However, thanks to the keen observation of the footplate crew on a third train, the 4pm Salisbury - Waterloo, a second rear-end collision was very narrowly averted. Having damaged the last two coaches in the Bournemouth train, the King Arthur class loco turned over on to its left and, as it did so, the coach following became wrecked on the tender. Fortunately, the presence of troops at the nearby Cove Camp helped effect a speedy rescue operation and many of the injured were given extensive first-aid at the scene by army medical orderlies.

Whilst the signalling system at Farnborough was approaching 30 years old, failures were rare and when it did go down it had failed safe. Therefore the signalling system was not at fault, but there was a serious error of judgement by the man in the 'box at Fleet. Once the problem became manifest, he should have commenced block working immediately, but in a desire to 'keep things moving' he began issuing the forms authorising drivers to pass the red lights. He further confused them by giving the impression that the line was clear as far as Sturt Lane Junction. It was a practice which he might have got away with, had not the Farnborough signalman delayed the Bournemouth train for so long. It was the last major disaster of the grouped era but it was a sad end to the Southern whose record was far from perfect, but even so it was nowhere near as bad as the LNER and the LMS (who seem to have suffered most of all out of the big four companies). Only the GWR could hold its head high, and that was thanks to its automatic train control system, but would nationalisation see a universal application of the safety field where the GWR were clear leaders? We will see the answer to that in the pages that follow!

It is, however, most ironical that the great safety improvements which could have come about on the railways as a result of the Grouping had not been really achieved. Only the GWR had escaped a string of catastrophes, and the LNER and Southern had suffered more than their fare share of problems. Unfortunately, the LMS had come off worst off all, and they seemed to have inherited the Midland's panache for wrecking its trains. As an ardent admirer of the LMS, I have to feel regret at making such a statement, but a glimpse at the pages in this past section will reveal that this is quite an accurate criticism. True, great advances had been made in addressing the effects of of accidents, primarily thanks to substantial improvements in coaching stock designs. The LNER had significantly advanced safety with its buck-eye couplings, the LMS had all but completely banished gas-lighting, and the Southern had significantly advanced its electrified suburban lines. Yet on their own, these improvements were not enough, the issues of full track-circuiting, train protection and of course Automatic Train Control were all needed to create a safe railway environment. As we now consider the next twenty year period, we must ask ourselves, how many lives could have been saved had the funding been found for such improvements?

PHOTOGRAPH: THE LATE ARTHUR TREVENA COLLECTION

WINSFORD

British Railways, London Midland Region
17th April 1948

British Railways had been in existence for just three and a half months when it suffered its first major accident, and where else would it happen but on the former metals of the LMS not many miles south of that double accident black-spot of Winwick. This time the culprit was a 19-year old ex-railwayman who was serving in the armed forces and travelling home on leave aboard the 5.40pm express from Glasgow, but progress was anything but fast and as it approached Winsford Junction the man decided to take a calculated risk so he could get home that night. His wife was living with his in-laws just a mile away from Winsford, but if he carried on to Crewe he knew there would not be a train back to the village until 7am the next morning so he sneaked into a toilet compartment and pulled the communication cord. The crew of No.6207 *Princess Arthur of Connaught* made an emergency brake application and when the train came to a halt, the soldier slipped out of a door and away over the fields to his wife. Now this was a trick which must have been well known amongst both railwaymen and servicemen, as many former drivers have written and told me of how common an occurrence it was. Normally it was a frustrating, but otherwise inconvenient stop, though on this occasion a signalman's error was going to compound the situation and create the first major disaster for the nationalised railway.

When a communication cord is pulled, the rules stipulate that the fireman must go back and protect the rear whilst the guard goes down the train to find out in which coach the cord has been pulled and then ascertain the reasons for this. However, on this occasion the guard thought that he would be better at protecting the train, so he sent the fireman to look for the indicator disc on the side of the coach where the cord had been pulled. It would have been better if they had followed the rules, for the guard had only managed to get 400 yards to the rear of the train, in which distance he had only laid two detonators. Yet it had been 17 minutes since the train stopped! Meanwhile he was not alone in his inactivity because the signalman at Winsford station was acting in a very wayward manner. It would appear that he was more preoccupied with getting his supper ready than protecting the trains, and he assumed the express had gone past whilst he had been at his stove. At 12.14am the Junction signalman rang him to find why he had not sent 'train out of section', to which the man in the Station 'box replied that he had missed its tail lamp. The first signalman assumed that his colleague was therefore 'holding the block' as the rules required, until he got clearance from Minshull Vernon the next 'box ahead. However, when it hadn't arrived there at 12.16am the signalman there rang up Winsford station and asked if the express was doing all right, to which he received the reply 'Yes'. He decided not to take any chances as the train was a long time in the section, so he put the Minshull Vernon signals at danger and brought a down post office train to a stop. It was a pity that the man at Winsford station was not as diligent, for he cleared back to Winsford Junction even though his section was far from clear. Accordingly, when the Junction offered him the late running No. 6251 *City of Nottingham on* the up Glasgow postal, he accepted it without hesitation. Two railwaymen and an ex-railwayman therefore contributed to that first major disaster on British Railways, and it cost the lives of 24 people.

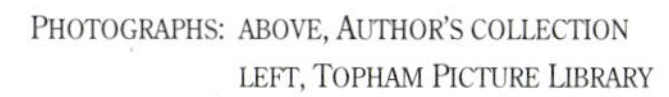

PHOTOGRAPHS: ABOVE, AUTHOR'S COLLECTION
LEFT, TOPHAM PICTURE LIBRARY

NEW SOUTHGATE

British Railways, Eastern Region 17th July 1948

If the London Midland Region was experiencing problems with its main line to Scotland, the very same difficulties were being mirrored on the ECML. Much of this centred around worn-out track which was right on the very borderline of safety, although few people would have admitted as much. Yet, as one ex-manager wrote to me 'the railway north of King's Cross was in an atrocious condition, with the badly-worn track being subject to a 60 mph speed limit.' The heavy wartime traffic and shortages of materials which had been evidenced since 1939 were continuing to plague the railways. Potters Bar was a classic example, because the station layout had long called out for remodelling and this work had been deferred as a result of the hostilities. However, it was in ordinary renewal work where the greatest problems were being noted. As reader John Aylard comments, 'A series of derailments at Marshmoor, Hatfield and New Southgate all testified to the poor conditions, but the issues of poor maintenance were clouded by the recall of the V2s to Doncaster Works for pony truck modifications as it was concluded that therein stood the cause of the frequent derailments.' However, the official report into the accident at New Southgate identified the real fault following the derailment there on 17th July 1948.

The accident occurred at 6am in the morning as the 7.50pm up express from Edinburgh was nearing the end of its long journey with a heavily loaded train of 11 coaches. The train was hauled by A2/1 Class 4-6-2 No.60508 *Duke of Rothesay* and it was running at a speed of about 70 mph. Whilst it was entitled to travel at this speed, we may well ask why the wartime limit of 60mph had been relaxed when so much of the track was badly in need of renewal. Arrears of track maintenance at this time were still continuing and only 35% of the track south of Hatfield was up to prewar standards. Chronic shortages of materials were compounded by a similar shortage of permanent way men, and the railways were having major difficulties in recruiting gangers. As a consequence there were serious track defects at New Southgate which presented a series of cross-level irregularities, and these combined to make the A2 roll as it entered the section at speed. Sadly the engine was unable to sustain this rolling as it had a weakened leading bogie spring (a common fault in the A2s in the postwar era), and after having the bogie completely derailed on a crossing near Barnet tunnel it finally turned over on to its right-hand side. Incredibly, quite unlike its Southern Railway counterpart at Sevenoaks, the A2 somehow missed becoming entangled with the piers of an over-line road bride. As it lay on its side, the engine slid along for about 100 yards passing between the piers of a 3-arch bridge. The official report notes that the fireman was killed in the accident, and this was recorded in Volume 3 of the original series; however several readers subsequently wrote in to correct this 'error' observing that it was the driver who was killed, a view also reported in one of the national daily newspapers of the day. On subsequent investigation all the official documentation notes the fatality as being the fireman, so we must take this as being our view. Whatever the case, later that same day, two more footplatemen were killed when an accident occurred to the West Coast Postal at Ardler Junction, after it collided with an 0-4-4T working a Dundee - Blairgowrie at 5.08pm.

PHOTOGRAPH; BBC HULTON PICTURE LIBRARY.

HARTHOPE VIADUCT, BEATTOCK

British Railways, Scottish Region 8th June 1950

One of the most intriguing railway disasters which I have ever examined was that which took place on the approach to Beattock Summit on 9th June 1950, for the events which happened in the few minutes before a blazing express train came to a halt at Harthope must ever remain a mystery. The story was told in depth in the May/June 1995 issues of *Steam World*, which was the culmination of four years investigation into one particular accident. The fire broke out on board the eleven-coach express, which had left Birmingham at 11am for Glasgow Central train, and it appears to have started in the second coach, No. 4851, a three year-old Corridor Composite Third built for the LMS at Wolverton. The cause was attributed to a carelessly discarded match or cigarette-end being dropped in the sixth compartment shortly before the train arrived in Carlisle, and then rolled into or under the seat. The doors of the compartment were closed some time afterwards and because the fire was starved of oxygen, slow-combustion began. Intensely hot gases then built-up inside the compartment, and though a few passengers thought they could smell smoke, it was put down as coming from the engine. Thus the fire went undetected until an explosion blew out the corridor-side window of the compartment, and was followed by a fire-ball which swept through the coach, claiming the lives of five passengers. Just one person managed to escape from the coach, and this was only because they were in the toilet at the time of the explosion. The train was brought to a halt on Harthope Viaduct, and the actions of all the railwaymen are to be highly commended, particularly those of Ganger Adam Moffat. It was he who entered the blazing coach to rescue the solitary survivor, and then went back inside to see if he could help anyone else - for this heroic deed, he was later awarded the British Empire Medal. The mystery of this accident concerns the inexplicable movements of those who died in this coach just prior to the explosion; furthermore, amongst the victims was a male passenger who's presence was not seen in the train before the fire broke out; and what part did several thousand pound's worth of missing jewellery have to play? That element was recorded in the press and it was notified to the Dumfries-shire police, but it was then handed over to the Lanarkshire force and thereafter all records of the investigation go cold.

PHOTOGRAPH; POPPERPHOTO LIBRARY

Fire has long been associated with railway disasters, but in reality, it is nearly always the result of an accident rather than a cause. There are a small number of incidents, however, where a fire has broken out in a moving train, Probably the worst example of such a disaster was near Westborough in 1941, when a coach was consumed by fire, claiming the lives of six schoolboys and injuring a number of others. In 1949, at Penmanshiel Tunnel north of Berwick, fire spread through a train with unbelievable speed because a nitrocellulose lacquer had been used to varnish the interior. Fortunately, though the train had actually stopped inside the tunnel, the coach in question was at the rear end and thereby had not actually entered it. If the train had progressed just a few more yards, there would probably have been a greater number of fatalities. It was the report of this accident that the late-Kenneth Hoole was reading as he travelled down the ECML when he smelt smoke coming down the train. Having discovered that the corridor connection between the first and second coaches was well alight, he pulled the communication cord and the A2 No.60503 *Lord President* screeched to a halt. The fire was duly extinguished by railway personnel, but as the picture shows the fire brigade were called out to check that everything was alright for the express to continue.

PHOTOGRAPH: THE LATE KENNETH HOOLE COLLECTION

PENMAENMAWR

British Railways; London Midland Region 27th August 1950

Just a few weeks after the Harthope Viaduct added its name to the list of railway locations which have witnessed more than one accident, so too did the tiny Welsh resort of Penmaenmawr. The first accident has already been discussed on page 35, and this second incident came 51 years later on the dark night of 27th August 1950. However, whilst that first accident was a shear freak of nature, what led up to the Irish Mail colliding with an engine and guards van could have been much more readily prevented but it still resulted in the death of five passengers. The light engine, Class 6P5F 2-6-0 No. 42885, had arrived at Penmaenmawr on the down line and was booked to work a goods train from the up sidings nine minutes before the arrival of the express. It had therefore crossed over to the up line, but due to a misunderstanding between the driver and the signalman, the engine sat on the main line for a good six minutes. As the driver had failed to carry out Rule 55, the signalman was blissfully unaware of the fact that the engine was not in the sidings and he therefore set the starter signal for the express. Meanwhile the light engine's driver, puzzled by the clearance of the signal, assumed he had been sent to Penmaenmawr by mistake and took it as a signal for him to return to the shed at Llandudno Junction. When he eventually began to move, he was running in a facing direction on the up line, just minutes ahead of the express. On hearing the sound of an approaching engine the alert goods guard showed a red lamp to the signalman, who in turn promptly dropped the home signal. However, the 16-coach express was fairly racing along behind No.46119 *Lancashire Fusilier* which was running at a speed of somewhere between 60 and 70 miles per hour.

Though the express driver promptly applied his brakes, the train was still doing around 45mph when it hit the the slow moving train, half demolishing its tender. The force of the impact was substantial, but other than the damage to its tender the light engine escaped serious harm even though it was driven back for a distance of 240 yards. The 83-ton Royal Scot was badly damaged in the collision, and the first two coaches telescoped into each other. The impetus of the train caused the next five coaches to derail and then scatter in a zig-zag fashion across the tracks, with the fifth and sixth vehicles being thrown on to their sides. The damage was severe, and with the sleeping car being almost completely demolished, it is little surprise that the attendant within was killed outright. Even so the drama had not ended, for an approaching down freight was racing towards the scene, and a double collision of the magnitude to Quintinshill seemed inevitable. However, this catastrophic event was prevented by the badly injured fireman of No.46119 who limped forward with his lamp and detonators. By his devotion to duty, the freight train was brought to a halt just feet from the scene of the collision. An interesting facet of the accident report is the fact that No.42885 is described as a 2-5-0!

PHOTOGRAPH: TOPHAM PICTURE LIBRARY

DRUMBURGH MOSS

British Railways, London Midland Region 23rd October 1950

Having already mentioned how bad the effects of continually deferred maintenance were on main lines in the post-World War period, we can only guess how poor the track renewal programme was in connection with secondary branch lines. Unfortunately, we have a quite graphic illustration with the accident of 23rd October 1950, which occurred on the former North British Railway branch from Drumburgh Junction to Silloth. The line which runs out to the small port on the Solway Coast is, with the exception of a few mole hills, as smooth as a billiard table. But it had seen track renewal repeatedly deferred over the years and this had led to a substantial decline, despite the fact that this was a very busy single-track branch to a busy docks and seaside holiday destination. Continual penny-pinching had left it in a very dangerous state, and it should have been completely renewed in 1928, but that was repeatedly put back in the 1930s, and then came a complete embargo on repair work during World War Two. Yet, through this period Silloth was classed as a safe port and millions of tons of trans-Atlantic goods, including large quantities of munitions, were landed at the docks. No renewal work was carried out after 1945, even though the traffic levels continued at very high levels. Silloth was a Class C line, which British Railways inherited from the LNER in January 1948, and six months later transferred to the London Midland Region as part of regional rationalisation. Coupled with this rationalisation came large staff transfers, regrading, and new appointments. Meanwhile, old traditional methods of track inspection were changed and P.W. gangs became smaller. From Drumburgh Junction to Silloth a gang of just 11 men (Ganger, sub-ganger, two patrolmen and seven others) now cared for the track, a drop of five personnel on prewar totals. Admittedly the gang was now provided with a motor trolley, which saved some considerable walking time, but one of the staff losses had been a patrolman, so the remaining two each had to cover a section almost 7 miles long. The ganger had been on the line since 1932, but only a few of the others had any long-term experience of it. This change of staff and maintenance procedure was a major element of the 1950 disaster! This, coupled with the deferred 1926-9 maintenance programme meant that by 1950 most of the track was rather superannuated. Whilst some lengths of 92lb rail had been laid west of Drumburgh, there were very long sections formed of 30' NBR rails - unfortunately the continual wear and tear had reduced their weight by an average of 10lbs per yard. The rail fittings were generally in good order, but the rails did not sit properly in the chairs and gaps were evident between the foot of the rail and the seat of the chair. The old ash ballast was dirty and deficient in the boxing and numerous voids were appearing below the sleepers as a result. The affect on the running of locomotives was quite noticeable, and coupled with cross-level irregularities, at certain locations, this had two effects; the first was nosing, where the engine would dip up and down as it crossed rail joints, further pumping the sleepers and increasing the size of the voids; the other affect was rolling, which became quite pronounced as the trains travelled at speeds above 40mph.

An official inspection of the line by the District Permanent Way Inspector on 22nd September 1950 awarded the line 850 marks out of a possible 1,000 which, for a 'C' class line, was 'very good'. From this it might be assumed that there was no need for renewals or a speed restriction, but at a meeting of the Local Staff District Council on 15th October, the Shed Master at Carlisle Canal MPD received a formal complaint about the branch. This was confirmed in writing by the ASLEF secretary three days later, who stated 'the question of the Permanent Way between Kirkbride and Abbey Town be raised with the Engineer's Department, the enginemen being of the opinion that the condition of the permanent way was not satisfactory for the running of freight and passenger trains.' No speed restriction was imposed however and, as it was, the letter was not passed on to the Divisional Motive Power Superintendent **until two days after the accident**. It was an ex-LNER class J39 0-6-0 No.64880 which came off, and it had done so whilst running with a normal four coach train at a speed of about 45mph. Though the speed limit on the branch was 60mph, later examination showed the permanent way was not fit to be worked at anything near that. As we have already seen, the drivers at Canal Shed had frequently experienced a rolling sensation with heavier engines, particularly the J39s. To safeguard themselves, it seems as though they had imposed their own speed limit of 45 mph. and it is significant that the train involved was going at that speed when it derailed on to its side and buried itself in the peat moss. The Inspector concluded that the accident had been caused entirely due to the result of a heavy engine being run over light and inadequately maintained track at too high a speed, though he attached no blame to the crew for this. The rails were clearly overdue for renewal but the work had been repeatedly postponed for lack of materials, but no speed restriction had been applied as a consequence. This was therefore entirely due to the mismanagement of the branch by the permanent way department, who were appropriately censured.

PHOTOGRAPHS: CUMBERLAND NEWSPAPERS GROUP.

DONCASTER

British Railways, Eastern Region 16th March 1950

It is yet another case of track failure which we must next discuss, although this one can not be directly attributed to wartime deferrals as the line in question had been completely renewed in January 1940. The fact that such work was carried out at all will indicate that the line was an extremely busy one, and had to be kept up to high standards whatever the cost. The location was the ECML just south of Doncaster station and only a few hundred yards from the scene of the 1947 disaster. Indeed, one of the signal boxes discussed in that accident, Bridge Junction, features heavily in the report into the terrible events of 16th March 1951. About 10.09am A2 class 4-6-2 No.501 *Cock o' the North* was derailed as it ran through a scissors crossover immediately next to Balby Road bridge. The engine, rebuilt Class P2 2-8-2, managed to keep upright as it pulled the first two vehicles on to the opposite side of the bridge. but the next eight came off the track and sustained considerable damage. The worst affected was the third coach where the bogies took two different directions, resulting in the vehicle being carried broadside into the substantial brick pier supporting Balby Road bridge. As a result the underframe wrapped itself around the pier and bent into a 'U' shape, with the body being completely wrecked. As may be expected the loss of life in this coach was very heavy, and it accounted for 14 fatalities and 12 serious injuries.

A rigorous investigation into the accident was undertaken to discover why this derailment had taken place, but no fault whatsoever could be found with the engine. Since its complete rebuild in 1943 the A2 had been well maintained, including a heavy repair the month prior to the accident. In the intervening time the engine had only run 3,000 miles and it was no worse than new. Attention had therefore to be centred on the track, particularly the crossing. On close examination it was found that the bolts holding the crossing rails together had become seriously fatigued and this automatically pointed at the cause of the accident being the collapse of the crossing as the engine went through. In fact, the speed of the engine appears to have been between 20 and 25 mph as it did this, despite the fact that a 10 mph limit had been imposed on this crossing. This excessive speed must have placed an even greater strain on the fastenings than they were able to bear, and they failed as a consequence. This did not auger well for the railways, and similar bolts were withdrawn from other crossings and sent to research department at Derby for analysis, Of the bolts examined, all were found to be badly corroded, and a third were found to cracked at the root of the thread. Others which had been sent for analysis after they had failed in service were all found to have fatigue flaws at the point of fracture, which again seemed to be at the root of the thread. From this it was clear how the derailment began, for some (if

not all) of the left hand wheels had begun to mount the rail just beyond the trailing end of the check rail. Whilst the speed of the engine undoubtedly contributed to the failure, the bolts were so seriously weakened by flaws that they might have broken at any time under normal traffic. Interestingly, despite the seriousness of the accident and the strict warnings about observing the speed limit, the *Railway Gazette* records; 'Timings and actual observations confirmed that drivers were not complying with the speed restriction. It is surprising that so shortly after such a serious accident trains were found to be travelling twice as fast as was permitted.' In discussing Doncaster, we might bear in mind that the state of the track on the ECML was far from adequate for the traffic which it was carrying. What's more, this is a situation which was sadly reflected throughout the country, following the severe abuse which the under-funded railways had been subjected to during the war years. At this point of time, it may seem hard to comprehend that for many years after the declaration of peace in 1945, a combination of deferred maintenance and shortages of materials that had resulted from World War Two presented a dangerous situation on many of the country's railway lines.

PHOTOGRAPHS: KEYSTONE PICTURE LIBRARY

FORD

British Railways, Southern Region, 5th August 1951

A further serious accident occurred on the Southern Region on 5th August 1951, when an EMU over-ran signals and collided with another train which was being shunted due to insufficient platform space. This disaster took place at Ford station in Sussex and claimed the lives of eight passengers and a motorman, in what was an easily avoided and most tragic collision. The station at Ford could easily accommodate the 4- and 6-coach EMUs which normally worked the stopping trains, but in the height of summer 8-coach sets ran regularly at weekends and on some weekdays. At 11.52am a Three Bridges - Bognor train arrived at the station two minutes late, where it was booked to wait five minutes to allow an 8-car Brighton - Portsmouth train to pass. This Sunday the Bognor train was also an 8-car affair, and thus too long for the loop platform so the signalman had to shunt it. However, as he had already accepted the other EMU into his section, he had to set his two home signals at danger. Though this would have delayed the Portsmouth train for a few minutes whilst the shunt was completed, it was a perfectly safe manoeuvre. Regretfully the motorman of the incoming train overran both outer and inner home signals, and ploughed into the back of the Bognor train. This is one of the many cases where an accident happened because someone saw (or thought they saw) what they expected to see. In this instance the motorman of the Portsmouth train would have expected the Bognor train to be safely in the loop and, as he was most probably under that impression he had clear signals, he drove his train into the station at about 25mph. As will be appreciated the 1937 stock, which made up both trains, did not stand up well to the resulting impact. The trailing coach of the Bognor train and the leading coach of the Portsmouth train telescoped into each other, causing the fatalities and 47 serious injuries. Fortunately police, fire, and ambulance services were on the scene inside ten minutes, along with doctors and nurses. Valuable assistance was also rendered by personnel from the nearby Royal Naval Air Station, including a number of men with special rescue equipment.

PHOTOGRAPH; TOPHAM PICTURE LIBRARY

NEWCASTLE

British Railways, North Eastern Region 17th August 1951

Twelve days after the accident at Ford, another collision took place between two EMUs, but this time we move well away from the Southern Region and visit the scene of the accident at the edge of Newcastle Central station. Whilst the electrical multiple unit operations of the Southern are well documented, few may realise how extensive electric services were to other provincial cities. We have already mentioned the early electrification of the coastal route north of Liverpool, and we have twice visited the Tyneside electric system in connection with the accidents at Manors. This system was introduced in the period 1904-9, with a circular service out to the Northumbrian coastal towns of Whitley Bay and North Shields instituted from 1917 onwards. A disastrous fire wiped out the Walker Gate car sheds in 1918, but by 1922 things were back to normal, however in 1967 the system was abandoned in favour of diesel multiple units. Unlike the fine dry weather in Sussex, it was raining cats and dogs around Tyneside on the Friday of the 1951 accident. Whether this had anything to do with the events which followed was never determined, but the British Railways internal report intimated it may have done. Whatever, an outgoing EMU set away from the station against the signals and collided head-on with an incoming train killing its motorman and two passengers as a consequence.

PHOTOGRAPH: THE LATE KENNETH HOOLE COLLECTION

WEEDON

British Railways, London Midland Region 21st September 1951

There is a saying that lightening never strikes the same place twice, but as we have already seen that statement is not true of railway accidents. In the incident of 21st September 1951 we have clear evidence of this, in that Weedon was the scene of an earlier derailment caused by inadequate maintenance, and what is more, the engine involved was one of the two Duchess class 4-6-2s that were participants in the first ever British Railways accident. At Winsford in 1948, still bearing its LMS number 6207, *Princess Arthur of Connaught* had been the innocent victim of a rear-end collision; it had escaped unscathed, other than a few small flats on its wheels which were occasioned when it was driven forward by sister engine *City of Nottingham.* It was quickly returned to service, and over the next three and a half years it ran many miles. On 20th September the engine was stopped for the routine 'X' examination which took place once a fortnight at its depot, Edge Hill, Liverpool. As the fitter went round the engine he noticed the leading left-hand bogie wheel was wearing sharp, so the axles and axle-boxes were swopped round and the front pair of wheels changed places with the ones behind it. Unfortunately when the rear axle was moved into the front position, the fit was far too tight to allow the wheels to rise and fall as normal under the springs and thereby made it difficult to follow any undulations in the track. With such a stiff axle as this, it is most surprising that the engine managed to get as far as it did when it re-entered service the following day. Tragically as it charged south with 8.20am Liverpool - Euston the defective axle decided enough was enough and it caused the train to derail - doing so on the very section of track where another fitter's error had caused a catastrophe 36 years previously.

As the 15-coach express approached Weedon it was about 11.15am, and the crew were fairly rattling along at 60 mph to make up a deficit of 15 minutes. As they went through the station the leading bogie wheels bounced up over the rails and were derailed to the right-hand side, this had no immediate effect and the train ran on for some distance without anyone realising that anything was amiss. However, having emerged from the southern portal of Stowe Hill Tunnel, the flat bottomed track gave way to the older bull-head type which was then awaiting replacement; and, as the derailed front axle encountered the cast-iron chairs it began to smash them systematically as it went along. Denied their fastenings the rails were unable to withstand the tractive effort of the driving wheels, and the permanent way began to collapse. The engine ran off to the left and plunged down a 12 foot high embankment before coming to rest in the soft ground below. The driver was buried under coal which cascaded out of the tender, but he was freed without suffering serious injury. Unfortunately the passengers in the train did not escape so lightly, as the train adopted the now familiar zig-zag pattern across the tracks. Seven people were killed, but the death toll would have been considerably higher if the signalman at Heyford had not put his signals against the down Royal Scot after hearing the sound of the accident; despite the fact that it was a good half a mile away. The engine was not badly damaged, thanks to the Pacific's soft landing in the boggy ground. However whilst that circumstance prevented serious injury, it also presented quite a major obstacle for the recovery crews who had to devise a most complicated arrangement for No.46207's extrication. A set of rails were laid down to the site where it lay, and two weeks after the disaster the engine was back on its wheels and bound for repair.

PHOTOGRAPHS: BRITISH RAILWAYS LONDON MIDLAND REGION

BLEA MOOR

British Railways, London Midland Region 18th April 1952

The problems of maintenance continued on BR during the autumn of 1951 and several minor accidents occurred due to failures in picking up mechanical defects during routine inspections and, of these accidents, that which occurred at Cowlairs Incline is most notable. On 14th November a light engine had got out of control on the incline due to a defective vacuum brake and it then collided with an ECS train being manoeuvred into the entrance of Glasgow's Queen Street station; seven railwaymen were injured, but thankfully no lives were lost. It was another Glasgow train that was involved in our next accident, which took place at Blea Moor on 18th April 1952. At 9.15am the up Thames-Clyde express left Glasgow (this time St. Enoch's) for St. Pancras and rolled south over former G&SWR metals to Carlisle where the train was prepared for its trip to Leeds. As it had been in 1910 and 1913, the practice of using pilot engines over Ais Gill was still as strong as ever. Assigned to assist train engine No.46117 *Welsh Guardsman* was an old Class 4P compound No.41040. It was a sister engine to that wrecked twice at Little Salkeld, but as the 4P rolled down the Eden Valley that spring morning nothing seemed wrong. Unfortunately, ignorance is bliss, for there was a rapidly developing problem beneath the engine's tender where the pin holding the front end of the right hand brake road was about to fall out.

The engine, like No. 46207 at Weedon, had undergone an 'X' examination the previous day, this time at Holbeck MPD in Leeds. Unfortunately, the round pin holding the brake gear was in a visibly distressed state, but this was not observed by the fitters. This round pin was held in place by a split-pin, but also like the engine involved in the earlier Weedon disaster, this pin was about to fail. Quite where it went we will never know, but many weeks later a broken split-pin was found between Long Meg Sidings and Long Meg Cutting and, if this was the one from No.40140, history had a very funny way of repeating itself when it chose the location around Little Salkeld to fail. Somewhere on the approach to Blea Moor the assembly failed and the leading end of the brake-rod fell to the ground and bounced merrily along as the train ran down toward the next set of points. These were the facing points leading to the up goods loop, and when the rod caught on the locking stretcher bar, it forced them open right in front of the bogie wheels of No.46117. As they were travelling at a fare rate of speed, the crew stood no chance, and without seeing anything had happened, they were derailed violently to the left. The Royal Scot slid on its left-hand side and buried itself in the ballast, whilst its train was brought up violently against the tender. In the now familiar fashion associated with rapid deceleration, the coaches zig-zagged across the tracks, some turning over on to their sides. In view of the devastation, it is remarkable to report that no passengers were killed in the crash, although 34 were injured. Prominent among those who helped in the rescue were Mr. J. B. Pearson, a director of breakdown crane manufacturers Cowans, Sheldon & Co. who was travelling in the train, the Dawson family who lived nearby, and a doctor who was holidaying in this part of the Yorkshire Dales.

PHOTOGRAPH: ABOVE AND RIGHT, AUTHOR'S COLLECTION
CENTRE: KEYSTONE PICTURE LIBRARY

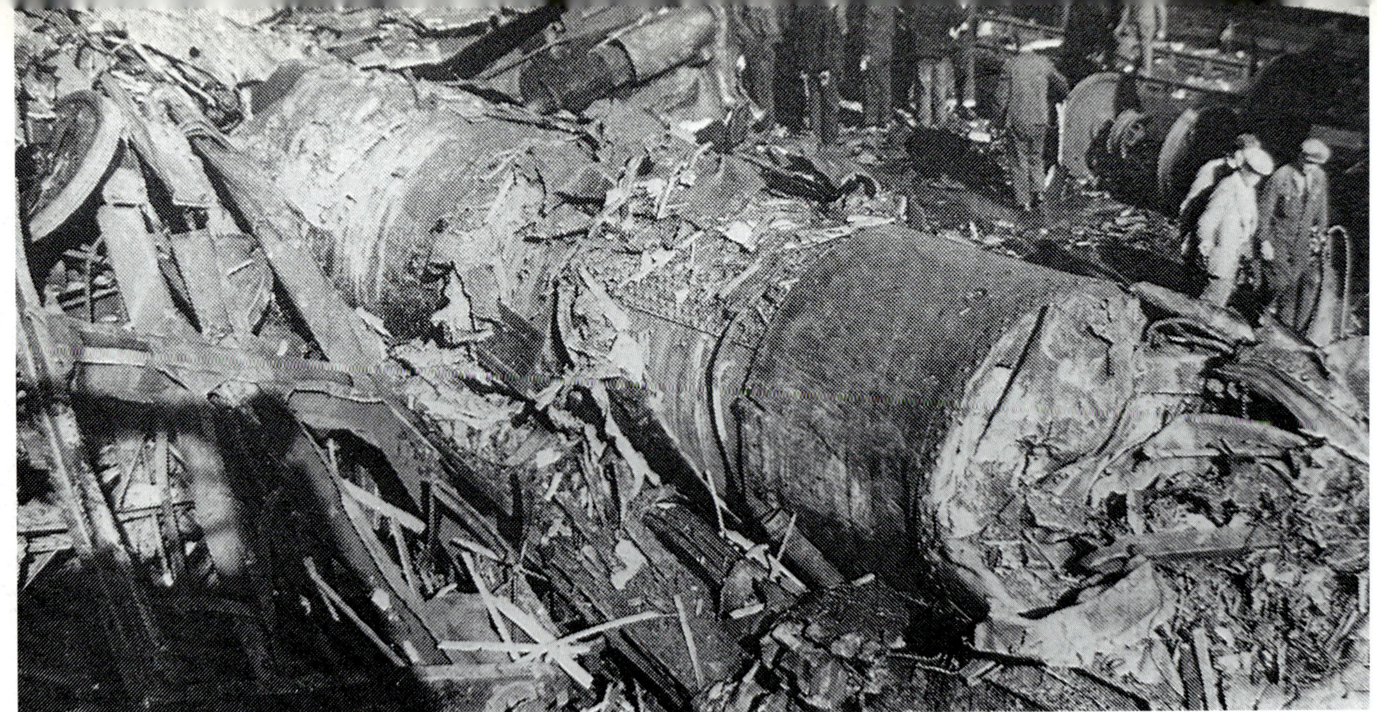

HARROW & WEALDSTONE

British Railways, London Midland Region 8th October 1952

It was without a shadow of a doubt the worst peace-time railway accident Britain has ever seen, and it came second only in magnitude to the awful events at Quintinshill in May 1915. It was also only the second time in the history of the railways that an accident in this country had claimed so many victims that the casualty list ran to three figures. It was, of course, Harrow & Wealdstone where 112 people died in an accident which would probably have been prevented if ATC/AWS systems had been in place. I was exactly two months old the day it happened, so my personal recollection of the events are nowhere near as comprehensive as those who have written about the event before me. But with the benefit of an unprejudiced viewpoint and an exhausting amount of research, I have been able to take a completely fresh look at the events. This was further aided by the screening of a Channel Four documentary in the series 'Rescue' which covered the topic extensively by showing hitherto unseen 'Movietone' news film of the event. The inescapable fact which emerges from this, is that Harrow & Wealdstone was a complete shambles. For years people had said it would happen, sooner or later, and it would happen on a line where ATC was not installed. Accidents like Charfield, Wembley Central, Ecclefechan and Bourne End had prefaced it, but the LMS had placed its faith in the 'indirect approach' to safety at signals and refused to adopt the GWR system. The same mentality had prevailed subsequent to nationalisation, even though the case for providing ATC was no less strong after 1948 than it had been when Colonel Pringle's report was published in 1930. This remains a matter of fact which can be confirmed by a review of those accidents which occurred between 1930 and 1960 when drivers overran signals set at Caution or Stop. By the end of World War Two it was already late in the day, but after Ecclefechan and Bourne End the Railway Inspectorate confirmed that it was desirable that ATC should be fitted to every main line in the country as soon as possible. However, no positive steps were taken towards a national system until a prototype train control system was duly devised for BR, but before tests began the colour light signals on which the LMS and (later) the London Midland Region had placed so much faith failed, on their own to prevent the terrible disaster at Harrow & Wealdstone.

So much has been written about this tragedy already that I felt it worth stressing the cause and the remedy, rather than just dwelling on the actual incident itself, but the bare bones I now relate. First of all we begin with details of the three trains involved, these being the overnight service from Perth to Euston behind No.46242 *City of Glasgow*, the northbound double-headed Euston - Liverpool behind No.45637 *Windward Island* and No. 46202 *Princess Anne,* and finally we have the 7.31am local train from Tring behind 2-6-4T No.42389. At a little after 18 minutes past 8 o'clock these were three complete trains, each in good mechanical order and each packed with passengers; then they were nothing but a pile of twisted, mangled wreckage. As the Perth express was running some 80 minutes late, it was quite in order for the signalman at Harrow to let the local train on to the up fast line in preference. Indeed such priority was given to the punctuality of suburban services at that time, so it was considerably more preferable to Control that the express should suffer the delay rather than the local. At 8.17am the local pulled into Harrow station, with 800 souls aboard it due to the fact that an earlier train had been cancelled on account of engineering work. Around the same time the signalman accepted the down Euston - Liverpool and Manchester express and he cleared his signals for it. He also accepted the Perth train but he kept his up signals on for this, preventing it from entering the station by means of his colour-light distant signal and the two semaphores behind this. Even though patches of fog were still hanging, fog-working had been suspended moments earlier, so the driver of the Perth train should have been able to see the aspects that were

showing. The local was still sitting in the platform a minute later, when out of the haze *City of Glasgow* charged into Harrow station.

There was nothing that the signalman could do to prevent the accident, and the Duchess buried itself into the back of the 11-coach local. At a speed approaching 60 mph, it is little wonder that the rear three coaches were completely wrecked, but it is surprising that even with its brakes off, the engine at its head, No.42389, was only driven forward a matter of feet. The Perth train was also badly affected, and the coaches slewed across the running lines in a similar fashion to Weedon and Blea Moor, but this time they were constrained in their deflection by the edges of the platform. Sixty-four people died in the local train, along with 23 in the sleeper, but more was yet to come. The first collision was a significant disaster in its own right, but within seconds the Liverpool train was upon the wreckage, hitting the debris with such force as to throw the leading engine on to the platform. In doing this the engine swept away 14 people waiting for an electric train, whilst seven more died in the coaches behind. The two engines, pilot No.45637 *Windward Isles* and train engine No. 46202 *Princess Anne* were utterly destroyed, and sixteen coaches were mangled in a mountain of debris which reached a height of 40 feet. Exactly when victims were claimed in this sequence of events may never be determined, but an interesting comment in the aforementioned Channel 4 documentary stated that there were casualties who perished that morning who would not have died had the accident happened today.

The rescuers being interviewed said that as this was a major operation, the policy of the emergency services were very much a 'scoop and run tactics', whereby patients would be extricated from the wreckage and whisked to the nearest hospital by ambulance. In fact it was not just ambulances that were used, as buses, private cars and even a furniture van were utilised. In this regard the rescuers admitted that not all the injured received the best treatment possible, but by contrast the first-aid that was rendered by medical teams from the American armed forces was completely different. For the first time ever in a British disaster, a system known as triage was applied, as the wounded were categorised according to the severity of their injuries, thus sorting out priority cases from the less urgent. A graphic illustration of this work was was later shown in newspapers around the world, with a press photograph of United States Air Force nurse Abbie Sweetwine, shown attending a British soldier who was badly injured in the crash. Whilst there may have been errors due to the sheer scale of the operation, rescue workers toiled without let up; a former divisional officer in the London Fire Service wrote to me saying 'few of my men took any rest in the 24 hours that followed, but it was a dispirited bunch of lads who finally stood-down back at the station at 4.30pm the following afternoon. The dramatic effect that Harrow had on us all will never be understood. We gave our all, but there was so little we could do.' There was also a profound effect upon the travelling public at large, and this incident did more for car and bus travel than any form of glossy advertising. A marked effect of how much this mentality prevailed was recently brought home to me by a family friend who visited our home whilst I was writing this book. She recalled that her mother had been due to travel by rail a few days after Harrow, but then promptly changed her plans and went by car. Even though they were involved in a motor accident on the substitute journey, the lady still vowed that it was no longer safe to go by rail.

I do not think any words could ever describe Harrow & Wealdstone, for it was quite unlike any other railway accident before or since. The circumstances may have been similar, the causes may have been similar, but no other accident would ever approach this in its effect. Even though it was second in causality figures to Quintinshill, it was more profoundly felt. First of all it was on the approach to London, not in an isolated passing loop in Scotland, and it was far more widely covered in news pictures, television and movie film. The other great factor in comparing the two accidents was that Quintinshill happened in a time of war, and most of the dead were soldiers destined for the battlefield. In those horrible, satanic days, the world had become used to death on a large scale; it was somehow different on a pleasant autumn day when people were travelling to work or on pleasure. It certainly changed many attitudes, from those like my friend's family to railway management who were finally stung into making improvements called for by the Pringle Reports two decades earlier. Harrow & Wealdstone also had another, less noticeable, effect; but it was one which, when implemented, would play a part in every major railway rescue and recovery operation that followed, for Harrow completely re-shaped BR's breakdown train policy. Just eight months later an Ad-hoc Committee was formed to determine a standard pattern for breakdown trains, recovery cranes, and the equipment used thereon. The policy was to determine a standard breakdown train (with varying categories depending on the size of the home depot), and a recommendation for a uniform list of tools, personnel and operating procedures. The idea behind this was to provide a standard arrangement where breakdown crane and recovery work was universal in its application, and thus enable several teams to work together if another accident occurred on the same scale as Harrow & Wealdstone - fortunately nothing was ever quite this bad again.

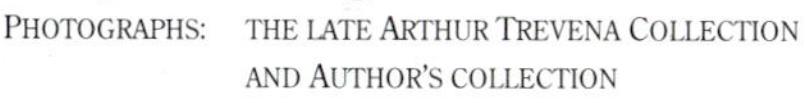
PHOTOGRAPHS: THE LATE ARTHUR TREVENA COLLECTION AND AUTHOR'S COLLECTION

STRATFORD

London Passenger Transport Board 8th April 1953

Thus far we have confined our discussion of British railway accidents to surface railways, strictly avoiding the subterranean lines which run in cities like London, Glasgow and (nowadays) many other locations. There has, for many years, been something of a taboo about discussing underground accidents and (to a lesser extent) those which take place in any tunnel, presumably for two very good reasons. First of all the sheer horror of an accident which takes place in a very confined space defies description, and secondly the opportunity to take a photographic record is considerably more limited than it is on a surface railway. The early books in the *Trains In Trouble* series steered well clear of the subject, but many readers wrote to me at Atlantic, asking why we never featured underground railways in the series. In deference to that request, and in our desire to present a progressive overview of the railway accident subject, we duly researched a couple of the more notable incidents with 'tube trains in trouble'. We begin with one of the most horrific collisions to occur on the Underground, which took place at 6.56pm on Wednesday 8th April 1953, when an east-bound train running under the 'stop and proceed' rule collided with a stationary train. The accident took place in the tunnel between Stratford and Leyton, resulting in the death of twelve people, along with four being seriously injured, and a further 41 being slightly hurt. Unfortunately, the wreckage at the front of the train was so bad that two of the victims were trapped for over seven hours and could not be released until 2.15am the next morning.
The accident happened on an extension of the Central Line to Stratford and Leytonstone which opened in 1946-7. At Stratford station the line came up to the surface, but beyond this it descended down a 1:30 gradient through a 12 feet diameter cast-iron tube. It was at a point 307 yards from the station that the accident occurred, as train No.59 ran into the back of train No.71 at a speed of 20 mph. The Inspector concluded that the driver of train No.59 had failed to exercise the caution which was explicitly required when applying the 'stop and proceed' rule. The driver claimed that he actually failed to see the tail lights of the stationary train due to a cloud of dust, but the enquiry dismissed this as being unlikely. However, the workings of the Underground were also to come into question, particularly the application of rule 55g. It was also clear that some very irregular instructions were being given to the drivers and some of these were in turn acting irregularly upon them. Additional confusion was being introduced, because Railway Executive staff working as controllers, did not fully know or understand the special rules of the London Transport Executive. Further questions were raised in the efficiency of detraining up to 1,000 from the two trains after the accident, and the delay that resulted was also severely criticised. The rear coach of train No.71 and the two leading coaches of No.59 were so badly damaged that it resulted in the tunnel being blocked for two days. Remarkably the driver of No.59 escaped from the accident with only serious injuries, when his cab had completely disintegrated.

Not all tube accidents were serious however, and by way of contrast our lower picture shows one which took place two years later at Aldersgate on the Metropolitan Line. Again it was a derailment on a set of points, but as the picture shows there were a number of impediments to hit the vehicle when it came off the rails. In actual fact the accident happened at 7am on 24th January 1955 (the day after the Sutton Coldfield disaster). However, on this occasion the train only had a few passengers, but many were reading the headline of the previous day's events in the Midlands. If this incident had occurred just half an hour later, there would have been many more people injured than the two passengers who filled in accident forms. Just two coaches of the set were derailed, but quite a length of track was torn up, completely blocking the line.
PHOTOGRAPHS: ALL ATLANTIC COLLECTION

MANCHESTER, IRK VALLEY VIADUCT

British Railways, London Midland Region 15th August 1953

In talking about the suburban electric services of Tyneside, Liverpool and London, we might as well mention those which served Manchester, as these were also the scene of a serious accident in the 1950s. One of the busiest lines in the North of England was the eastern approach to Manchester Victoria, where lines from Bury, Yorkshire, Oldham and Stalybridge merged. One of these lines, the Bury route was so busy that a new loop had to be opened in 1904 to take passenger trains into the suburban bays on the south side of Victoria Station. Known as the Collyhurst Loop, it diverged from the 1879 Prestwich/Bury railway at Queens Road and climbed over the Cheetham Hill line which was used predominantly by the Yorkshire trains, before diving under the Miles Platting Incline. There was a connecting spur from the Collyhurst Loop on to the Yorkshire line, allowing suburban trains from Manchester to reach places like Middleton and Heywood and yet avoid the Miles Platting Incline. The direct line to Bury was significantly improved by the introduction of a third-rail 1,200v dc electrified service which employed rather attractive EMUs. It was on this electrified line that the serious Irk Valley accident took place on 15th August 1953.

The junction for the spur between the Collyhurst Loop and the Yorkshire lines was situated on a viaduct above the River Irk, and it was towards this junction that the 7.10am electric train from Bury Bolton Street was carrying around 100 passengers early that Saturday morning. Most of the people were on their way to work, but a few were making their way to Victoria to catch an early train for their annual holidays. The second train to play a part in the affairs was the 7.44am to Bacup (via Bury Knowsley Street), which was to depart from Victoria behind Stanier 2-6-4T No.42474. It would leave Manchester via the Collyhurst loop, then drop on to the Yorkshire line by the Irk Valley Spur. At 7.40am the electric train from Bury approached Irk Valley distant signals at caution, which should have indicated to the driver that the junction signals could have been at danger. However, for some reason this failed to register with the driver (who is reported as being a very experienced man), probably because he was used to always getting a clear road through the junction. He ran through the junction at the usual speed of 35 mph, then collided with the Bacup train which was just going over the diamond crossing at a speed of around 15mph. The ex-L&YR electric motor car struck the Stanier 2-6-4T and overturned it, then hit the leading coach of the steam train which was derailed, before it cannoned into the second coach. The leading car of the EMU then bounced off to the right, smashed through the parapet of the viaduct and plunged into the River Irk below. The motorman lost his life because of his momentary lapse, but he took with him 9 others and injured 58 more. Rescuers were quickly on the scene, rendering assistance to the survivors on the viaduct, whilst others dived into the murky waters of the Irk in the vain hope of finding people alive.

PHOTOGRAPH; ABOVE, ATLANTIC COLLECTION
RIGHT, MIKE BLAKEMORE COLLECTION

KINGSBURY
British Railways, London Midland Region 16th August 1953

In a number of accidents discussed in this book, we have seen the tragic consequences when derailed trains plunged down embankments and suffered serious damage as a result. However, the accident that happened at Kingsbury on 16th August 1953 was fortunate in the fact that the coaches were saved from serious injury by the nature of the railway's formation, as they were prevented from completely over-turning by the steep sides of a 25 feet deep cutting. The train involved was the 9.28am Bradford - Bristol express, which was carrying 456 passengers when it came to an abrupt halt at Kingsbury around 1.20pm. Having left Tamworth, it was travelling at about 55 mph, well below the permitted speed limit of 75 mph, when it suddenly broke in half. The engine and two coaches ran away for 116 yards before turning over, but the seven remaining coaches were also derailed. Fortunately they turned over to the left and came to rest on the side of the cutting, and our picture shows them propped against the banking. The driver and fireman managed to jump clear, and despite heavy landings they both busied themselves in their duties to protect the train and managed to stop the oncoming traffic. The guard and ticket collector went to the assistance of the passengers, but only a few were found to be suffering from shock and none were badly injured. Evacuation of the passengers and their luggage was handled to by two officers and 23 men from the 18th Parachute Battalion (TA) who had been travelling on the train at the time. It turned out to be a text book operation, and disaster was duly averted by the prompt action of those involved. The investigation found that the division and subsequent derailment had occurred because the train engine, 4-6-0 Jubilee Class No.45699 *Galatea* had distorted the track by behaving in an unusual manner known technically as hunting. Briefly described this is a combination of transverse oscillation of an engine on the track about a vertical axis (nosing), and a transverse oscillation of an engine on its springs, about a longitudinal line (rolling). Such an instance had occurred due to three distinct factors: 1. a broken bogie spring on the locomotive; 2. lateral play between the wheels and the frame of the tender, and; 3. wear and cross-level irregularities in the track. None of these were serious in themselves, but combined they presented a lethal combination and it is extremely fortunate that the consequences were so light indeed.

PHOTOGRAPH; KEYSTONE PICTURE LIBRARY

WATFORD JUNCTION
British Railways, London Midland Region 3rd February 1954

The accident which occurred at Watford Junction station on 3rd February 1954, is of extreme interest because of its technical considerations rather than the seriousness of the event. Fortunately, despite the severity of the crash no-one was killed or badly hurt and only 15 people suffered minor injuries or shock, though it could have been much worse. As the 10am 'Royal Scot' from Glasgow, headed by 8P class 4-6-0 No. 42650 *City of Lichfield* passed through Watford Tunnel, a rail broke as the 10-coach train passed over it. The trailing wheels of the ninth coach were derailed, and this was noticed by a passenger who pulled the communication cord. However, the train failed to stop, and the engine did not come to a rest until 1 mile 1,604 yards further on.

On reaching the point-work at Watford Junction station, the rear part of the train broke free, and the trailing bogie of the eighth coach was pulled away. The ninth and tenth coach became completely derailed, and grazed the sides of the second to fifth coaches in the 4.37pm Euston - Wolverhampton which was passing through the station on the down fast line. At first examination, it would seem that the permanent way staff had been negligent in allowing the track to deteriorate to a point where it was unsafe, and then that the driver and guard were at fault for allowing the train to run on for almost two miles after the initial derailment. Yet, the 25-page report into this accident did not reach that conclusion, although it did make a few minor observations in those directions. It would appear that the rail failure was due to a combination of design problems, both in locomotives and the permanent way. Whilst in simulated tests after the accident, it was discovered how difficult it was to notice the 'gradual' brake application of the communication cord on a falling gradient.

PHOTOGRAPH; OPPOSITE PAGE TOP ATLANTIC COLLECTION

PLUMPTON

British Railways, London Midland Region 8th May 1954

Being in the right place at the right time is the main ingredient for a successful railway accident picture. The press could usually do this at any time, but in view of the scale of charges that these organisations now make, they have tended to price themselves completely out of the market as far as railway publishers go. It is therefore most welcoming when readers come forward with excellent illustrations which have hitherto been unknown; this helps writers like myself to disseminate the history of railway accidents and disasters much more readily. It is even nicer when the contributor turns out to be an old friend, as was the case with Frank Alcock who was the former headmaster of Plumpton School just north of Penrith. On Saturday 8th May 1954 he had gone into work to catch up on some outstanding jobs, when news of an accident at nearby Kitchen Hill was conveyed to him by a young pupil. Frank set off with his camera and captured the scene of the derailment which involved a Class 8F 2-8-0, No.48463 and 37 mixed freight vehicles. As the train neared Plumpton the driver noticed that it had parted behind the 18th wagon, a problem which occurred due to a drawbar failure. The rear half of the train then piled up and debris littered the line with wreckage up to a height of 30 feet, blocking the WCML in both directions. Express traffic was diverted over the Settle & Carlisle line, whilst slow freight was routed via Wigton, Workington, Cockermouth and Keswick, to rejoin the WCML in Penrith.

PHOTOGRAPHS; THE LATE FRANK ALCOCK COURTESY JOHN ALCOCK

SUTTON COLDFIELD

British Railways, London Midland Region 23rd January 1955

The accident at Sutton Coldfield is one of the peculiar cases found in the annals of railway history, to the extent that it is in many ways quite a mysterious event. The train involved was the 12.15pm express from York to Bristol, drawn by a Stanier Class 5MT 4-6-0 No.45274 which was giving a rough ride to the crew as it made its way south. When it arrived at Derby it was 3.09pm, and the train was some 30 minutes late due to engineering work on the line. When the Sheffield crew gave the engine over to the Derby men, they told them that the Bristol-based engine was riding roughly, and knocking in the axle boxes. Even so, by Burton-on-Trent the time had been cut to just 17 minutes down, but more engineering work lay ahead and the train was to be diverted through Lichfield and Sutton Coldfield. This line was not usually used for express traffic, and it was normally closed on Sundays, so it was not a route which the Derby men knew sufficiently well enough to have signed the 'route card' for. Accordingly a conductor driver came on the footplate at Burton, and he was well used to taking slow freight trains and 2-6-4T tank engines across the route with local passenger trains. Complaining that an old leg injury had been aggravated by the rough-riding engine the driver decided to leave the footplate and take a rest on the 'cushions' in the coach behind the engine; this was something which he was not entitled to do even though there was a conductor-driver on board. Whether his continued presence would have affected matters or not we shall never know, but in his absence the conductor took the train on from Lichfield at a very fast speed, proceeding past Four Oaks in excess of the 40 mph limit. On his approach to Sutton Coldfield (where a 30 mph limit existed through the station), the guard realised they were going too fast and made a gentle application of the brake. It had no appreciable affect, but instead of making a longer application he obviously hoped this would 'make his driver take notice'. The line through the station was on a radius of 15 chains, and entirely unsuited to the 57 mph at which the train entered the curve. The train derailed and smashed up against the down platform, and the wreckage blocked both lines. Despite the severe experience they had just gone through the ticket collector and an off-duty fireman who were travelling in the train, realised that the down 1.20pm from Bristol to York had not yet passed them. They ran to the nearby signal box (at the time switched out), and broke open the door to set all the signals to danger. Had they not succeeded in doing so, the disaster might have approached the magnitude of Harrow and Wealdstone. Even so, of the 300 passengers on the train 17 were killed; the conductor driver and fireman also lost their lives, and a further 64 people were injured - 23 seriously so.

PHOTOGRAPHS; THOMAS MOUNSEY

WORMIT

British Railways, Scottish Region 28th May 1955

Our penultimate consideration of a Scottish accident in the steam era takes us back to the side of the Firth of Tay, on the afternoon of Saturday 28th May 1955. At this time there was still an alternate route between the south end of the Tay Bridge and Leuchars Junction, which cut across the north east corner of Fife through Wormit and St. Fort. In the days before the opening of the Tay road bridge, it was an exceptionally busy line and regularly carried through services which were not booked to call at stations on the coastal route. On the day in question, however, it was being used by two trains which were carrying groups of children to organised picnic parties at Tayport and East Newport. After arriving at their respective destinations, the trains then ran ECS to the sidings at Tayport, and some members of the crews went to join the Tayport picnic. Before returning to their trains, some of the men went off to a local pub and both guards ended up being late back. As a result of this the departure of the trains was delayed, and both were worked back running tender first. The first train made a normal journey back to Dundee, but problems were soon to face the second. The boiler of class 5MT locomotive had been overfilled before departure and as a result the engine was priming. This caused the driver to be distracted, and the presence of an unauthorised adult and child on the footplate can not have helped either. As the train descended the incline towards Wormit the speed began to rise to about 55mph as it reached the station, even though a 20 mph restriction was imposed over the facing points which lay just ahead. As the engine raced into the southern portal of Wormit Tunnel, the tender became derailed and when they emerged from the portal, both engine and tender turned over on to their left side and the coaches piled up around the wreckage. Of the 500 passengers aboard the train 40 were injured, but on the footplate the fireman and the two unauthorised passengers were killed. This accident was caused by nothing other than sheer recklessness, and was a sad blight on the good record of Scottish railwaymen in general.

PHOTOGRAPH: AUTHOR'S COLLECTION

BARBY

British Railways, Eastern Region 7th August 1955

Another accident in 1955 to occur due to excessive speed was that which took place at Barby near Rugby, when the 10.35 am train from Manchester to London rolled over as it was crossing from one line to another at a point where engineering work was under way. The weekly printed notices for the period 6th - 12th August informed drivers that a crossover between the up and down lines at Braunston & Willoughby was being used to facilitate single-line working south of that point. However, on Friday 5th August, the permanent way teams decided that points at Barby would not be affected by the work, so the section of single-line working was shortened, and the crossing to the ex-WD depot at Barby used instead. The pilot man who had joined the engine at Rugby said he told this to the driver, but the fireman claims that he never heard this said at all. In any case it is evident that the Neasden-based crew were expecting to cross-over where the weekly notices said they would, for they never slackened off their speed at all as they approached Barby. It was considered that the problems began because the train was 1 hour 26 minutes late in starting from Rugby, and apparently the driver may have been trying to make up some of the lost time. As the V2 turned into the crossover, the engine's estimated speed was 75 mph. Not surprisingly it became derailed and then rolled over on to its side and landed on the embankment, killing the driver. Seventeen passengers, the fireman and pilot-man were all injured, in what the Inspector called 'serious failure of the human element'.

PHOTOGRAPHS; HERBERT COLLECTION, COURTESY NATIONAL RAILWAY MUSEUM

MILTON, Near DIDCOT

British Railways, Western Region 20th November 1955

Sundays have traditionally been a time for railway engineering works, with the engineers taking possession of stretches of track at their quietest times to carry out vital maintenance. For the average passenger, such work meant frequent delays, slow journeys and late arrivals; however, for one group of travellers on Sunday 20th November, 1955, the consequences were far more serious. Their day had begun at 8.30am at Treherbert and, on arriving at Cardiff, Britannia Class 4-6-2 No.70026 *Polar Star* was coupled on for the journey to London. Along its route the train encountered a series of frustrating diversions and the next one of these was to be through the up goods loop at Milton, but the driver had failed to notice this restriction in the 'Weekly Notices' and he was expecting a clear run on the main line. Regretfully, he also failed to see both the distant and home signals for Milton until the engine was almost at the crossover which gave access to the loop. As it reached the facing points the Britannia's speed was far too fast for the sharp radius and because of this the engine was instantly derailed and it careered away to the left. With two of the coaches, the second and third vehicles in the train, *Polar Star* ploughed down an 18 foot embankment and came to rest on its side against the boundary fence. The first coach broke away from the tender and was thrown clear, but the others were completely demolished as the accompanying pictures show only too graphically. Of the 293 passengers on board, 11 lost their lives and a further 157 were injured, many seriously. Of the railwaymen working the train, six were injured, including the driver and a travelling ticket collector who were both to receive serious wounds. Fortunately the accident occurred close to the Didcot Central Ordnance Depot and it sent out rescue teams and fire engines, as did a nearby Royal Air Force base. Ambulances from at least ten surrounding towns were sent to the scene, whilst fire appliances came from Didcot, Reading and later Oxford. Local GPs, St. John's Ambulance and a strong contingent from the Berkshire County Police force all rendered their own particular skills to assist in the rescue work.

After four months of examination and testing, the Inspector issued his report, concluding that the derailment was solely due to the excursion train's taking the Milton crossover much too fast. Though most of the criticisms would be levelled at the driver, the guard was also censured for not applying the brake when he realised that they were approaching the crossover at too fast a speed, whilst the District Permanent Way Inspector was reprimanded for failing to appoint a hand signalman at the points. The track was in good condition and in no way contributed to the failure. The driver's estimated speed of 40 mph was well below what he had actually been doing, which was probably in excess of 50 mph when the limit was 10 mph. Although the crossover was protected by signals equipped by ATC apparatus, the driver claimed his siren had not sounded. There was no proof that the ATC had failed (and every indication that it hadn't), even though the siren may not have sounded clearly. Therefore the train should have been stopped by the apparatus and this suggested that the re-setting lever had been lifted, so the Inspector concluded that the driver had probably lifted the handle without realising it.

PHOTOGRAPHS; KEYSTONE PICTURE LIBRARY.

BARNES

British Railways, Southern Region 2nd December 1955

Less than a fortnight after disaster struck the Western Region, it was the turn of the Southern Region to face a terrible railway accident. Once again it was the misuse of the Sykes Release Key which led to a rear-end collision, but on this occasion it was attended by a fierce fire in which the leading coach of a four-car EMU was completely destroyed. The 11.02 pm train from Waterloo to Windsor and Chertsey, was travelling towards Barnes station under clear signals at a speed of 35 mph when it collided with a freight train which was moving slowly in front of it. Drawn by an 8F 2-8-0, the 42-wagon freight was running from Battersea to Brent along a route which saw heavy night-time freight traffic. It had just recommenced its journey after a stop signal at Barnes Junction when the EMU drove into its rear, demolishing the guard's van and killing its occupant. The motorman must also have been killed at the same time as well as some of the eleven passengers who died in the crash, because the front end of the EMU and its leading compartments were completely destroyed. If this was not bad enough, the body of the EMU fell over on to its side and landed on the down through line, where the electric supply failed to trip out. Fed by a supply from Clapham Junction substation, the third-rail caused a severe arcing and the wooden body of the EMU began to catch fire. Regretfully this arcing continued for six minutes after the collision, until an off-duty motorman who had been travelling in the wrecked train managed to find a short-circuiting bar and apply it to the down through.

Emergency calls were made to the rescue services by the signalman at Barnes Junction, but due to a misunderstanding the Barnes fire and ambulance station only sent an ambulance at first. The first fire-fighting appliance to reach the scene came, in fact, from Wandsworth and it arrived at 11.44 pm; two more fire engines arrived from Barnes around the same time, and these were followed by a further five machines from other fire stations in the area. The nine appliances soon got the blaze under control, but by then it had completely consumed the leading coach. The fire was one of the most serious of the post-war period, and it considerably worsened the situation; the effects of the collision, whilst bad, were not very severe because the freight train was on the move when the passenger train hit it, but the fire undoubtedly played a major part in the casualty figures. In addition to those who died, twenty passengers were seriously hurt, and another 21 sustained minor injuries and shock; two of the rescuers (both police officers) who had battled to free a seriously injured passenger, suffered injuries which kept them off duty for a considerable time. The construction of the train undoubtedly played a major part in the accident, for the wooden bodies of the 1935-built stock were no protection against fire. However, it will become even more disconcerting when I reveal that the bodywork of these EMUs was even older than the build date of 1935/6 suggests. These bodies were, in fact, former steam-hauled stock which had been built in 1895 and were thus 60 years old at the time of the accident. When the EMUs had been built, these bodies had simply been adapted to fit on the new steel underframes and bogies which the Southern Railway had constructed. True, the framing of the coaches was of hardwood, but there was a great deal of softwood in the construction and this ignited rapidly when the arcing began. The flames were also undoubtedly aided by the wax wrappings round aircraft aerials which were being transported in a container on the freight which smashed open in the collision.

In his summary the Inspector attributed the fault to the signalman accepting the EMU from Barnes Junction when the freight train was still in the section. Had berth track circuits been installed on the local lines at Barnes as they were on the through lines, this acceptance could never have happened. However, in their absence the signalman at Barnes Junction made an irregular use of the Sykes Key, but it was a sad reflection that 57 years on from St. John's, this situation was still occurring. Even so the Sykes system, although very dated in 1955, was still an effective means of controlling traffic on intensified suburban routes. The accidents at Battersea Park, South Croydon, and at Esher on 28th January 1945, were just three disasters caused by the ability of a signalman to use the key to reset the equipment without reference to any other authority. The necessity to have a more modern, tamper-proof system, was clearly demonstrated and the official report drew out this point stating 'the time has come when the concentrated suburban traffic on this route should be controlled by modern colour light signalling coupled with the continuous track circuiting which eliminates the possibility of block working mistakes.' The Inspector also commented strongly on the ongoing use of wooden-bodied stock, but continued 'it is estimated that under the Modernisation Plan all of the 13,900 wooden vehicles which remained at the end of 1955 will have been eliminated within seven years'. Of final interest is the fact that in view of the confusion in the telephone request for emergency services, the General Post Office (fore-runner of British Telecom) significantly improved the way 999 calls were handled, and the saying '999 which service do you require' became standardised throughout the country!

PHOTOGRAPHS; ABOVE: ILLUSTRATED LONDON NEWS
BELOW: BBC HULTON PICTURE LIBRARY

WELWYN GARDEN CITY

British Railways, Eastern Region 7th January 1957

A little after 7am on the morning of Monday 7th January 1957, the staff of Newmans Newsagents in Welwyn Garden City were treated to a most bizarre sight when a customer walked into the shop bleeding profusely from a wound in his forehead. After calmly purchasing a packet of cigarettes, he lit one up, then left the shop and crossed the road to the railway line. The customer was, in fact, one of the first survivors to leave the 7am local train to King's Cross to arrive back in Welwyn Garden City after it had been struck in the rear by an overnight express from Aberdeen. His train was the 6.18am from Baldock (on the Cambridge line), comprised of six coaches and headed by Class L1 2-6-4T No.67741. As it was booked to run fast to Finsbury Park, it had been allowed by Control to run on the up fast line, in preference to the late running express. However, the L1 had just negotiated the crossover and was about half a mile from the station when the express caught up with it at a speed of 60 mph. At the controls of the express locomotive, A2/3 Pacific No.60250 *Owen Tudor,* was a driver from the New England Depot, Peterborough who only had a limited experience of driving fast expresses. He had come to driving late in life, and only been passed out at the age of 47. His first years as a driver were spent on local workings and freight trips and he had only driven south of Hitchin a few times, so most of his route knowledge to King's Cross had been gained as a fireman. His course of action that day is inexplicable, because he ran past the outer distant at caution and then continued for 1½ miles through the outer and inner home signals which were all set at danger. He even exploded two detonators that were placed on the track to warn that the signals were not clear and also failed to react to the red hand lamp which was shown to him by the telegraph lad assisting in the Welwyn Garden City 'box. Why he made such a lapse is quite beyond comprehension, but it was to have tragic consequences.

Having only just got up to 30 mph, the local train had no chance of pulling away from the express which was running twice as fast. The last coach of the local was a brake third No.61617, and normally it would have had the brake compartment at the trailing end, but on this occasion, abnormal working over Christmas and the New Year holidays had resulted in the passenger compartments being at the tail. With exceptionally violent force *Owen Tudor* smashed into the compartments of this 28 year old wooden-bodied coach and in so doing caused most of the twenty-five injuries (five serious) and the one death that are recorded in this accident.

Nevertheless, Welwyn demonstrated only too clearly the need for ATC/AWS. The driver at once tried to shift the blame from himself to the Welwyn Signalman and claimed that the signals had been clear but were altered after the express had gone through. Now here is the strange facet of this accident, for the Welwyn Control system which had been born out of one signalman's inadequacy now exonerated his successor in the same 'box twenty-two years later. The system had saved the signalman because, under Welwyn Control, it was proved that he could not have done what the driver claimed. Another irony of the 1957 accident is the fact that whilst, only one passenger died in the accident, two more lives were to be claimed by the end of the day. In a tragic sequel to the events just after 7am, at 10pm a ganger walking home after working at the site all day noticed what he thought were two bundles of rags, or pieces of debris laying across the tracks. Thinking it was something that had fallen off one of the trains which had cleared away the wreckage, he went over to move it to the cess. One can imagine the man's horror to find that the rags were the remains of two of his colleagues who had also been working at the crash site that day. The Coroner's Inquest later concluded that the men, aged 60 and 52, had been struck and tragically killed by an unidentified train whilst walking home. The final twist of fate in this whole story is the fact that Welwyn was part of the 105 miles of the ECML which was then equipped with the BR AWS equipment, but comparatively few of the engines which worked between London and Grantham were fitted with receiving equipment - *Owen Tudor* was one of those which had yet to be equipped. Thirty-five years after the first Pringle Report, train control had still to be universally introduced. Once again, Welwyn Garden City demonstrated it was a case of too little, too late! In terms of fatalities it could have been much worse, and before the year was out, it was to be overshadowed on 4th December.

PHOTOGRAPH; BBC HULTON PICTURE LIBRARY

CHAPEL-EN-LE-FRITH

British Railways, London Midland Region 9th February 1957

This is another of those railway accidents where I have chosen to include the names of the crew, as their actions demonstrate the high traditions of the railway service and not the foolishness or unwise actions found in many of the incidents we have thus far discussed. Similarly, like Driver Ben Gimbert and his Fireman Jim Nightall, and shunter Norman Tunna from Birkenhead, the driver of a Buxton - Warrington freight train, John Axon, was to be awarded the George Cross for displaying devotion to duty far above what might be reasonably expected. The accident in which he lost his life was one of those which falls into the one-in-a-million category, for it was an instance of when something completely unforeseen went wrong. It occurred at Chapel-en-le-Frith, Derbyshire, on 9th February 1957, when a class 8F goods locomotive got out of control and ran into the back of a preceding train. Working a Buxton - Arpley (Warrington) train, No. 48188, was handling an unfitted freight comprised of 24 loaded coal wagons, 5 wagons of freight, 2 empty tank wagons, 2 loaded flat wagons, and a 20-ton brake van. As far as Bibbington's Sidings, the train was being banked by another class 8F, but on board the footplate of the train engine Driver John Axon and his fireman R. Scanlon were having problems with steam escaping from the driver's steam brake handle. This brake had leaked on their journey to Buxton, but it had been attended to by a fitter who tightened up a nut on the pipe which had apparently cured the problem. Now all they hoped for, was to get into the sidings where they could get assistance, then came a deafening bang and an explosion of escaping steam. This drove both men back to the tender, and though they tried to get to the controls they could neither make a full brake application or sound the whistle. The banker was still pushing hard at the rear, so Axon told Scanlon to jump off and drop as many wagon brakes as he could, whilst he tried to get to the control.

Scanlon managed to drop a few brakes, but the train was going too fast and it sped away down the incline. On its arrival at Dove Holes loop, the signalman was faced with the unenviable choice of either letting the engine crash there (and probably demolish his 'box in the process), or letting it run on in the hope that the driver could regain control. He chose the latter option, and then telephoned Chapel-en-le-Frith Central station to inform them of the run-away; staff there acted with all promptitude and evacuated passengers from a 2-car DMU waiting in the up platform. Regretfully, the preceding down freight train, working from Rowsley to Stockport was just passing through the station, and there was little they could do to help them escape from Axon's train which was fast overhauling them. The 8F smashed into the back of the Rowsley train, killing the goods guard and demolishing a number of wagons, whilst the vehicles in the Buxton train piled up in a 25ft high heap behind No. 48188. Despite the opportunity to jump out of his cab, Axon displayed great courage and stayed with his train even though he must have been well aware of the danger. The accident was later attributed to a faulty braised collar on the steam brake pipe union, which had finally collapsed after it had been tightened at Buxton. The courage of the driver was not only recognised by the posthumous award of the medal, but also in the naming of a BR electric class 86, No. 86261, *Driver J. Axon GC* in the 1980s

PHOTOGRAPHS; R. LEECH COLLECTION

LONDON; ST. JOHN'S

British Railways, Southern Region 4th December 1957

At 3.15pm on 4th December 1957 a Battle of Britain class light pacific, No.34066 *Spitfire* left the Stewart's Lane Shed in Battersea for Cannon Street station which was slightly under four miles away. The engine was due to take out the 4.56pm for Folkestone and Ramsgate, in effect the same train which had been wrecked at Sevenoaks thirty years earlier! However, that night it took its time in reaching Cannon Street due to the severe fog. Upon leaving the shed it travelled over the Nunhead - Lewisham loop, through Blackheath, Charlton and Greenwich to the Rotherhithe Road carriage sidings where it was attached to its train; then with an engine at the opposite end, it was drawn through London Bridge into Cannon Street where it finally arrived an hour and a quarter late. The Ramsgate shed crew who were due to take the train out stood waiting its arrival on the fog-bound and freezing platform. At 6.08pm they finally got away, some 72 minutes late and completely displaced from their original path, mind you they were not unique in that position as dozens more trains were running around the metropolis in no particular order, and it must have been a signalman's nightmare. Even so, after the driver of *Spitfire* stopped to notify the signalman that he intended to take on water at Sevenoaks, he had a good run all the way to New Cross with green lights shining out through the fog. He must therefore have fully expected to be given a clear run due to the fact that his important train was so far behind schedule. However, in advance of him was Parks Bridge Junction, where the mid-Kent line diverged for Hayes and Addiscombe Road. Standing at the signals was one of the new Hastings line diesel-electric multiple units, which the signalman had mistaken for a Hayes train. There was, in fact no need for the DEMU to be held, but the signalman had become confused by the passage of trains out of sequence. The mistake would not have happened if the man had been provided with the booking lad he was entitled to, but there was a great staff shortage in such grades and recruitment was very slow. Behind the stationary DEMU the Hayes train was also drawn up, but signals behind it were denoting the fact that it was stopped; L18 showed red, L17 a single yellow, and L16 double yellow. Unfortunately, near to L16 was New Cross signal A42 which was showing green, and with the limited visibility from the narrow cabbed 4-6-2 being hampered by the streamlined cab sheets and the dense fog, there is little wonder that the Ramsgate driver took the green as referring to him.

Indeed, he fully expected a clear road, and from his statements to the Inspector one can only feel sorry for him when he continued past the signals at caution. It would seem unlikely that this was a deliberate act of overrunning signals, nor is it even a case of negligence, it would just seem as though the idea that they were at caution never entered his head. Having missed the two signals, only L18 now stood in defence of the standing train and *Spitfire* was running at a speed of over 30 mph. The fireman saw the red light shining through the fog and called out a warning to his mate, but although the driver applied the brakes the train could not be brought to a halt in time. The 4-6-2 buried itself into the back of the Hayes train, forcing the ninth carriage to override the eighth, but the offending train was damaged even more severely. Having struck what amounted to a 400-ton obstacle, the Battle of Britain class engine was derailed, and the tender and leading coach were flung against a stanchion supporting the Nunhead - Lewisham loop girder bridge which spanned the main line at this point. This two-span girder bridge, which *Spitfire* had travelled across only a few hours earlier, then came down and crushed the second and third carriages of its train. The driver was found on the footplate badly shocked, but not seriously hurt, though his fireman nearby had suffered severe injuries. The guard of the Hayes train, and 37 of his customers were killed by the rear-end collision which, in itself, was a serious enough accident. Unfortunately another 52 people also died, most of whom were crushed by the falling girders of the bridge. Even then, the death toll could have been much higher, as a train travelling over the loop line was brought to halt with its leading bogie actually resting above the mangled wreckage of the Ramsgate train. The sad driver of *Spitfire* was given very fair treatment in the official report, but he was nevertheless brought up on a charge of manslaughter by the Coroner's Jury. He came to trial on 21st April 1958, but the jury could not agree and a re-trial was ordered for 8th May, though when it came to court the Crown offered no evidence and the driver's ordeal was over. The enormity of a simple mistake must have lain heavy on his conscience ever after, for with 90 dead and 109 injured it became Britain's third most serious railway disaster.

PHOTOGRAPH; KEYSTONE PICTURE LIBRARY

DAGGENHAM EAST

British Railways, Eastern Region 31st January 1958

With the disaster which was experienced at St. John's in December, the minds of railwaymen of all grades were concentrated on safe operations in fog. A circular was even issued to shed-masters in all regions, warning of the attendant dangers associated with fog and fog-working on 10th January 1958. This document drew special notice to the working of lines not equipped with ATC/AWS, and was particularly relevant in view of difficulties associated with getting personnel to undertake fog-signalling duties. The accident at Gidea Park in 1947 had shown that recruiting men of the right calibre was not easy, and I also think that the withdrawal of fog signalmen immediately prior to the Harrow & Wealdstone disaster had left a lasting impression in the minds of senior railway management. The fact that St. John's had also happened in the fog had done little to restore confidence in rail travel. It also has to be mentioned that fog problems were particularly bad in cities such as London, Birmingham, Sheffield and Manchester, and the 'clean air' legislation which was then working its way through Parliament was seen as an essential means of creating improvements in the situation. Nevertheless, despite the bad fogs that were experienced over the winter of 1957-8, some railway lines were considered considerably safer than others; primarily because they employed train control systems. The former London, Tilbury and Southend section of the LMS was one such line, even though peak traffic might result in the headway between trains being as little as five minutes. Yet the enviable record of the Hudd Electro-Magnetic Automatic Warning System offered a great degree of protection for trains, as it provided an audible siren in the cab if a distant signal was passed at danger. Obviously, such a system should also have been applied to home signals as well, because failure to equip all signals was eventually bound to lead to disaster.

When it came, the disaster stuck on 31st January 1958 after a BR Standard Class 4MT 2-6-4T, No.80079, left London's Fenchurch Street station for Shoeburyness. As it approached Upney in dense fog, the driver apparently missed the home signal and entered the next section where an 11-coach passenger train had been halted by the signals of Daggenham East 'box. Though the driver later claimed he was running under clear signals, the Inspector found that this was impossible because at the time the Becontree signal box was in the process of closing down for the night. As the 'rush hour' was coming to an end the signalman began the process of switching out his 'box, and to do this he would have to ensure that the 'Train on the Line' indicator was showing the correct reading before he could physically turn the switch linking his block instruments to those at Daggenham East. In view of this there was no way in which he could register a 'false 'line clear signal and his starting signals would have to remain at danger. Once this was done, only the signalman at Daggenham East could operate the Upney signals, and even he would not be able to release them until the train standing at his signals had been passed through into the next section. Unfortunately the signals at Upney were of the semaphore type, and the dull oil lights would not have been very effective in a thick fog where visibility was down to just a few yards. It is quite evident that, rather than having a clear signal at Upney, the driver of the 2-6-4T had missed seeing the signal altogether and he had somehow deluded himself into thinking he had a clear road. In the end his progress was only impeded when he ran into the rear of the stationary train. This was the 6.20pm stopping passenger train from Fenchurch Street to Thorpe Bay, which was heavily loaded with commuters who were packed into wooden bodied coaches. Once again this wholly inadequate stock failed to offer the protection demanded by passengers, and ten people were killed as the rear two coaches were completely demolished by No.80079. Another 89 people were injured, with some being quite badly hurt. Our picture shows that the offending engine was only slightly derailed, and with the exception of a badly battered trailing bogie, it was not too seriously damaged. Looking at workmen cutting away the rear buffer beam with oxyacetylene torches, it may be difficult to comprehend that this engine was eventually preserved. Built in March 1954, it was withdrawn after just eleven years and three months duty and sent to Woodham Brothers, Barry in January 1966. After languishing there for five years, it was taken to the Severn Valley where it was rebuilt, and eventually steamed again in April 1977.

PHOTOGRAPH; KEYSTONE PICTURE LIBRARY

PAISLEY

British Railways, Scottish Region 20th May 1958

Moving into 1958 we come to the collision at Arkleston Junction, near Paisley, on 20th May, in which one person was killed and 97 people injured after an inexperienced driver drove his engine and brake van into a heavily loaded passenger train. As the 8-coach 7.15am train from Gourock to Glasgow headed towards the city, packed with commuters it proceeded through Arkleston Junction where an 0-6-0 tender engine was waiting to cross the four running lines with a 20-ton brake van. The driver of the 'J' class engine was a young, passed-fireman and his mate was a passed-cleaner, and both were quite inexperienced. Due to an error of judgement the driver took his engine across the path of the 2-6-4T on the passenger train, and the two collided at a combined speed of about 35mph. It came about because the movement of the engine and van was a very complicated one, perhaps best illustrated like a pedestrian trying to cross a busy road in the rush hour. Naturally it required the observation of both fixed and hand signals, a difficult enough job for any driver but a nightmare for one with only limited experience. However, such movements were frequently assigned to very inexperienced drivers, who in turn were only assisted by passed-cleaners and junior guards. Such work was often given by shed-masters to new drivers as a prelude to yard shunting duties, but it was almost akin to letting a learner driver on to the M25 on a Monday morning. A moment's lapse in concentration, a misunderstood signal, or just lack of attention could lead to disaster - and at Paisley it did! The newspapers were quite critical about a system which placed so much responsibility on a novice driver, and in the official report the Inspector commented; 'It is all the more necessary, therefore, that the dual responsibilities of enginemen and guards on these occasions for observing signals should be brought home to junior men, both during teaching and examination, and during footplate supervision. It may be advisable to give more weight to this aspect of instruction for firemen and guards, and I would also suggest that some emphasis might be laid by supervisory staff.'

PHOTOGRAPH: ATLANTIC COLLECTION

HOLLAND PARK

London Transport 28th July 1958

Illustrated at the top of the opposite page, is the disastrous tube train fire which was experienced at 7.14am on the morning of 28th July 1958, when a Central Line train from Ealing Broadway to Hainault came to a stop 23 yards short of Holland Park. Whether the stop was caused by a passenger pulling the emergency handle or the fire is not known, but severe arcing had developed due to a fault in the back of a power receptacle box at the rear end of the leading motor car. Built in 1928, the wooden body of No.3645, was soon affected by the arcing as the intense heat caused a 'torch-like' flame to burn through the bulkhead and enter the guard's compartment. As the fire did not have the time to build up in the confined space, there was no fireball or explosion, but there was exceptionally intense heat and smoke. This swept through the carriages forming the first four cars of the eight-car train set, choking passengers and reducing visibility to zero, before spreading through the tube tunnel into Holland Park Station.

The driver acted with commendable effort, and after detraining the first batch of passengers he went back twice to assist in the rescue of the others, but the London Fire Service was not called until 8.04am. They got to the scene with two appliances at 8.09am, but the delay in calling them out meant that almost half an hour had been wasted. In all 48 passengers and three railwaymen were seriously affected by the fumes, and unfortunately one of the passengers was later to die in hospital. As might be expected the Inspector heavily criticised the delay in getting passengers to safety, but concluded that the driver had shown considerable devotion to duty. It is quite clear that he had got the seven people out of the leading car only seconds before it was engulfed by a blast of scorched air, which would surely have taken the lives of all concerned.

PHOTOGRAPH; OPPOSITE PAGE TOP, ATLANTIC COLLECTION

LONDON; BOROUGH MARKET

British Railways, Southern Region 12th August 1958

The problem of worn track which we discussed in the accident at Grendon, bears a great similarity to the one which occurred at Borough Market in 1958; for, in both instances, the Permanent-way Inspector miscalculated the life span of the track involved and, as a result of excessive wear, a train was subsequently derailed. The junction was the point where the line from London Bridge Station diverges for Cannon Street and Charing Cross, which had no less than 275 booked train movements every weekday. In such locations it was desirable to install longer-lasting manganese-steel switch rails, but difficulties in supplies had meant that when the switches were replaced on 16th March that year, ordinary 95lb bull head carbon steel had to be employed. Previously, such switches had lasted between 12 to 14 months compared with the 17 to 22 months for manganese steel. Yet, following the introduction of ten-coach (4-car + 4-car + 2-car) EMU sets, the wear became even more rapid and a set of manganese steel switches installed the previous June had lasted just 9 months.

Within five months the new switch rails had worn away, and they effectively turned themselves into a ramp. On 12th August the first seven vehicles in the 6.52am from Sanderstead to Cannon Street managed to negotiate these points safely, but the eighth coach was deflected. The rear two-car set was completely derailed and bounced against the parapet of the viaduct. Power supply to the tracks was cut off inside a minute, and all the passengers emerged little the worse for their ordeal.

PHOTOGRAPH; BELOW, ATLANTIC COLLECTION

EASTBOURNE

British Railways, Southern Region 25th August 1958

On 25th August 1958 a 12-car EMU pulled into Eastbourne amidst a heavy rain shower in readiness to form the 7.25am departure service for London Bridge; a train which its regular passengers called the 'friendly train' because so many of them were on first name terms. Indeed, as one passenger wrote 'we had a little joke every morning; if it was a fine we said good morning to each other, if not we just said morning. That day we had said bad morning', little realising how prophetic the statement would be just a few minutes later as our day turned to disaster with the death of four people.' The agent of destruction was the 7.45pm car-sleeper express from Glasgow, which was running southwards in atrocious weather behind BR Standard Class 5, 4-6-0 No.73042. Despite being twelve minutes late in starting and the weight/length of the train, the timings were not too difficult to prevent them making up time, so when it arrived at Polegate Junction the deficit had been cut to six minutes. The time was now 7.21am, and for operating reasons an 11 minute stop was booked at the junction, giving a scheduled departure at 7.26am. However, if 'line clear' was given by Hampden Park Box, the train could be passed on earlier, as it was at 7.23am that morning. Around this time the signalman at Eastbourne box had watched the electric train enter platform four and restored levers one and two in the frame and gave 'train out of section'. He then restored number three lever to the frame and the No. 3 signal went back to danger. In order not to delay the late-running electric service, he began to set the road for its departure, this meant obtaining clear on the up line from Hampden Park, before setting starting signal No.36 and its platform repeater. The route out of the platform was duly set, and the London train would have to negotiate this before lever No. 36 could be released. So the Hampden Park signal would be locked at danger by the Eastbourne block commutator until this was turned to clear, even after this Eastbourne No. 3 down home signal would remain locked against incoming traffic. However, this was no protection against a train not responding to the signals, and in his own evidence the driver of the incoming train said that as they ran towards Eastbourne he was looking out of his cab, straining his eyes to watch out for the down home signals. He said he was braking slightly as he did so, and estimated his speed at about 20 mph, but he drove past the signal protecting the station approach. He later stated that he must have blinked because of the bad weather as he passed it, but when he straightened out of the curve he saw the EMU in the platform ahead. He applied his brake, though he failed to see the signalman frantically waving a red flag from his box as the train burst through the end of the points and travelled towards No. 4 platform by means of the cross-over. A collision was now inevitable, but the station foreman standing on No. 4 platform realised what was about to happen and he ran to his office to alert the emergency services without waiting for the disaster to take place. The steam train driver readily admitted his error, and cooperated fully with a team of British Transport Commission doctors who were researching the phenomena of drivers passing signals at danger. Unfortunately, no firm conclusions were ever reached and similar incidents continue down to the present day.

PHOTOGRAPHS; KEYSTONE PICTURE LIBRARY

SETTLE

British Railways, London Midland Region 21st January 1960

From the rainy shores of the south coast, we move to the snow covered fells of the Yorkshire Dales, once more up to the lofty heights of the Settle & Carlisle line. Almost a year and a half had passed since Eastbourne, and thankfully 1959 was one of the less troublesome years for BR. However, 1960 was to start out with an incident which was all too similar to the last fatal crash on the Settle & Carlisle for, like the high-speed derailment at Blea Moor, another Scotch express was about to be derailed due to faulty maintenance. The train was the 9.05pm from Glasgow (St. Enoch) to London (St. Pancras) which, like the 9.12am in 1953 was routed over the former G&SWR line to Carlisle, but this time the main difference was that no pilot engine was required for Ais Gill . The locomotive assigned to the job was one of BR's powerful new express engines, Britannia Class 4-6-2 No.70052 *Firth of Tay,* but these were not well-liked engines amongst many of the drivers who travelled the Settle & Carlisle. Whilst not as problematic as the Clan Class 4-6-2s, they were rough riding engines which were prone to suffer heavy knocking in their big ends. They were also known to lose their side-bar assembly bolts, which were difficult to reach and tighten; in fact so serious was this problem that the 'Brits' were being progressively modified when they went in for major overhaul or repair, but it is not likely that the driver of the ill-fated train on 21st January would have thought much about this problem as he pounded up the S&CR after restarting from Appleby.

The signal post which sent him on his way, once stood just a few yards from our living room window, but as he went on his way few people would have noticed his passing on that vile winter's night. He had travelled but five miles when a nut and bolt fell off the right-hand assembly near the 270 mile post, half a mile further on another nut came away, followed by the loss of the inner-slide around the 267 mile post (a mile in advance of Kirkby Stephen station). As the train began the harsh ascent to Ais Gill, the front packing piece dropped off just north of Birkett Tunnel then, when the Britannia crested the summit a final nut and bolt failed and the bottom outer slide bar fell away. The vibration that began between the top slide bar and what was now a loose cross head, was sufficiently loud enough to be heard on the footplate. The driver eased up his speed as they ran past the site of the 1910 crash and eventually made an unscheduled stop at Hawes Junction, by now renamed as Garsdale following the closure of the line to Hawes nine months earlier. The driver went round his engine with a small battery hand lamp, but in the raging storm it is little wonder that the problem was not seen. Climbing back on to the footplate he decided to take the engine on cautiously to Hellifield, where he would get a replacement for the trip into Leeds. However, he failed to let Hellifield know this intention, and as No.70052 began the descent down towards Settle the speed of the train began to creep up, although they probably did not realise that this had happened. The driver was adamant that he had proceeded cautiously, but from the records kept in the signal boxes on the route, it was discovered he had averaged 40mph on the 20 miles from Garsdale to Settle Junction. As the train ran up towards the distant signal for Settle station, ballast suddenly began to spray up against the side of the cab. The right-hand piston rod, cross head and connecting rod had finally come away, but as these were still attached to the driving wheel they were flailing round and round and digging deep into the ballast. Unlike the locomotives at Weedon and Blea Moor in the 1950s, the Britannia remained upright and disaster was seemingly averted. Unfortunately passing by on the down line was a Carlisle Kingmoor 2-6-0, No.42881, on a freight train, which was derailed when the Britannia's cross head damaged the track immediately in front of it. The freight train ripped open the carriage sides in the Glasgow train just like a can-opener and five of the 75 passengers were killed outright, with eight more being injured. The guard of the freight train had a lucky escape as his van piled up into the wreckage, but he escaped alive although badly injured. It was to be the last bad accident on the Settle and Carlisle, but 35 years later (and almost to the day) disaster once again struck the high fells not far from where the No.70052's slide bar assembly had eventually failed.

PHOTOGRAPHS; K. & J. JELLEY

ROYTON

British Railways, London Midland Region 8th February 1961

The year 1961 was another bad one for accidents, and it got off to a poor start, at 6.21am on the 8th February on a rainy day in Lancashire. The steeply graded Royton branch which diverged off the Oldham - Rochdale line was notorious for runaways as it descended down one long gradient to the terminus. An L&YR 2-4-2T picked up on the incline in 1906, and an 0-6-0 A Class followed suit in 1917. In LMS days a 2-6-2 tank on a passenger service to Manchester began skidding back down the incline, its wheels unable to grip the rails after a fine rain shower froze on touching the ground and rendered the surface like glass. That incident damaged a brake-third coach at the rear of the train, but this was not as bad as the covered carriage truck which was completely demolished whilst standing at the end of the platform road in January 1940 after an 8F got out of control on the descent. The introduction of DMUs on the branch reduced the number of incidents, but early in 1961 it was realised that even new forms of traction were not infallible. As a two-car unit made its way to the town to form the first working of the day it too ran away down the grade at an alarming speed, the driver sounding his horn to warn those standing in the station awaiting its arrival. It hit the stop blocks with force, smashed through the wall and careered over the road and buried itself into a row of terraced houses opposite. It then burst into flames as the house collapsed around it, but although the driver was badly hurt he escaped with his life. In staying with his train he had exemplified remarkable devotion to duty as he could easily have jumped out when the train began to run away.

PHOTOGRAPH; RICHARD S. GREENWOOD

RUGBY

British Railways, London Midland Region 11th February 1961

Just three days after Royton, in the early hours of the morning another driver was killed when an express from Swindon to York ran into an obstruction across its path between Rugby and Lutterworth Central. Having left Swindon at 10.23 pm the express was running north behind an ex-GWR engine at a speed of about 60 mph when the crew saw the obstruction in their path, but it was far too late to do anything and they struck the wreckage with sufficient force to turn the express locomotive on to its side. Although the driver was tragically killed, it is gratifying to report that even in such a serious accident only two passengers suffered slight injuries. The obstruction was, in fact, a derailed pallet van which had become thrown across the tracks when the 1.50am Woodford - Mottram express freight train suddenly divided just before 3am. The freight train was comprised of a Class V2 engine, 36 wagons and a brake van. The first 12 vehicles in the train were vacuum braked, whilst the 23rd to 29th were 12-ton pallet vans, all of which were empty at the time. About 1 mile 220 yards north of Rugby the 26th vehicle became derailed, whilst it was travelling at a speed of about 50 mph. This probably occurred because the design of the van meant it was not heavy enough for such a speed, and other derailments to similar vehicles were already demonstrating their inherent dangers. Anyway the van travelled on for just over 1 mile before it parted company with the one in front, and it then piled up. The crew of the V2 failed to realise that anything untoward had happened and they travelled on towards Lutterworth, leaving the guard to protect his stranded portion of the train. However, he acted in a most lethargic way and for 6½ minutes he seems to have been singularly inactive because he considered that the train had come to an ordinary stop at the signals. When he discovered that this was not the case, his attempts to protect the rear of the train were far too belated and he was unable to stop the express. Once again a call was issued by the Inspector and the rail unions for train guards to be issued with warning flares in preference to standard oil lamps, but despite tests being undertaken by the British Transport Commission that year, this area of protection once again went without any further development.

PHOTOGRAPH; KEYSTONE PICTURE LIBRARY

BASCHURCH

British Railways, Western Region 13th February 1961

With the exception of a handful of accidents, most notably at Milton near Didcot in 1955, the Western Region of British Railways had a record which the other regions could rightly be very envious of. This was, undoubtedly due to the Automatic Train Control systems, but even so in some other areas the GWR did not take associated steps in railway safety which might have made the system as near fool-proof as possible. For example it did not fully adopt the track circuiting systems widely employed by the other railway companies; had they done so it would have prevented a serious accident at Baschurch on the evening of 13th February 1961. That evening an unfitted freight train, which was equivalent to the length of 46 wagons was being taken from Coton Hill to Saltney by an ex-GWR 28XX class. When it arrived at Baschurch (between Oswestry and Shrewsbury), it was to be shunted to allow a following down express to pass. Whilst setting back the driver had felt resistance to his train and, having thought that the brake van had reached the buffer stop, he stopped even though the engine was still foul of the main line. What the driver did not know, was that the resistance was caused by a newly appointed guard screwing down his brake prematurely, because he was apprehensive as to whether his train would fit into the siding. On stopping the driver got down and started to walk to the rear of the train. However, he had barely walked down the length of four or five wagons when he saw that the inner home and starter had been cleared and he assumed that there had been a change of plans and the signals had been cleared for him to go on. Regrettably, the annals of railway accident history are littered with wrong assumptions! Worse still, as the driver hurried back onto the footplate, he failed to see disc signal No.9 was at danger as he passed it. In his own mind he was confident that the signalman would know he was not in a place of refuge, because he had not 'popped' his whistle to signify he was fully in the siding. Interpreting the signals as being meant for him, he slowly put on steam and began to draw forward. He was just doing so when the engine of the express, running at between 40 and 45 mph, caught the leading vehicle in the goods train. Seeing danger bearing down upon them, the crew of the 2-8-0 quickly baled out of their cab, an action which probably saved their lives.

With the freight train foul of the main line, the crew of the express could do nothing to avert disaster; accordingly 4-6-0, No. 6949 *Haberfield Hall,* caught the leading vehicle in the goods train (a bogie bolster wagon) and then struck the rear of the 2-8-0's tender. The express engine overturned on to the up line, and a stores-van next to the engine mounted the platform whilst the next vehicle (a corridor brake second) was thrown partially on top of the van. Coals from the engine must have fallen out into the wreckage, because the stores-van (a converted coach of 1908 vintage) caught fire. Two storesmen were riding in the van, but rescuers were only able to release one of them before the fire completely consumed the wooden shell. The driver and fireman of No. 6949 were also killed in the collision, but only two of the 22 passengers on board the six-coach train were injured, and then only slightly. The cause of the accident was entirely due to the failure of the signalman to ensure that the freight train was in the siding, but the driver and guard of that train also ought to have been more diligent. Understandably, it was the signalman who was to bear the brunt of the criticism, but the Inspector hinted that the railways were at fault for not providing track circuits; 'This human failure would not have occurred in a modern signalling installation because the line on which the freight train was standing would have been track circuited, and the occupation of the track circuit would have prevented the home signal from being cleared. There are, however, a large number of installations where there are as yet no track circuits, and a great many of them will remain so and in use for a long time. The safety operation at such places depends to a large extent on signalmen complying with the Rules and not making foolish mistakes, such as the signalman at Baschurch made in this case. I hope that it will serve as a useful lesson generally.' Under such circumstances, even the GWR's highly-efficient signalling system was unable to prevent a human failure of this type. Continuous track-circuiting would have made such an error highly unlikely, as would the provision of a loop siding rather than a refuge - both of which were installed shortly after the event!

PHOTOGRAPHS: ELTHAM TIMES COLLECTION

LONDON, CANNON STREET

British Railways, Southern Region 20th March 1961

The year 1961 continued to witness a number of serious railway accidents, and these seemed to affect every part of the country. Some were minor and trivial, others were much more serious. A contrast in the two types was noted on the Southern Region within a three week period that spring, the first of which occurred at Cannon Street on 20th March 1961. Whilst it was not a serious accident and no-one was hurt, it was one which looks as though it could have been. An incoming EMU heading for the city overran two successive danger signals because the driver failed to realise that they applied to his train, meanwhile the road was set for an outgoing DMU which was running empty to the carriage sidings. The errant driver finally realised his mistake and he applied his brakes, but it was too late to prevent the two trains meeting in a side to side collision and carriages in both of them were overturned to varying degrees. The lack of injury demonstrates the way in which carriage design had so significantly improved to such an extent as to prevent serious harm being sustained, even though our picture reveals just how bad the overturning was. The overturning of the coaches was so great as to completely wreck two of them, and four others were completely rebuilt. It was one of a series of semi-serious accidents to affect the Southern Region in the late-1950s and early 1960s, other less serious accidents such as Staines, Maze Hill and Croydon all featured in Volume 6 of the original series.

PHOTOGRAPH; KEYSTONE PICTURE LIBRARY.

LONDON, WATERLOO

British Railways, Southern Region 11th April 1961

Regretfully just a few short days after Cannon Street, the Southern Region suffered another accident, this time with fatal consequences at the approach to Waterloo Station. As the evening rush hour progressed on 11th April, precedence was being given to departing trains over those ending their journey. Though delays only averaged about three minutes it was felt acceptable, so when an 8-car multiple unit arrived from Effingham Junction it too was ordered to a halt by red signals. However the EMU failed to stop at this signal and it ran through the point-work at about 25 mph. Reversing out of the station at the same time (under clear signals), was a modified West Country Class 4-6-2, No.34040 *Crewkerne.* It had brought in the 1.25pm train from Weymouth, and was now running 'light engine' back to the motive power depot at about 12mph. As it was being driven tender-first, the driver had a restricted view and only saw the EMU just before the collision. Though the EMU was of all-steel construction, the driving position offered little protection when it was hit head-on with such a considerable force.

The motorman was killed outright, but in the train itself there were few casualties; of the 100 people on board only 14 reported any form of injury, and none were serious. However, something potentially more dangerous took place after the accident. When the accident occurred at 5.26pm, the circuit-breakers at Queens Road Sub-station tripped, and power to the line was cut off. Yet, the down train to Horsham had been brought to a stand at the advance starting signal and by accidentally bridging the current-gap, it was allowing current to pass from the platform roads onto the supposedly 'safe' section. This was not discovered for some time, and during the intervening period all the passengers had been safely detrained. Though no-one was injured by this omission, the methods which were adopted after this accident took place were completely contrary to the procedures laid down in Southern Region's manual 'Instructions Applicable to Electrified Lines', and apparently no-one even thought of ensuring the safety of those walking around the crash-site by using short-circuiting bars. Quite why the motorman, who had an excellent record, over-ran the signals remains a mystery, though it is assumed he was simply not sufficiently observant. Just five days later the problems continued, when disaster struck at Pitsea after 'an experienced and properly equipped man' made an error which derailed a ten-coach train to Shoeburyness.

PHOTOGRAPH; ATLANTIC COLLECTION

SINGLETON BANK

British Railways, London Midland Region 16th July 1961

Our next accident in 1961 is the outcome of a signalman's error, that led to a terrible rear-end collision when a holiday-special smashed into a stationary train. The weekend of 15th July 1961 was the start of the annual 'wakes weeks' in parts of Lancashire, a traditional time when the mills and factories closed their doors and the local populace migrated westwards to the coast. For one group of holiday-makers, the destination was Fleetwood, where a boat would convey them over the Irish Sea to the Isle of Man. To transport them a special express passenger train was arranged from Colne, from where it departed on Sunday 16th July. The route took them west through Burnley, Blackburn and Preston, towards Blackpool and Fleetwood. Along this line it would traverse Singleton Bank, where engineering work was shown in the 'Special Weekly Notices' for 15th - 16th July, as being subject to 'single line working. The driver of the 'express', (three 2-car diesel multiple units), knew of the restriction but as he approached the scene of the permanent way work, he was signalled to continue on the down line, and was not crossed over on to the up line as was intended. However, as the train rounded the bend at Singleton Bank near Weeton, the driver was confronted by a ballast train sitting on the track ahead of him. Despite braking hard for over 800 yards, the impetus was just too great to prevent a collision. The leading car smashed through the brake van with a blinding blue flash followed by an explosion, then leap-frogged over the ballast wagons and plunged down a 15 feet high embankment. The driver was killed instantly along with six of his passengers, whilst 116 others were injured; many seriously, for out of the 312 people on board, only 59 were fit enough to carry on to their destination. The fact that the permanent way gang were still on the scene when the accident happened undoubtedly helped to save lives, as did the presence of two ambulance drivers who lived nearby and were able to provide immediate first-aid. An RAF officer saw the accident occur, and he immediately summoned aid from RAF Weeton from where 100 men rushed to help. Fortunately none of the dead or seriously injured were children, even though a third of those holding tickets were under 16 years of age. The Inspector attributed the cause of the accident to the premature withdrawal of single-line working by an inexperienced signalman and a confusing telephone call, but he further added that it was an indirect result of 'atrociously sloppy working practices' among both senior and junior members of railway staff.

PHOTOGRAPH; LANCASHIRE COUNTY RECORD OFFICE

BODMIN GENERAL

British Railways, Western Region 8th December 1961

It is always nice when there is some cross-pollination between railway historians and railway preservation groups, and I am therefore pleased to report the assistance of the Bodmin & Wenford Railway in the recording of the accident which occurred at 6.15am on the approach to Bodmin General station. The engine concerned had come to grief whilst working an early morning train on a cold frosty morning, when it collided with a shunting engine. The driver was killed in the accident after he overran a signal which was supposed to be at danger, but which had actually been pulled off slightly by tension in the wires. The weight of the evidence suggests that the signal was properly set at danger, and that the angle was such that it should not have been accepted as a clear signal. However, the warning given by the distant signal at Boscarne Junction was such that the crew should have had an idea that they would not, in all probability, have had a clear road in to the terminus. The fireman may have failed to understand its actual position but the driver also failed to cross the footplate to observe the true state of the signals. Unfortunately in the half-light he failed to see a shunting engine which was running across his path in order to enter Bodmin General. Following the accident, the signal was repositioned on the recommendations of the Inspector and its sighting distance thereby improved. Some months afterwards, the engine is pictured at Exmouth Junction shed. By now the the 57xx Class 0-6-0PT has actually become an 0-6-0 having lost its pannier tank. Meanwhile the wrecked engine is sheeted over with a tarpaulin, a typical practice following an accident, whilst a decision is taken about its future.

PHOTOGRAPH; T.W. NICHOLLS

CONNINGTON

British Railways, Eastern Region 21st December 1961

A series of three inter-related collisions occurred in an 8 minute spell, commencing at 10.15pm on 21st December 1961. The ECML at Connington was provided with four running lines which extended four miles to the south at Abbots Ripton (itself the scene of a frightful crash on 21st January 1876). Running on the up goods were three trains, each moving south under the permissive block working arrangement; these were an unfitted goods train, a fully fitted goods train and an empty coaching stock train from Scotswood (Newcastle) to Holloway (London). In charge of the ECS train was Deltic class D9012 *Crepello,* then one of BR's newest and most powerful locomotives. Whilst this train should have been signalled through on the up fast line, it had been put on to the slow line; even so the driver should have been observing the signals, but this appeared to be far from the case in view of what happened next. As the V2 got under way after a signal check, it had just reached a speed of around 10 mph when the Deltic struck its guards van at a speed of around 30 mph. As a result of this collision the wreckage of the brake van and the rearmost pair of wagons spilled over on to the up and down main lines. Some three to four minutes later another fully fitted freight train, behind a Class A3 with 34 empty wagons bound for Newcastle, hit the wreckage whilst travelling on the down main line at 50 mph under clear signals. The engine turned over on to its side and 32 wagons were derailed but within another three minutes a third fitted freight had ploughed into this wreckage as the crew of the Class V2 locomotive had no chance of seeing the debris in the dense fog. There was no serious injury to any of those involved, and only the guard of the first fitted freight was detained in hospital for treatment, and then only for a couple of days. The driver and fireman (secondman) of the Deltic were also shocked and bruised, but they were allowed home from hospital the following morning. The official report took a detailed view of the circumstances, particularly the working of the permissive block system under foggy conditions, but whilst it concluded that such an arrangement was not really desirable, it was the only practical alternative to delaying or cancelling trains. That said, the driver of the Deltic should have been more observant of the signals, and not travelled at such an excessive speed when visibility was down to between 30 and 50 yards in places. He had not long before stopped his train at Connington South signals, and then drawn his train slowly forward until he saw the signals for the goods loop were clear. In view of this, he must have been aware that there was another train ahead of him on that line, and he should therefore have exercised much more caution as he moved off into the fog. However, the Deltics were exceptionally powerful and it is most likely that the driver grossly under-estimated the way the engine's speed built up.

PHOTOGRAPHS; COURTESY P. N. TOWNEND

LINCOLN

British Railways, Eastern Region 4th June 1962

To some hardened steam enthusiasts the sight of a diesel or electric locomotive remains an anathema, and some may question why we should incorporate views of accidents featuring 'modern traction' in a book which is primarily concerned with disasters in the age of steam. Firstly I have included them because these were serious events which fall into our time span of 1868 to 1968, and secondly they also play a very important part in the story of transition from steam to diesel/electric operation; the most notable example of this was the incident which occurred on the approach to Lincoln station when 4th June was only a few minutes old. Every night sleeping car trains traversed the length of Britain, and with only a few exceptions (notably Harrow & Wealdstone) most travelled in perfect comfort and safety. With their gentle swaying motion deepening slumber, passengers usually arrived at their destination having had a good night's rest, unfortunately this was not the case for travellers who boarded the 10.15pm Night Scotsman at King's Cross on 3rd June 1962. The train was formed of an English Electric Type 4, one composite coach, three first class sleeping cars, three second class sleepers, two corridor brakes and a GUV van. Normally this train worked north up the ECML, but due to engineering work it was being diverted via Lincoln. As the rostered driver did not know the diversionary route, a conductor driver was appointed to take the controls at Peterborough; however, there were soon to be parallels which would lead many to compare the disaster which followed with the one that had taken place at Sutton Coldfield seven years earlier. It is strange to report, however, that the man given the duty of conductor work had never been passed out for diesel locomotives and, although he had some experience with shunters and DMUs, his normal work was on steam-hauled freight trains. It is evident that he completely misjudged the speed of the Type 4, as he took it at a considerably fast pace all the way to Lincoln, averaging 60 - 65 mph all the way. Indeed, had he not overturned on the approach to the station, he would have arrived there a full 21 minutes early. Though the regular driver would have been reluctant to interfere with a conductor, he should have exercised much closer supervision particularly where the speed was concerned. As a result of the negligence by the two drivers and the fact that the locomotive department at Peterborough had not checked out whether the conductor was capable of driving a train of this type, three people were killed and 49 passengers injured when the engine took a 15 mph section of track at four times the permitted speed.

PHOTOGRAPH; KEYSTONE PICTURE LIBRARY

BARNHAM JUNC.

British Railways, Southern Region 1st August 1962

The next 'modern traction', that which occurred at Barnham , was another of those 'one-in-a-million' accidents, when an EMU was derailed at partially open facing points and deflected on to the platform. The EMU rolled over on to its side, but none of those on board were seriously injured. The cause was eventually traced to the electric point motor, which had been wrongly energised because a small washer had slipped from the switchgear and bridged the gap to make contact for the reversing circuit, and this allowed current to run via the point rodding from the running rail. The heavy current taken by the train as it started from the home signal was sufficient to bring the rail's electrical potential above earth, which in turn energised the points and partially opened them. It was impossible to discover how long the washer had been loose, but the danger could have lurked unseen for years; when it finally made contact with the electrical supply, it led to the injury of 37 passengers and the driver of the EMU.

PHOTOGRAPH; KEYSTONE PICTURE LIBRARY

MINSHULL VERNON

British Railways, London Midland Region 26th December 1962

We have visited Winsford and Minshull Vernon signal boxes before, when we examined the tragic case of a soldier who wanted to get home early and a signalman wanted to make his lunch. The results of their actions were such that a tragic accident needlessly occurred, but in its aftermath, the line upon which it happened was significantly improved and equipped with the most modern signalling and safety devices then known. The signals were 4-aspect multi-lens colour lights and the lines were fully track-circuited; the aspects of the signals normally showed green, but controlled by the track circuits to show double yellow, yellow or red according to the occupation of the track circuits ahead of it. These systems were designed to prevent, as far as possible, accidents occurring from human errors, but they could not prevent a disaster which resulted from gross mistakes on the part of a driver on the Mid-day Royal Scot. On a cold, snowy Boxing Day 1962 severe weather conditions had resulted in some of the points at the approach to Crewe being rendered inoperable, so trains arriving from the north were beginning to build up a back-log. Each time one of these trains came to a halt, the crew would leave their engine and telephone the signalman for instruction in accordance with Rule 55. South of Winsford, the trains were moving one block section at a time, and at the back of this queue came the electric-hauled 4.45 pm Liverpool - Birmingham express. It had been stopped at signal No.114 and then moved south, under caution, to signal 110. The next train to come to a halt at signal No.114 was a Type 4 1 Co-Co 1 diesel locomotive from Polmadie Depot in Glasgow, which was conveying 500 passengers on the 1.30pm Glasgow - Euston Mid-day Scot.

When the crew tried to use the signal telephone to contact Coppenhall Junction signal box, they found the line to be out of order because the switch had not returned to normal when the crew of the Birmingham train had used the telephone. When one telephone went down, all the others on the same circuit also failed and the up 'phones went dead. However, the down lines were on another circuit, and these could have been used by the driver of the Mid-day Scot, but he decided not to do this and under his own initiative he took his engine past the red danger signal. In doing so the driver contended that his train was never running faster than 2-3 mph but the evidence suggests that, like the driver at Lincoln, he grossly underestimated the speed they were actually going as this must have been at least 15 mph. As the train ran on into the dark night, the crew of the English Electric locomotive saw the red light ahead changed to yellow, and notched up to a speed which must have been approaching 20-25 mph. Unfortunately that signal had actually changed for the Birmingham train standing near signal 110 which was just about to move forward. However, before it could do so the Mid-day Scot was on it, and the crew of that engine failed to see its tail-light until the very last minute when the buffers were about to meet. The force drove the Birmingham train forward; despite the fact that the coaches were of all-steel construction and fitted with buck-eye couplings, the coupling between the 7th and 8th coaches fractured and the two were telescoped into each other. Eighteen passengers were killed, and 34 other people were seriously injured, including the guard of the Birmingham train. The time was 6.01 pm and emergency services were summoned by the driver of the Birmingham train about three minutes later, but despite this the police, fire and ambulance services did not get to hear of the accident until 6.34 pm, even then the seriousness of the situation was not fully appreciated until 6.45 pm. An immediate rescue operation swung into being, the services were not on the scene until after what is now known as 'the Golden Hour'. This hour is the most vital period after a major disaster, for in this time it was decided whether people lived or died depending on the treatment they received. Harrow & Wealdstone had shown that people needed treatment where they lay, and that first hour was crucial, but the 'Golden Hour' failed them at Minshull Vernon because of delays in getting emergency aid to the scene - had Minshull Vernon station not been closed in 1942, help would have more readily available. A great many of the injured were treated on the spot, others were tended to in the refreshment and waiting rooms at Crewe which remained open all night to meet the needs of passengers. The incident was due solely to the negligence of the driver on the Mid-day Scot, who failed to obey the rules governing the observance of signals. He also failed to observe the conditions (h) and (i) of the extended Rule 55. Ironically, the offending engine D326 was to become even more notorious, for this was the very same engine that was brought to a halt by the Great Train Robbers.

PHOTOGRAPH; AUTHOR'S COLLECTION

CHEADLE HULME

British Railways, London Midland Region 28th May 1964

I have already spoken in great depth about the inadequacies demonstrated in the staffing of some special trains, with the case at Wormit being a very sad example. Indeed, any accident where children are involved is particularly harrowing to research, but that which happened at Cheadle Hulme in 1964 is especially so for it befell a school trip. The weather forecast for 28th May was good and the platform of Gnosall station (between Wellington and Stafford) was packed with over 200 excited school children. As teachers and parents fussed about, a Stanier Black 5 No.45222 bustled into the station at the head of a nine coach special. The train was of the usual type found on many excursion trains of the era, and therefore made up of 'special' stock which was somewhat aged. All the coaches dated from the period 1937 to 1950 and all, except the fifth (a brake corridor second), were of the open type; the seventh and eighth coaches were an articulated pair sharing a common central bogie. The train crew were not exactly what could be described as 'top link' either, as it comprised a passed fireman as the driver, a fireman who did not know the road, and a goods guard. Once under way the train made a fairly quick journey, and as they reached Bramhall Loop signalbox it was running at a speed of 40 to 45mph, but the driver then failed to see the Advance Warning Board that had been erected to advise drivers about a speed restriction ahead. It was not without good reason that advanced warning had been erected at Bramhall Loop 'box, as a temporary bridge had been installed at the southern approach to Cheadle Hulme station in connection with modernisation work going on there at that time. This work involved the widening of a road passing beneath the Macclesfield branch platforms which necessitated the removal of the old steel superstructure and the creation of new abutments and a new bridge. In the meantime, the District Engineer had installed a temporary bridge, but as this was both on a skew and a curve, the waybeams had to be specially constructed.

Normally Cheadle Hulme had a permanent approach speed of 45mph which was advised by means of a metal cut-out sign 360 yards south of the bridge. However, in view of the fact that there was a more limiting speed restriction, the 45 sign had been covered over with canvas sacking and was no longer in force. Yet despite the Weekly Notices which carried details of the Cheadle Hulme speed limit, it would appear that the driver had somehow failed to appreciate that such a restriction was in force. Unfortunately he was not aided in his recollection because the new speed limit sign was not of a standard type, and it failed to attract the attention of several drivers on preceding journeys, but none had reported the fact. So, at 9.40am that Thursday morning (the children's first week back at school after the Whitsuntide holidays) the York-bound train was derailed as it crossed the temporary bridge at Cheadle Hulme. At its excessive speed the 126 ton loco and 258 ton train had burst the track and derailed against the side of the platform. Under the stress of the derailment and the subsequent dragging against the platform edge, the drawbar of fifth coach sheered off and this caused the train to divide into two portions. Two of the young passengers were killed outright, as was the railway representative who had organised the trip. Twenty-seven other children were injured, four of them seriously. Of these three made a good recovery, but one young girl was still receiving constant medical attention six months later. It was a tragic end to a day's outing and one of the last really serious incidents in the days of steam.

PHOTOGRAPHS; ALL AUTHOR'S COLLECTION.

THIRSK

British Railways, North Eastern Region 31st July 1967

As the British Railways Board began to consider placing orders for the second generation diesel locomotives, a number of firms showed an interest in producing the new Type 4s. One of these, English Electric, developed its 16-cylinder CSVT engine which had been installed in the LMS prototype diesels Nos.10000-1 and placed this in the body shell of a Deltic locomotive. The resulting Co-Co 2,700 hp was well within the 18-ton axle load imposed by BR, and when the prototype was introduced on the WCML in May 1962 it rapidly began to prove its worth. It then transferred to the ECML, but a decision was already being taken to purchase 50 similar locomotives in view of the difficulties then being experienced with the Brush-Sulzer Type 4s. In an earlier Atlantic book, *Diesel Pioneers* by Robert Stephenson, it was recorded that the prototype DP2 ran 100,000 miles without incident, but this failed to take into consideration an incident at Edinburgh Waverley station in August 1966. Pictured top right, DP2, is seen straddling the points where it had become derailed. It was a minor incident, but before long a much more serious problems were to befall this attractive engine. At 02.40am on 31st July 1967 a train of 26 4-wheeled bulk cement wagons and two 20-ton brake vans left Cliffe in Kent for Uddingston near Glasgow. As it made its way up through North Yorkshire on the down slow lines, the cement train was being followed by the 12 noon King's Cross - Edinburgh express passenger train which was on the down fast line. It was due to pass the cement train before they reached Northallerton, but as the driver of DP2 came up to its rear he suddenly saw a cloud of white dust go up in the air. Knowing something had gone drastically wrong, he applied the brakes at once, but this was not sufficient to prevent an accident because he was then going at a speed of around 80 mph. The cement train was running at around 45 mph when the axle of the 12th wagon in its train derailed, and the coupling on the 11th wagon suddenly failed. Subsequent investigation revealed that the axle had built up wear in the UIC link-type suspension and was thus prone to lateral oscillation; in turn this may have exploited a defect in the track. Having jumped the rail, CEMFLO Bulk Cement wagon No. LA233 ran on partially derailed for a distance of 250 yards before the coupling gave way under the strain. The front portion of the train ran on for quarter of a mile before coming to a halt, but the continuous brake on the rear portion was applied at once. The 12th wagon turned round to its side and spread across the down slow line, whilst the 13th to 22nd vehicles turned to the left and ran down an embankment. The 23rd wagon unfortunately failed to follow them, and it slewed round at right angles and fouled the up fast line and the path of DP2. When the prototype engine hit the wreckage it was still running at a speed of 50 mph, and the damage it sustained was exceptionally heavy. The bulk of the damage to the engine was around the front left-hand nose, and the rail unions were quick to point out that had this locomotive been one of the flat-fronted cab types which were coming into vogue with the BR design team, the consequences for the driver would have been very severe indeed. Unfortunately, the train behind DP2 did not withstand the impact as well, and in the mangled wreckage seven passengers were killed and 45 injured. This was the end of the road for DP2, for after a month under sheets at York it was returned to English Electric's factory at Newton-le-Willows where it was broken up.

PHOTOGRAPHS; ABOVE, THE LATE KENNETH HOOLE COLLECTION
BELOW, COURTESY JOHN M. BOYES

HITHER GREEN

British Railways, Southern Region 5th November 1967

In the final years of steam on British Railways, the last three major accidents were all sustained by the newer types of traction which were being introduced to replace traditional forms of motive power. The first of these serious accidents was the accident to DP2 at Thirsk, the second occurred at 9.16 pm on Bonfire Night 1967, when the 7.43 pm train from Hastings to London (Charing Cross) was derailed at high speed as it approached Hither Green station under clear signals. Comprised of two Hastings line diesel/electrical multiple unit sets, Numbers 1007 and 1017, it was packed to capacity with passengers standing in the corridors. As it ran on to a diamond crossing at a speed of around 70 mph, the leading wheels of the third coach struck a small piece of rail which had broken away from a rail end, and this caused the bogie to become derailed towards the down fast line. It ran on in this condition for about a quarter of a mile, when the derailed wheels struck a diamond crossing in the up fast line. The leading car negotiated the crossing safely, but the derailed third coach caused the car in front of it, and two more behind it to become completely derailed and turn over on to their sides. The coupling behind the leading coach broke, and it ran on into Hither Green station unharmed, but in the wreckage behind 49 passengers were dead or dying, another 78 were injured, 27 seriously. Fire, police and ambulance were all on the scene within a matter of minutes, and first aid was being given to passengers where they lay, the lesson of the 'Golden Hour' now being applied for the first time in a major disaster since Harrow & Wealdstone. It was not a perfect rescue operation by any means, but it was proficient; 33 ambulances and 28 fire appliances attended the scene, and doctors rendered immediate care to the patients where they lay before they were transported off to hospital.

There is no doubt that the initial derailment was caused by the fracturing of a rail-end joint, which was situated on a section of 'closure rail' between two sections of continuously welded rail (CWR). Ironically, only the Southern Region used 'closures' and it is strange that the practice was maintained there, because the very purpose of CWR track was to eliminate as many rail joints as possible. Indeed, as a result of this accident the practice of using 'closures' was also abandoned on the Southern, and existing closures were progressively replaced in the next four years. The rail fracture came about because of the unsatisfactory condition of the joint, which had a void underneath the sleeper due to the ballast being old and compacted. However, from the surface the sleeper looked in good order, and it had a good top; but when under load, the sleeper would have been 'pumping' and this in turn would have worked the rail joint to the point of fracture. It is not likely that this fracture would have been evident to the naked eye, but it was recommended that more frequent testing be undertaken using specialist equipment. Unfortunately, much of the Southern Region's track was found to be in a condition that was less than desirable, and when the Hastings line DEMUs were tested by the Inspector he found the riding 'not so good'. Admittedly they were not outside the acceptable limits, but compared to the riding qualities which were observed when they were tested on the Eastern Region, they were way below what they should have been. Obviously all possible steps were being taken to improve the quality of the permanent way on the Southern Region, but this was going to be a long process as the Inspector acknowledged. He did, however, recommend the premature replacement of old track panels with CWR as a matter of urgency, particularly on heavily used lines as this was seen as the best way of eliminating dangers from defective track joints. Obviously blame for an incident of this magnitude had to be apportioned to someone, and it fell upon the heads of the Southern Region's Permanent Way Department, notably the Chief Permanent Way Inspector, the District Engineer and the Chief Civil Engineer. It was a damning indictment, but it was the last serious accident in the age of steam where the passenger death toll reached double figures. Unfortunately, there was yet one more awful tragedy which we will have to discuss, and this took place just 62 days later, a little over eight months before the end of steam.

PHOTOGRAPH; ILLUSTRATED LONDON NEWS

HIXON

British Railways, London Midland Region 6th January 1968

In 1880 the first Public Inquiry into a British railway disaster was held following the collapse of the Tay Bridge on 28th December 1879, in which 75 people died. The terms of reference for that formal inquiry were constituted under Section 7 of the 'Regulation of the Railways Act, 1871' and differed considerably from the normal type of investigation into railway accident carried out by the Railway Inspectorate. It was rare for an accident to be investigated in this way, but that which occurred at Hixon Green on 6 January 1968 was so serious in its nature, and caused such a high level of public concern, that a second Public Inquiry into a railway disaster was authorised by Mrs. Barbara Castle, Minister for Transport just ten days later. The bare bones of the accident are very well known now, as is the procedure for conduct expected of road drivers at automated level crossings, but back in 1968 it was a much different story as road-users struggled to come to grips with the new technology. The accident occurred on the former North Staffordshire Railway at the level crossing in Station Road, Hixon, where the station had closed precisely 21 years earlier on 6th January 1947. The automated level crossing in question was on the road connecting the A51 with a disused airfield, and had come into operation in April 1967. It was operated by treadles on the railway line 1,000 yards from the crossing, and situated on an overhead electrified line where the maximum permitted speed was 85 mph. Going south there was a gradient of 1:600 which meant that a train of 400 tons going at maximum speed would need a minimum of 1,520 yards to stop. There was also a sign-posted minimum headroom of 16' 6", and two warning signs which read **'In emergency or before crossing with exceptional or heavy loads or cattle phone signalman'**. Unfortunately both of these were set at such an angle as to make them hard to read by road users. In December 1967, English Electric Limited applied to the Ministry of Transport for 'the Authorisation of Special Types General order for an abnormal indivisible load' in compliance with Section 64(4) of the Road Traffic Act 1960; in order to move a 120-ton transformer from their factory at Stafford to store on the former airfield at Hixon. The contractors, Robert Wynn Limited provided a specially strengthened 32-wheeled, self-steering trailer, with a 'Conqueror' tractor unit at either end. Staffordshire Police sent along a patrol car and two constables as an escort. At around 12.20 pm the slow-moving convoy was nearing the end of its journey, when it encountered the AHB crossing at Hixon. The police car went across first and waited on the opposite side, but in view of the fact that the height of the load was 16' 9" it did not have sufficient headroom to cross in safety. However, most drivers of abnormal roads knew that the notices often erred on the side of caution and the height of cables was usually two feet more than it said on the warning plate (as was the case at Hixon). Even so the driver took no chances and proceeded taking his 148 feet long vehicle slowly across the level crossing at a speed of 2-3 mph with men walking alongside to ensure that the transformer did not foul the 25 Kv catenary above. Unfortunately, none of them had seen the signs warning about slow moving vehicles and telephoned the signalman as advised. Therefore, as it was crossing, the 11.30am Manchester - Euston express behind E3009 came on to the scene at near to maximum speed and the treadle sequence was initiated. Twenty-four seconds later the express had struck the transporter at its rear end, just where the 'swan neck' connected the low-loader to the rear tractor. The engine and the first five coaches were severely damaged, and the next three vehicles were all derailed. The driver, second-man and a spare driver travelling in the cab were all killed, as were eight passengers in the train behind them. Forty-four more passengers and a restaurant car attendant were injured, six of these quite seriously. Upon coming to a rest, the surviving member of the train crew, the guard, undertook his duties to protect the train in a most commendable manner. He first of all ran northwards for a mile to place detonators at the prescribed intervals, and upon coming to a working telephone he called the electric traction room at Crewe and advised them of the accident. He then returned south, running all the time, to a point a mile in front of the train in order to protect the down line. A railway fireman travelling on the train commandeered a passing motorist to drive him to the A51 where he made a call to the emergency service. The two police officers also used their radio telephone to summon emergency aid, including two helicopters which the Army had loaned to the Police for trials.

PHOTOGRAPH; COURTESY STAFFORD/STONE NEWSLETTER

INDEX

POSTSCRIPT

To conclude a story such as this is no easy task, and from the outset I have been troubled over what my final words should be. It is no light matter to talk about death and destruction page after page, and not be affected by it. It has always been my aim to take a detached view of the subject, for the sheer enormity of the death and injury caused in 170 years of railway operation is hard to describe. Yet, describe it I can, for if you were to visit the reading room of the National Railway Museum in York, you will find a set of wooden index card drawers which list all known accidents in geographical order, each drawer is filled with hundreds of cards, and each card is but one record of disaster. Nearby stand the bound volumes of all the annual accident reports, some of these are slim volumes (the good years) others are the bad ones. Look at 1910, 1915, 1961 etc. and you will see what I mean. It is possible to enure one's self against words or frozen images on a printed page, but it is no easy task to steel oneself to watch moving pictures of the aftermath of a rail disaster. Such was the case with the video of the Clapham and Harrow railway crashes which was sent to me for review by Channel 4 Television; even more poignant was my inspection of the wrecked 'Sprinter' trains which were mangled pieces of metal following the Ais Gill disaster of 1995. Both of these were items which led me to reflect on the severity of it all, indeed, it would be an insensitive person who could not. Yet, I strongly feel that it is still a very important subject which should be covered, for there is much to gain from going over old, painful ground such as this. A quotation in the Hixon report was most apposite, in that it stated 'from this nettle, danger, we pluck this flower, safety.' The catalogue of accidents and disasters such as we have recounted herein should be, in my view, essential reading to all railwaymen, managers and the hierarchy who administer the Department of Transport. As railways enter the 21st century, we are undoubtedly going to see more accidents, and I dare say the claim will be made that 'we never knew that could happen', it has certainly been said often enough before! But, like the problems of landslides on the Settle & Carlisle line or the Cambrian coast, some dangers are as old as the lines themselves. As privatisation comes, it is perhaps inevitable that corners will be cut and old safety techniques abandoned in favour of less-proven, but newer (more cost-effective) innovations. As I write these words, the rail unions are demanding a public inquiry into the Ais Gill accident of 1995, on the basis of just those sorts of issues. As a regular rail traveller, I wish them well.

Steam came to an end almost three decades ago, and this book tells the story of accidents in the most important hundred year period of British Railway history, spanning the consolidation period of the 1860s, to the near abandonment of our national system under Beeching in the 1960s. As we take a further step towards the ending of a truly nationally owned and operated railway in the mid-1990s, it is fitting to look back for a moment to what we believe to be the very last railway accident in the BR steam era. It was not a serious event, nor was it any way newsworthy, but a friend, Barrie Woods, happened to record it on film at Rose Grove Shed on 3rd August 1968. This was just before the final elimination of steam, when Stanier 8F No.48666 decided enough was enough. Bearing the so called devil's mark, she tried her own fiendish antics to protest at her demise, by splitting the points and dropping between the rails. At the time she was being taken on her last short trip under steam, heading into the road where the other 'dead engines' were being stored prior to disposal. It was recovered from this predicament by sister engines 48775 and 48191, but all were soon to go for scrap; a picture of them resting at Rose Grove before the final journey is shown on page 159 of my book *Steam For Scrap.* With that little bit of trivial nostalgia, it is fitting to draw the story to its end with our final picture taken in the car park of the Old Blacksmith's Shop at Gretna, showing the memorial erected in memory of the Quintinshill victims by the Western Front Association in May 1995. It took 80 years to get the memorial, as the Caledonian, LMS and BR all refused permission for a lineside plaque. However, when this one was erected just over the fields from the disaster site. The last remaining survivor of the crash was in attendance at the ceremony. Like myself, all who have visited the site will no doubt find comfort in the words of the Apostle Paul in the Acts of the Apostles Chapter 24 verse 15.... if you have a moment to spare on conclusion of this book, you too may care to take a reflective consideration of the words therein.
Safe travelling where ever you go.